Safe

Safe

A MEMOIR OF FATHERHOOD,
FOSTER CARE, AND THE
RISKS WE TAKE FOR FAMILY

Mark Daley

ATRIA BOOKS

NEW YORK   LONDON   TORONTO   SYDNEY   NEW DELHI

An Imprint of Simon & Schuster, Inc.
1230 Avenue of the Americas
New York, NY 10020

First Atria Books hardcover edition January 2024

ATRIA BOOKS and colophon are trademarks of Simon & Schuster, Inc.

Simon & Schuster: Celebrating 100 Years of Publishing in 2024

For information about special discounts for bulk purchases, please
contact Simon & Schuster Special Sales at 1-866-506-1949 or
business@simonandschuster.com.

The Simon & Schuster Speakers Bureau can bring authors to your live event. For
more information or to book an event, contact the Simon & Schuster Speakers
Bureau at 1-866-248-3049 or visit our website at www.simonspeakers.com.

Interior design by Kyoko Watanabe

Manufactured in the United States of America

1   3   5   7   9   10   8   6   4   2

Library of Congress Cataloging-in-Publication Data
Names: Daley, Mark (Foster child advocate), author.
Title: Safe : A Memoir of Fatherhood, Foster Care, and the Risks We Take for
Family / by Mark Daley.
Description: First Atria Books hardcover edition. | New York : Atria Books, 2024. |
Includes bibliographical references and index.
Identifiers: LCCN 2023029083 (print) | LCCN 2023029084 (ebook) |
ISBN 9781668008782 (hardcover) | ISBN 9781668008799 (trade paperback) |
ISBN 9781668008805 (ebook)
Subjects: LCSH: Foster parents—United States. | Foster children—United States. |
Gay-parent families—United States. | Foster home care—United States. |
Child welfare—United States.
Classification: LCC HQ759.7 .D36 2024 (print) | LCC HQ759.7 (ebook) |
DDC 306.8740973—dc23/eng/20230830
LC record available at https://lccn.loc.gov/2023029083
LC ebook record available at https://lccn.loc.gov/2023029084

ISBN 978-1-6680-0878-2
ISBN 978-1-6680-0880-5 (ebook)

For Jason, who brings love, kindness,
and great hair to our world.

Contents

Safe

Prologue

I want to write this story like a fairy tale.

I want it to be a love song. Something Taylor Swift would write.

I want to romanticize the plight of a young woman on a bus that smelled like diesel and potato chips, alone and pregnant, a five-month-old baby asleep on her lap.

I want her to be the heroine, riding toward the unknown with all the virtue and strength and resilience we automatically ascribe to mothers, with no thought of the burden.

I want to imagine the husband she left behind, endowing him with the will and power to move heaven and earth to keep his family whole.

I want to write this story so that it's clear who is the hero and who is the villain. Who deserves to parent and who does not.

But in real life, those things are rarely as clear as in fairy tales.

This is what I know: A pregnant woman with a five-month-old baby got on a Greyhound bus to California with no money, one diaper, no food, and no hope. She felt broken. She didn't know her family was about to crash into a child welfare system that was just as broken.

And I had no idea her family was on a collision course with mine. Or that life is rarely as simple as a love song.

Chapter 1

Protection

No matter how hard we tried, we just couldn't get pregnant," I said, winking at Jason, my husband of four months. The six other couples— one also gay, the rest straight—stared blankly at me, trying to determine if I was joking or a complete idiot. I smiled and let out a small laugh to assure them of my humor and that I understood the basics of reproduction. Jason smiled, but didn't laugh. He'd heard me deliver that joke a few dozen times before and it was apparent by the look on his face that he didn't believe our first class to become certified foster parents was the best place to recycle it.

"Both of our families have a history of fostering and adoption," he chimed in. "We just feel like we want to start our family the same way." Jason delivered our canned response and I nodded in agreement. The truth was a little more complex but there was no reason to spill the tea to a bunch of people we'd just met.

The class was held in the brightly colored conference room of Children's Bureau, a nonprofit located between Koreatown and downtown Los Angeles that recruits, trains, approves, and supports foster parents. The tables were arranged in a semicircle with each couple occupying their own table; a piece of paper with our names handwritten on the front was folded to stand upright. Sonja, a woman in her twenties with the longest and most intricate eyelashes I'd ever seen, shared that she and her husband had just taken custody of their school-age nephew and were now required to get certified in order to keep him. "My sister was a teenager when she got pregnant," Sonja said. "She wasn't ready to be a mom and now she's dealing with some addiction and mental health issues." She paused for a second, likely questioning if she'd just overshared. "But she's starting to do some work and taking her meds, so we are all hopeful."

As a gay man, I never had to worry about an unplanned pregnancy, morning sickness, or the lifetime of responsibilities that go along with having a child. I could brunch, blissfully unaware of the hours-long dance recital at the theater on the corner, sipping mimosas while parents reapplied sunblock at soccer games in the park. I have never had a pregnancy scare force me to ponder important questions like: Am I ready to be a parent? What does it mean to be one? What makes a good parent or even an acceptable one?

There are only a few roads leading to parenthood for couples like Jason and me: surrogacy, private adoption, or foster to adopt. I don't recall exactly when we first talked about our options, but I'd always assumed we'd foster-adopt a child at some point. Three of my cousins had come into our family through foster care, and I'd also consulted for a few child welfare nonprofits, which gave me some familiarity with how many children across the country were in need of foster homes. I knew that over four million children come to the attention of child welfare agencies each year on concern of abuse or neglect,[1] and that on any given day, roughly 120,000 children are waiting to be adopted.[2] In California, one in five children entering foster care were babies under the age of one.[3] And that is what we wanted, a baby. We didn't care about race or gender. Give us a boy or a girl or one whose gender would be determined later in life. None of that mattered. We were in love and we had two big, loud, supportive families and a huge community of friends in our corner.

I'd skipped into the first of four intensive foster parent training sessions like Belle in the opening scene of *Beauty and the Beast*—one hand clasping my husband's and the other tightly wrapped around a Starbucks. "Bonjour. Good day." We were newlyweds, living our fairy tale. And like the heroes at the beginning of every classic quest, we were excited and naive. Our love for one another and desire to grow a family overshadowed the truth of what we'd just signed up to do.

We were less than fifteen minutes into class when Cindy, the social worker with tight, curly hair and glasses who led the training, crushed my "infants-only" stance. "The county allows families to set age ranges like zero to three for the children they are willing to foster, but infants-only isn't an acceptable range," she said. That was news to me. We expected a child entering our lives from foster care to carry a history of trauma, but we had hoped to intervene early enough to spare them from any significant harm or abuse. I thought more about Cindy's words and realized they couldn't just force us to take in whatever child they want. When they would eventually call and tell us about an available child, we could still say no and wait for them to call back with an infant. But, like a bartender with a heavy pour, Cindy kept serving truth bombs, hell-bent on making sure the entire class understood the realities of fostering.

"There are normal losses almost every one of us experienced growing up, like going to day care or starting school and being forced to be away from our parents for the first time," Cindy said. "These are relatable, common experiences we call *maturational* losses. Children in foster care, however, often experience unpredictable, traumatic life events, called *situational* losses." She asked us to name examples of situational loss and wrote the list on a whiteboard: divorce, death of a parent or child, sexual abuse, mental illness, job loss, natural disaster, loss of a home, food insecurity, community violence, incarceration, drug addiction and alcoholism, witnessing or experiencing physical or emotional abuse or neglect. She went on to talk about these adverse childhood experiences (or ACEs) and how they can lead to depression and anxiety, and may have long-term effects on our emotional well-being and physical health.[4]

"By a show of hands, how many of you have experienced one of the losses on this list?" Cindy asked, looking around the room. Most people's hands shot up. "How many have experienced two? How about three?" By the time she got to five there were no hands in the air.

I looked around the room, at the other families. The couple next to us, who had jokingly told the class they were done having babies and wanted to foster and possibly adopt a teenager, was no longer smiling. They were inspired to foster when they learned that teens account for less than 10 percent of all adoptions.[5] They had two adult children. "What's one more?" the husband had joked. But in that moment, their good intentions were blindsided by the realities of childhood trauma.

Everyone was silent, imagining the horrors our future foster children might have endured and the resulting behavioral issues that might emerge. Cindy had deflated our cheerful optimism with the sharp edge of truth. I looked around the room and tried to guess who might not be back the following week—who was up for the challenge and who was not.

The couple who wanted a teen looked especially grim.

Next, Cindy the Dream-Slayer asked us to track how many situational losses had been experienced by a seven-year-old boy in a video she screened from a warbly VHS cassette. When the video was over, I had to count again, sure I'd made a mistake. I hadn't miscounted. In just seven years, he'd endured thirteen of these losses, a number Cindy told us was not unusual for a child in foster care. She'd seen five-year-olds who'd entered care with scars from cigarette burns, had cases with kids as young as two who'd been molested. I could feel my stomach turning. Cindy had just said our baby could be a victim of sexual abuse. Where would I begin to help that child? What would they need? The questions in my mind raced as fast as the adrenaline in my veins. Will the baby act out? What sort of behavioral issues might they have? What if my little girl is afraid of men? She's going to have two dads. I feared what I didn't know—the past of a child, a victim, who was about to enter my life, to become my world, and I was completely unprepared. I wanted to watch them shine, but first I'd have to help them heal.

I looked back at the list on the board and thought about my mom. She was the same age as the boy in the video when she lost her own mother to a hemorrhage caused by an ectopic pregnancy. In a sense, she lost her father that night too. His battle with grief was roiled by alcoholism. Mom was bounced from one living situation to another. A series of people incapable of caring for her and her younger siblings.

I estimated she had experienced at least seven situational losses before the age of ten. It was hard to know for sure. She was always careful when she talked about her childhood, never wanting us to be encumbered by the pain of her past. But over the years I had collected the slivers she let slip and assembled them, along with the fragments I gathered from my aunts and uncles, in meticulous fashion, like piecing together the shards of a broken lamp.

Despite, or maybe as a result of, her childhood, Mom loved and watched over her three children with the ferocity of someone who understands just how delicate life is, how one tragedy can upend everything in a matter of seconds. She mastered the balance of protecting her children, while teaching us to survive. She gave us experiences she had only dreamt about. But most importantly, she provided the one thing I needed above all else: a safe space. Whether we were alone talking in the kitchen or belting along to Rod Stewart in her Monte Carlo, the pressure I felt around others to be someone else was never there. It always felt like she saw me, the real me. And she loved me just the same.

———

The biggest trauma of my childhood was coming to grips with being gay. My parents had never physically hurt or abandoned me. I never worried about my safety the way Mom had or the way my future child may have. How would we build trust with a child who'd endured so many losses? We wouldn't just be first-time foster parents—we would be first-time parents, period. My baby fever had suddenly been interrupted by the heavy recognition of all the hurt our future child might have experienced, and of all I didn't know about nurturing any young person, much less one who'd faced trauma.

"What is the most common reason a child enters foster care?" the woman at the table next to ours asked.

"That's a great question," Cindy replied with a smile, "and it's also a very difficult one to answer." She took a deep breath, removed her glasses with one hand, and rubbed her eyes with the other. "Neglect is the box that gets checked most frequently by investigators, but neglect can mean different things to different people. If there's an allegation of abuse, a judge may want evidence and an investigator can't always prove how a bruise ended up somewhere. Neglect, however, can be subjective, relying on the opinions of investigators or the agency's definition of neglect. Sometimes neglect gets selected simply because it's easier than proving abuse."

Cindy's answer was yet another curveball to my foster-adopt strategy. I'd done a lot of homework before arriving in class. I knew there were factors that increased the likelihood of a child not returning to their birth parents. When a parent has already lost a child to the system or has a history of drug use or mental health issues, the odds are not in their favor for reunification. When the call would come, and Jason and I would be presented with the facts of the case, we planned to ask a series of questions to screen out the children with the highest likelihood of reunification. We wanted to adopt a child in need and I wasn't sure I was emotionally prepared for reunification. I thought, by doing my homework, I could increase my chances of winning the jackpot, the perfect baby ready to be adopted. But what Cindy had just said meant that the data used to inform my research might have been a bit murky. I was beginning to believe it was all muddy, a swamp.

Cindy returned the conversation to trauma and how foster parents can best support children who've been traumatized. She must have mistaken my wandering thoughts for an expression of boredom because she called on me for her next question.

"Mark, what are you going to do if you have a Black daughter?" she asked. "How are you going to help her maintain a connection to her culture of origin? How are you going to learn to do her hair?"

"I'm a gay man in Hollywood," I joked, trying to deflect the question and hide my growing insecurities. "Do you really think I don't know a hairdresser?"

Everyone laughed. But her point wasn't lost on me. We were navigating challenging terrain, and understanding how to care for and style a child's natural hair was just the tip of the iceberg. As foster parents, it would become our responsibility to instill a child with a sense of pride and cultural context. There was also the legacy of social injustice. Poverty, mass incarceration, and other social endemics adversely impacting communities of color have led to a population of Black and Indigenous youth in foster care that is far greater than their portion of the general population.[6] It was unlikely, given the demographics of Los Angeles County, that the child we'd receive would look anything like us.

A few months into our marriage, and we were about to open our hearts and our home to someone with a host of needs and experiences we couldn't predict—or in some cases, even fathom. I had no idea exactly what kind of parents we would be, but I did know we had both the time and love to share.

I figured that was as good a place as any to begin figuring it out.

Chapter 2

Husband and Husband

Four months earlier, I stood in front of the big leaning mirror in our guest bedroom, my mom and best girlfriends crowded around me in a panic like a scene out of *Father of the Bride*. Jason had gone ahead to the venue to greet guests and play host, and I was trapped with confounding flaps of silk around my neck, watching the eighth pointless YouTube video, listening to a smugly dapper man chastise, "Every man should be able to tie his own bow tie."

"I got this," Trisha said. "I totally got this." She pursed her lips and squinted her green eyes in determination.

My mom, sitting on the bed beside me, squeezed my hand. She claimed to have flown out from Boston almost a week early to help with the last-minute wedding prep, but I knew the real reason she'd come to LA days before my father arrived: she was here to keep an eye on my anxiety. Jason was the even keel in our relationship. I was the hot mess.

Shrieks shot upstairs from the front entryway. In a flash of long limbs and blond hair my friend Buffy raced down the hall, stopping at the guest room door to blow me a kiss, her face flushed.

"How is it this hot in October?" she groaned.

She was training for an Ironman, but Jason and I had joked that her true athletic feat would be traveling from another wedding in Copenhagen to LA on a red-eye via London, fighting traffic to our house, and getting dressed and done up in time for pictures before the ceremony.

"You've got twenty minutes," Trisha warned, lifting and resetting my collar to take another go at the tie. In the precise clockwork of wedding planning, we'd figured out how to get Buffy here from a different continent in time to shower, steam her dress, and do her hair and makeup. Our calculation hadn't taken into consideration the possibility that *I'd* be the one who was unprepared.

My stomach lurched with nerves. And there was something else— the feeling of wanting something so much that the strength of desire made me afraid it was out of reach.

—————

Jason and I had met the traditional way.

On Tinder.

I'd had a pair of meaningful relationships, each lasting three years, and opened my heart and bed to an embarrassing number of others. I'd been ghosted, breadcrumbed, and borderline stalked. But at thirty-six years old I had finally confronted the monster of internalized shame that spawned from a childhood in the closet. Straight people typically figure out who they are while coming of age and hopefully begin to love and respect themselves around the same time. Gays of my generation— we tended to lag behind.

I remember hating myself after my first few hookups. I was terrified of someone finding out. *My future would be ruined. I was a sinner, a deviant, a fag, or whatever other names the Westboro Baptist Church lobbed at boys like me.* Night after night, I sobbed myself to sleep, wishing I was anyone other than who I was. Shame squeezing every ounce of self-love out of my soul. I allowed shame to win for way too long.

But I was in a different place in my life when I met Jason.

Tinder had just been released, but I didn't know about it until I met my girlfriends for our regular Sunday night dinner. When I arrived at the restaurant, they were all on their phones, swiping left and right with the excitement of children on Christmas morning.

"It's this new dating app," one friend said, barely prying her eyes away from the screen to update me on the new and highly efficient way to cruise. "If you and the person you're into both swipe right, you're able to message one another. It really cuts through the noise," she said.

"Are the gays on it?" I asked, intrigued.

She shrugged and kept swiping.

In the early days of Tinder, they sent you male and female candidates indiscriminately, regardless of your orientation. My first day on the app I hilariously matched with Trisha and two other girlfriends, and I was so busy taking screenshots of the bogus matches that it took a minute to register a real one: Jason, whom I could swear I'd seen before, maybe at the gym or one of the parties in the Hills that every gay in LA attended—the Super Bowl (what we called the Beyoncé Concert in the Middle of a Football Game), or one of the legendary Cupid's Stupid Valentine's Day parties. Jason suggested Eveleigh on Sunset for drinks at 7:00 p.m. Did seven o'clock mean dinner, or just drinks? Was I supposed to eat first? I polled the girls and we agreed I'd better eat before I got there—they'd all seen what being "hangry" does to me.

When I arrived, Jason was sitting at a small bar on the French-cottage-inspired covered back patio. I slid onto the stool next to him and ordered a glass of red. He stuck with sparkling water, asked the bartender to bring us olives, and told me he'd been sober for fifteen years.

Great. I'd already flubbed the date. "Does it bother you if I drink?"

"No," he reassured me. "I used to be a bartender."

When he ordered a charcuterie plate that I was too full to help him finish, I asked if he'd eaten dinner.

"No, have you?"

"So, by 'drinks at seven' you actually meant 'dinner and *no* drinks at seven,'" I joked.

He wasn't from LA either—he'd grown up in Pittsburgh—and soon we were talking about our favorite things to do in our chosen city.

"I like to ride the trains," he said. "When people visit me, I always take them downtown on the subway."

"LA has trains?" I asked. "Are you sure?"

"We should go do it. Right now."

"But I live in LA because I don't want to live in New York," I said. I told him I always took visitors to the beach.

"Then let's go to the beach," he said.

We dropped his car off at his house by the Grove, an LA shopping landmark, which meant we had to go by Doughboys for cupcakes. We ordered a giant red velvet cupcake to share and then drove to Malibu. It was pitch-black on the beach. Jason walked ahead of me, holding the box with the cupcake, and I was right on his tail. Just as my eyes were starting to adjust to the dark, my foot landed in a hole in the sand, and I pitched forward. He stopped short, turning toward me, and suddenly I was Kate Hudson in an early 2000s rom-com. I fell into him, and we kissed for the first time by accident. It was a fantastic kiss. Surprising. Electric. New. Had this been an actual rom-com, fireworks would have spontaneously lit up the Pacific sky. We would have held still, clasping hands, watching the explosions dance overhead. And as the night air filled with the crescendo of our film's score, we'd embrace once more as the camera panned down to the sandy cupcake at our bare feet. But this was no movie. We kissed in the dark to the sound of crashing waves. His arm around my back and the other, thankfully, still clutching the cupcake.

Jason took the games out of dating. He called when he said he was going to call. He texted to check in. He made plans. Other guys had traded me in for a go-go boy or an after-hours party. Jason made himself available and that made me feel wanted.

A few months after our first date, I watched him wind up and pitch a Wiffle ball to his friend's six-year-old, and I knew. I snapped a picture of him, baseball cap on backward, the sun bringing out the gold in his ginger beard, and texted it to the girls. *FYI*, I wrote, *I'm going to marry this man.*

And I was right.

But first this stupid bow tie.

In an hour and a half, we'd get married in front of three hundred guests, a celebration of commitment and vision and partnership. Also a celebration of the fact that we *could* get married. When I came out in my twenties, gay marriage wasn't legal. I didn't grow up seeing gay couples grocery shopping or picking their kids up from school. In fairness, I was raised in Brockton, Massachusetts, a working-class city south of Boston, and didn't see a lot of straight husbands or dads pushing grocery carts or running car pool either. I'd come of age in a culture with a narrow vision of what it meant to be a couple or a family. The roles were defined. There's a husband and a wife, no exceptions. It didn't matter that Patrick Swayze in a tank top made you feel things you'd never felt before; there were norms. Norms that left kids like me feeling isolated, lonely, and depressed.

While my parents had never uttered an unkind word about gay people, we were a blue-collar Irish Catholic family during the height of the HIV/AIDS epidemic. I didn't know anyone who was gay. The only time I had heard the word used was as a punch line. I didn't realize it at the time, but each crack, each cruel joke, added a new pound of shame to my young, weary shoulders.

Sometimes I felt disappointed—no, angry—that I, and everyone in my generation, were given such limited models of who we were and who we might become. Sometimes I just felt grateful for the cultural shifts and change-makers who paved the way, who'd made it possible for Jason and me to become husbands and, we hoped, dads.

———

We piled into separate Ubers and rode a mile down the street to the Ebell of Los Angeles, one of a number of women's clubs that had been built along the California coast in the late 1800s to give women more access to the arts and cultural events. I'd like to believe we'd chosen this place for its history, but the elegant chandeliers, sweeping staircases, and ornate, gilded plaster ceilings hadn't hurt my vision of a fairy-tale wedding.

"Someone's getting *married*," the Uber driver sang, pulling up to the curb.

My mouth felt like it was full of sand, dry and scratchy with nerves. Inside, caterers bustled around in aprons, setting up tables and stainless-steel serving trays. Our videographer ran up with his camera, filming my arrival. The knot in my stomach tightened. For a closet introvert, there's no worse hell than hosting in public.

I stood still and let Trisha fix my collar, my eyes roaming around the room. My mom in her taupe dress stitched with pearls, her hair in a loose chignon, joined a clutch of aunts and cousins, and with a lump in my throat I thought of the two most important people who weren't with us today. My cousin Jaime and my aunt Cheryl. Jaime was three days younger than me and my closest friend. She passed away suddenly when we were twenty-three. She should have been riding over in the Uber with me and her sister Keli today. I looked up at the ornate ceiling in hopes gravity would pull back the tears forming in my eyes.

Auntie Cheryl was Mom's sister and Jaime's mother. She had died of cancer a few years earlier. For fourteen months she'd fought for her life, and every single day of her illness, her husband of thirty-plus years brought fresh blueberries into the house, convinced the antioxidants would keep her alive. As she lay dying in the home they built, he stood, knelt, and slept beside her, his devotion my personal image of love in action. Before Jason, I'd just kept breaking my own heart. Jason had opened it. How, I wondered, would our love be called to action?

That's when I noticed the tablecloths. They were laid two to a table, one lighter and one darker green. I knew marketing, policy, and strategy, but Jason knew event planning, and he knew tablecloths and centerpieces and what looked right. He'd been very particular about the look he wanted for the tables—but the cloths were on backward. The lighter green was supposed to go on the top, the darker on the bottom. There were at least thirty-five tables—there was no time to fix them. I looked down at Trisha in a panic.

Just then she stepped away from me, hands overhead, raising the roof. "Check you out!" she said, distracting me from the tablecloths. "The perfect bow tie."

She was right. She'd nailed it. I kissed her cheek and took the stairs two at a time to find Jason. I was finally ready.

"You prepare, you do your best, and there are things you can't control," Jason had said that morning in bed when I checked the weather report for the fiftieth time and confirmed that we'd be marrying in unseasonable triple-digit heat. "You decide whether it gets to ruin your day." Sometimes it was a real pain in the ass to live with a wellness coach who taught workshops like *Meditation for Assholes . . . and People Who Don't Want to Act Like One*. A little part of me wanted to see him undone by the tablecloths, not because I wanted him to be upset, but because I wanted him to be like me, someone who could become a basket case over a small thing.

Jason stood with a group of groomsmen, everyone else sipping champagne in T-shirts, waiting till the last possible minute to put on wedding clothes. Jason looked completely relaxed and at ease in his black tux. My chest bounced with nervous energy. Jason lazily turned his gaze my way and smiled, his blue eyes washing me in sudden calm.

"Hey, babe," he said and moved across the room toward me. He kissed me on the lips, and I knew I wouldn't say anything about the tablecloths.

Just before four thirty, when the ceremony was scheduled to begin, the string quartet started playing arrangements of Tupac songs and guests began filling the seats.

"Welcome, everyone," our dear friend Peggy, the officiant, began. "On behalf of Jason, Mark, and their families, I thank you for stepping out of your busy lives and into their love story on this beautiful, *brisk* day."

Jason stood across from me on the landing at the top of the stairs. Together we watched our giant wedding party—our siblings, cousins, closest friends—process up the aisle, followed by our dads, each escorting two nieces, our ring bearers. He winked at me.

"Here we go," he said.

In minutes our mothers would walk us down the stairs and up the aisle and he would become my husband. I'd been to so many weddings, celebrated couples I cherished, but this was Jason and my day, the celebration of a love I never thought I'd find.

I took a deep cleansing breath and Jason gave my hand a quick little squeeze. My brother had joked that Jason was "just what every middle-aged, fat guy longed for—another younger and more handsome brother." Jason wasn't perfect. I hated the way he insisted on putting almond milk in my coffee, or teased me for being a typical youngest sibling, something only an oldest sibling like him would scoff at. But we had fun in all parts of our life together, even in traffic—which made Los Angeles paradise. I respected Jason's steadfast commitment to his sobriety, admired how even after fifteen years sober, he continued to honor that commitment with humanity and humility by sponsoring others in recovery. Most of all, I loved his kindness and attentiveness, the way when we had a misunderstanding, he always reached to fill the crack in our relationship with love.

I squeezed his hand back.

———

"Mark and Jason want to start a new tradition right now that is based on one of our most sacred rituals during this season," Peggy continued from below us. "The ceremonial coin toss to see who will take the field first."

My friend Kim came forward, a referee jersey pulled over the top of her dress.

"Forgive me," she said. "This is my first time refereeing a wedding." She tossed the coin, and I held my breath. I didn't care who walked down the aisle first. But it was my habit to stop breathing when the odds were wide open, the outcomes unknown. Jason's proxy called heads and won the toss, and suddenly the string quartet was playing Jason's processional music, "Falling Slowly," the Glen Hansard song from the musical *Once*, which we'd seen together in London the year before. He glanced at me and started down the stairs, arm in arm with his mom.

My mom grabbed my hand like she had a million times before. Walking me into kindergarten on the first day, and the second day, and the last day. I was not a very brave child. She gave me strength and eased my fear with her soft voice and unwavering love. Now, with her stance tall, shoulders back, smile bright with joy, she was ready to escort her baby down the aisle.

My song was playing, "Halo," by Beyoncé. Mom and I started down the stairs, three hundred faces lifting toward us. I was smiling and crying at the same time.

"Mom," I said as we reached the aisle, love on all sides of us, Jason beaming at me, "thank you for making all my dreams come true."

Then I was standing with Jason, my hands in his hands.

"Lovely men," Peggy said. "The moment has arrived."

Now I know that at 5:10 that October afternoon, as I vowed, "I promise to be honest, kind, patient, and forgiving—and sometimes admit I'm wrong," and Jason said, "I promise to let you love me like you love me, even when there are times when I don't feel like I can let you love me like you do," a bus pulled into the Greyhound station three miles away and a pregnant woman with a baby in a soaked diaper stepped into the hot evening sun.

As I said, "I promise to be your partner in life's adventures—and to always make sure we have protein bars so no one gets hangry," and Jason said, "I promise to continue to sign up for the many incredible adventures we bring to each other's lives, whether that be a journey across the world or bringing home a dog from a charity auction, and I promise to be there alongside you, cleaning up after any of the things left behind from the many adventures we have," the woman in the bus station waited for her mother-in-law, who was supposed to pick her up.

As I said, "I promise to support your ambitions and aspirations because your gifts make our world so much better," and Jason vowed, "I promise to hold your heart in my hands, and never squeeze it too tight, and never hold it too loosely, but to let it grow, beat, breathe, all the while knowing it always has my protection and care," the woman was alone.

At the Ebell, the string quartet launched into "Crazy in Love" and Jason and I practically levitated up the aisle; husband and husband, cheered on by the joy and affection of our dearest family and friends. It was the fairy-tale moment we had imagined and planned for. But we'd forgotten how grim and terrifying fairy tales can be. How their protective alchemy works through caution and warning.

As Jason and I bathed in the warmth of our community's love, a young woman got into the car of the only person she had to call, the mother of the man she was escaping.

We didn't know how complicated a happily ever after could be.

Chapter 3

Baby Fever

A couple of months after saying "I do," Jason and I sat side by side on a couch in the San Fernando Valley, in a house converted to an office, with the mauve-and-white minimalism of a Botox clinic. It smelled faintly of cats. The owner, a willowy platinum blonde with a Zen smile, introduced us to her employee, a former surrogate mother.

"I had two kids of my own," the surrogate mom said. "I just really wanted to help another couple experience the same happiness of being parents."

"There are other families ahead of you in line," the owner said, "but we have at least two surrogates who I'm sure would be excited to meet you. We can get you started on the matching process as soon as you're ready."

I smiled and nodded, but it blew my mind to think there were people who were willing to do this. It wasn't like donating blood. It wasn't even like donating a kidney. I was sitting in a room with someone who was willing to put her whole body, her life, on the line so that people like Jason and me, who couldn't have biological kids on our own, could be parents. It didn't seem possible. And it didn't seem exactly fair. I wasn't like a lot of my friends who always imagined they'd be parents or Jaime, who had dreamed of becoming a mom ever since we were little kids.

Thinking of Jaime made my breath hitch and my smile falter. Every milestone in my life was marked by her absence. Even visiting this office, contemplating such a monumental and happy decision, made my heart ache because she wasn't here to share it with me.

A few weeks after we turned twenty-three, Jaime's intoxicated boyfriend drove their car into a tree, and she died. I thought a lot, too much maybe, about all the important experiences she'd never have, including the one that mattered to her the most: having a child. She would never get to build a life and a home, to protect and care for another soul, to love and be loved. I didn't grow up with the same desire. Jaime's childhood dream of marriage and parenting was unattainable for a boy like me.

I didn't dream of someday getting to be a father. I was too busy dreaming of someday getting to be me.

The few times I had thought about having a biological child I wondered if I could handle parenting a kid like me, one who constantly lived in fear of having his secret discovered; one who believed he only had permission to be himself at home, that his personal safety stopped at his front door. Or one who had to step into costume and assume a role every time he left the house. The idea of watching a child live out my insecurities was excruciating. It wasn't until I had finally shoveled aside the mound of shame and self-loathing I had been living under that I began seeing myself and parenting differently. Beneath that pile of negativity was a strength, an ability to empathize and relate to a child struggling for acceptance.

It wasn't just me who changed. As I got older and braver, the whole world changed. The early 2000s, when I came out, saw a rapid upswing in gay rights. We went from closets and clubs to boardrooms and stages, from "don't ask, don't tell" to "here and queer," and from shame to pride. I found and freed myself in time to love and be loved. But Jaime would never get to know who I became or that I'd get to live out her dream.

On the ride to Malibu, on our very first date, Jason asked if I'd ever thought about parenting. "Yeah, but not until recently," I said, honestly. "Marriage and kids; it's all new to us." He nodded slowly in agreement.

"What about you?" I asked.

"I want to have kids," he responded without hesitation. "My sister had a baby, a girl, last year and she's changed the way I see everything." Smiling, he added, "I can't get back to Pittsburgh often enough to see her."

The more time we spent together I could see what an amazing father Jason would become. We visited his family and I watched how effortlessly he engaged with his nieces and coddled his newborn nephew. He was a natural. Perhaps having a brother who was fifteen years younger had given him a leg up. His prowess gave me confidence, knowing I would be tag-teaming parenthood with an all-star. And having a baby quickly became a question of *how*, not *when*.

We wanted two or three kids and ruled out private adoption from the start. We had friends who had waited years to be selected by birth parents, and we were impatient. I wanted a timeline, something that felt like we were working toward the end goal. Jason also loved the idea of foster-adopting, but we wanted to see *if* and *where* surrogacy would fit into our plan. We knew surrogacy would take time. We'd have to find a surrogate and select an egg donor long before we would even start the nine months of gestation.

Before the wedding, surrogacy was our "someday, maybe, who knows" option, but now, suddenly, I felt different. To be married. To be married to a man. To be married to a man I loved who was obviously born to be a father, and with whom I could have biological kids. It was more than the twenty-five-year-old me who had confessed to his parents he was gay could have ever dreamed possible.

When I made that call thirteen years earlier, I was so terrified it took two vodka tonics and an hourlong pep talk from Buffy to work up the courage to dial my parents' number. I had moved to Des Moines, Iowa, six months earlier to work on a coordinated campaign for the state's incumbent Democratic senator and governor—and I'd met someone. I had been skating along the edges of my sexuality, never allowing things to progress far or long enough for a relationship to form. But this time was different.

I was already crying when my mother picked up the phone, and when I heard her voice the floodgates opened. I tried to speak, but I could barely catch my breath between sobs. "Mark? What's wrong? What happened?" her pitch rising with alarm as I struggled to get the ragged sounds coming out of my mouth to resemble words.

Finally, I sputtered, "I'm gay."

Her response was immediate, unequivocal: "Nothing you could ever say or do could change the way I feel about you. Nothing." I sat still, quietly replaying her words in my head.

She exhaled. Relieved, she added, "Oh honey, I thought you were going to tell me you were hurt or had been in an accident and hurt someone else."

I asked her to tell Dad. I wasn't ready to say it again. She agreed and said she'd call me back.

I closed my flip phone and sat in the dark, trying to process the irrevocable shift I'd just made to my world. Coming out to my parents was also coming out to myself, which made it all real. Now that I had said the words aloud, there was no going back. This was one of life's nonrefundable, no-money-back declarations. It meant I was accepting gay as a part of my identity. A brand I would wear for life.

Waiting for Mom to call back, I stared out the window and watched the snow falling under the soft glow of the streetlights outside. I had heard stories of people whose families stopped speaking to them after they came out, but I had no reason to expect or even fear the worst from my parents. I knew there were no disclaimers to their love. I felt lighter, like the Buick I'd been carrying on my back had finally been lifted. I wasn't sure if this lightness would last, but I wanted it to. The snow continued to fall, dusting the hoods of the cars parked below. The moon glowed in the distance, just as it had the night before and the night before that. I leaned closer to the window, my breath fogging the glass. I may have shifted my world, but as far as I could tell, nothing else was changed.

My phone rang. Only a few minutes had passed. Mom handed the phone to Dad and he opened with a joke. In tense or uncomfortable situations, he becomes Jerry Seinfeld—either a gift or a curse, depending on the moment. I don't remember exactly what he said, because all I heard was "I love you."

Coming out was the scariest thing I had ever done for myself, and I wanted to share the peace I had found. By 2004, Lambda Legal had filed a lawsuit in Iowa that would eventually lead to the 2009 court ruling making Iowa the third state to recognize same-sex marriage. I wanted to be a part of the fight and so I founded One Iowa, a grassroots organization working to increase public support for marriage equality. I didn't know it then, but this was the first step in my journey to this moment, sitting next to my husband on a couch flecked with cat dander, about to make our first major parenting decision. I wasn't sure whether it was allergies making my eyes water, or my overwhelming emotions.

There was something else too. Something my neighbor Joe had reminded me of a few days earlier when we were bringing our trash barrels in from the curb. He mentioned how much he and his wife had enjoyed our wedding. "We were late getting into the room for the ceremony," he said. "We sat in the back, and I was thinking, if this were twenty years ago, how many of these men would be sick or dying?" Joe bought his house the year I was born. A professor and musician, he'd loved and lost more friends to AIDS than I would ever know.

———

Sitting in this office, I wanted to be a father more than at any point in my life. I wanted to see the reflection of myself, the strengths and the flaws, and be there to comfort my child if they inherited my fears. It was also a way of honoring the men who'd wanted the opportunities Jason and I had, but who'd been born at the wrong time, or whose lives had been cut short. I saw our choice to marry and parent as a way to celebrate our place in a generation that was changing the landscape. The *Leave It to Beaver* hetero gender roles that had dogged our culture for decades wouldn't even remotely apply to our family. And if surrogacy could help Jason and me have biological children, maybe Jaime's dream would live on through our family too.

"Would you like us to add you to the list of families looking for a surrogate?" the woman asked.

Jason squeezed my hand, and I squeezed back.

"Let's do it. Let's get on the list," I said.

A few weeks later, Jason and I were in North Carolina for a New Year's Eve wedding. We had breakfast with my friend Mariah, whom I'd met a few years earlier through my work with Youth Villages LifeSet, a program that provides support to some of the roughly twenty thousand young adults who age out of the foster care system each year.[1] Mariah was twenty and a freshman in college when her group of LifeSet youth scholars was brought to Los Angeles on an enrichment trip. My assignment was to help match each young person with a mini internship that supported their dreams and ambitions, not simply those in areas they were familiar with.

When I first met Mariah, she'd been friendly but guarded. Over time I'd earned her trust. Now she was a senior in college and as we ate our omelets and avocado toast in a strip mall diner, her warmth and liveliness bubbled over.

"How long till you two are toting around a car seat and a pack 'n' play?" she asked.

Jason smiled and gave me a happy wink. "We're hoping soon," he said.

As we continued to laugh and chat, Mariah confided that someday she wanted to write a book about her experience growing up in foster care. I was struck by her resilience and grit in the face of so much adversity; hers was the kind of success story every social worker hopes for in the children they serve.

"I grew up without my biological mom," she said. "I had foster moms. Lots of good maternal figures. But they all had kids of their own before they met me, and I never quite felt like I came first."

It was the first time she had spoken so openly about her past. Her words, between bites of eggs, revealed the pain of a little girl missing her mother. As she recalled the discomfort of school projects—the family tree assignment or the papier-mâché Mother's Day flowers—I saw that hidden behind her infectious smile was the broken heart of a child. All these harmless school activities were reminders that she was different. That belonging, for her, was always just out of reach.

It occurred to me, maybe for the first time, that any child raised by two dads would also grow up without a mom. How would we explain this to a child? For a child adopted through foster care, it seemed obvious. They'd come into our lives with a history and the truth of their journey could be spoon-fed in age-appropriate portions over time. They would, most likely, have a mom. She just wouldn't be raising them. But, for a child born through surrogacy, how would we help them make sense of a process I barely understood? I thought of how a friend's daughter who was born through surrogacy describes her surrogate as "some nice lady in Palm Springs."

We wouldn't be the first men to raise children without a mom, but the gravity of what that might mean for a child had never crossed my mind. We didn't have a robust generation of same-sex parents ahead of us we could learn from and look to for guidance. The gay men I knew raising kids had all been married to women prior to coming out. They all shared custody of their children with highly engaged mothers.

But, more than any of that, I now couldn't help but wonder, if Jason and I had a biological child first, would a foster child inevitably share Mariah's feeling of always coming second?

After breakfast we climbed into our rental car—a cheesy black Mustang convertible, somehow the only option available when we'd arrived—and Jason spoke the words we were both thinking: "What if we waited on surrogacy and fostered first?"

As we drove to the airport my mind buzzed with the question. I'd gotten swept up in the possibility of bringing home a tiny infant, a little person who would carry Jason's genes or mine, whom we'd think about through the months of gestation, wondering whether our baby would have dirty-blond hair like me or be a ginger like Jason. I'd caught baby fever and somehow compartmentalized what I knew through my work in child advocacy: that more than 400,000 American children are in foster care on any given day,[2] roughly the same population as the number of residents of Miami, Florida. That each year in the US alone, more than 1,700 children are killed for reasons connected to abuse and neglect.[3] That too often, the cycle of abuse continues: parents who abuse their children are more likely to have experienced abuse in their own childhoods.[4]

I thought about Mariah's words, as if she were warning us about the unintentional harm we could cause for another child. About how our good intentions could leave one of our own children feeling like they never truly belong. Belonging to my family was my safety net, my foundation, my shield. I wanted more than anything to ensure all our future children knew they belonged.

By the time we were checking in for our flight, we had a new game plan. We would foster-adopt one of the more than 100,000 children already born who needed loving, capable parents and a permanent home.

———

We wasted no time. Two weeks later we had an informational meeting at our home with Cathy Allan, the program coordinator for Children's Bureau, one of a few dozen nonprofit foster family agencies contracted to support Los Angeles County's Department of Children and Family Services. I could hear Jason upstairs talking when I opened the kitchen door. Then I heard a woman's voice with that loud, grating, painfully familiar accent say, "That's wicked awesome."

What was going on? Was one of my aunts in town? That was Boston. That piercing shrill of an accent I'd beaten out of my system was a symphony of nostalgia. I raced to the hallway to see Jason and a woman I'd never met, but already felt a connection to, walking down the stairs.

As we made our way to the living room Cathy said she'd been in Los Angeles for twenty years, but her accent hadn't faded a bit. If she traded in her pantsuit for a Patriots hoodie and a Dunkin' Donuts iced coffee she could easily pass as a member of my family. There was no need to meet with other agencies. My mind was made up.

"Mahk, how are you from Brockton? You don't even have an accent," she said.

I smiled. The way she butchered my name reminded me of home. "One of my first jobs out of college was as a press secretary for a congressman from the panhandle, back when Florida elected Democrats," I explained. "Reporters would call all the time and ask to speak with 'Mack' or 'Max.' That's when I knew I had to do something about it."

We sat down in the living room and Jason left to bring coffee and tea in from the kitchen. Cathy turned to me. "You've got plenty of room, how do you feel about siblings?"

"Great," I said. It didn't take much thought—it was certainly in our plan to reconnect with the surrogacy agency within the next few years so the siblings could grow up together.

Jason ran back into the room, a dish towel over his shoulder. "What did you just say?"

"That we're good with siblings," I said.

I couldn't tell by the look on his face or the tone of his voice if he was shocked or faking it to amuse Cathy. He and I had discussed having more than one. She had asked me a hypothetical question, and I couldn't see us turning away a second child down the road.

I'd watched my sister and brother and cousins become parents. I'd seen my friends have children. I wondered if the next baby I held would be my own.

Chapter 4

Love and Risk

By the end of foster parent training, I was no less passionate about the path we had chosen, but I did feel overwhelmed by the huge list of unknowns, including the most foundational reality of fostering: that you don't know how long the child will be in your life. The whole point of fostering is to care for kids when their biological parents or other family members are unable to do so. It's not meant to be a permanent arrangement. Ideally, the biological parent takes an anger management class or enters recovery or finds a home or comes out of prison, and the child reunifies with the parents. But reality and the ideal don't always align. We were told that 55 percent of kids in foster care in California reunify with their birth parents.[1] The others either move on to adoption by an extended family member or foster parent, or they age out of the system.

We had signed up to foster-adopt with the belief that it was a surefire way to start our family. I had this rosy vision of celebrating our adoption ceremony in a courtroom filled with all our friends and family and a judge smiling brightly, holding up a signed certificate. We would all marvel at how the universe had conspired to bring Jason and me and this perfect baby together for a joy-filled life. I had yet to confront the obvious reality that for us to foster and eventually adopt a child meant that other parents would have to lose their children. And a child, no matter how hard we tried, would have an indelible bond to parents who were unable or deemed incapable of properly caring for them.

During our home inspection and disclosure meeting, the last stage of our certification, a social worker walked through our house with a ten-page checklist:

- Walls and ceilings are clean and in good repair.
- Doors are in good condition and operate properly.
- Room temperature is a minimum of 68 degrees and a maximum of 85 degrees.
- Knives, scissors, razors, and other sharp objects are inaccessible to children.
- There is a working phone on premises.
- Home is free of flies and other insects and woodpile has been re-stacked and checked for spiders in the last six months.
- Building and grounds are free from hazards and rubbish.
- Powdered milk is not used as a beverage.

When she placed a thermometer under the kitchen faucet to inspect that the water temperature did not exceed 120 degrees, I thought, *I really hope it doesn't because I don't know how in hell to turn that down.* Then came the disclosure questions. The social worker interviewed us separately about our relationship history, our sex lives, past drug use, and our family backgrounds.

"Has anyone close to you died?" she asked. "Has anyone been a victim of abuse? Has there been a murder?"

I talked about my aunt Cheryl's death to cancer, about the car accident that took Jaime.

"Anything else?" she prodded.

I shook my head.

"Are you absolutely sure?"

Then I realized what she meant—that Jason must have told her about my cousin's daughter Joanna, whom I'd only met once or twice. About an incident so horrific it was both impossible to forget and impossible to think about.

It happened in early August 2007, when I was living in Iowa, working for Hillary Clinton's presidential campaign. On a campaign, every day is Monday. I spent my weeks traveling the state in a motorcade, four or five large events a day, eating at Maid Rites and Dairy Queens, any topic that didn't pertain to precinct captains or ethanol policy a blur. Though she found out early Sunday morning, my mom knew I'd be working through the weekend and waited until later that night to call. Her voice was thin and shaky.

"Honey, it's bad news. It's really bad."

She told me to pull up the *Boston Globe* headlines, and there was my cousin Heather, standing outside of her home weeping, flanked by her husband and other family members and friends.

On Saturday night, Heather had brought her six-year-old daughter, Joanna, to a sleepover at the safest place in the world—Heather's mom's house in Weymouth, Massachusetts. Joanna bounced in through the door of her grandmother's house, carrying her Disney princess sleeping bag and chattering about movies and pancakes. Early Sunday morning, she was found wrapped in a comforter in the back seat of a stolen car, her body naked, badly bruised, and showing signs of sexual assault. There was blood in her mouth; her legs were gray and discolored. She'd been abducted from the room where she was sleeping, her assailant climbing on top of a car to cut the window screen. Her grandmother didn't even know Joanna was missing until police arrived in the morning to report that she'd been found dead. If my aunt had woken up, she may have been killed too.

And the police told her it wasn't a stranger who'd raped and abducted Joanna.

It was Joanna's twenty-year-old cousin and former foster brother, Ryan.

Now, almost nine years later, preparing to become a parent myself, the pain and grief of Joanna's murder struck me anew. I remembered hugging Heather at the wake, how she called out "Mah-key" when she saw me, how she couldn't believe I'd flown all that way. "We're family," I'd told her. "That's what family does."

But that was the irony. Joanna's death made it plain that being family doesn't guarantee love or safety. Love is inherently risky. In love there are no contracts, no assurances. Extending your heart to someone, a partner, a friend, a child, is the ultimate act of vulnerability. The universe makes no promises. Yet, to fully love, you must accept the risk and proceed anyway.

I've often thought of Heather and her husband, Jerry, in the same light as parents of school shooting victims. They were all trying their best to love and protect their children. They did everything in their power to do right by their kids. But unlike a parent's love, which can have no limits, their ability to keep a child safe is bound. You can't plan for the unimaginable.

"Heather didn't do anything wrong," I told the social worker. "She's a great mother, who protected her babies with the vigilance of the Secret Service." I found myself tensing up, the pain of nine years earlier resurfacing. "Ryan was an addict. He broke into his grandmother's house probably to steal some cash. When he found Joanna lying there . . ." I stopped to catch my breath and realign my words with my thoughts. "What he did is incomprehensible."

Jason and I were ready to love and risk our hearts for a child. We wanted a baby, one who hadn't experienced whatever pain or trauma Ryan had endured before he was sent to live at a facility for teens with behavioral issues. We would build a safe home and environment for our baby to grow up, free from abuse and neglect. We'd teach them to be aware in public, like my mom had taught me. We'd do our best to mitigate danger, and if we were lucky, we would be spared the horrific fate Heather and Jerry had endured.

———

By the end of April, we were officially certified to foster a child. We had formally checked the box indicating we'd accept babies ages zero to three because, as we'd learned, newborns-only was not an option. It all happened so fast. We didn't have a crib or any of the essentials expectant parents usually stockpile, and we were both in the middle of major projects: Jason had been working with Harry Belafonte to promote awareness of social justice issues, which culminated in a music festival in May, around the same time I would be traveling to the Cannes Film Festival to enlist celebrity support for the Brady Campaign to Prevent Gun Violence. We needed the month to get ready and I wanted to take two weeks off work when the baby arrived. We were frantic to finish our work and excited about our looming parenthood.

Jason and I were like kids counting down the days until summer vacation. We didn't know enough to be scared.

We told Cindy we would be available to take in a baby starting on June 1, and I left for Europe knowing that upon my return, life would never be the same.

After my work in France was done, I stopped over in London to visit my friends Oscar and Kristin, who had just given birth to their third child, a boy named Harry. Oscar, a US government employee working in Kenya, was given the option to temporarily relocate his family as Kristin's due date approached, so they had settled in England.

I exited the Baker Street station at half past twelve in the afternoon. We had planned to meet at one o'clock and I knew better than to mess with the schedule of new parents. Regent's Park was just across the street from the Underground station, so I took a walk through Queen Mary's Gardens to kill time. I'd been so consumed with getting my work in order, making sure my clients were aware of my situation and

that my staff was ready to pick up the slack in my absence, that I'd
spent little time processing my excitement and fears around parenting. Stopping to admire the roses, blooming in harmonious shades of
pink, yellow, orange, and white, the rewards of a caretaker's love and
nurturing, I thought about parenthood and what excited me about
it—selecting the best schools and encouraging their creative or athletic
interests, the pride I'd feel in their accomplishments, large and small. I
wanted to provide for them, like my parents had provided for me. The
allure of parenting has a spellbinding effect, like the head of a rose,
distracting your eye from thorns—the diaper changes, the tantrums,
the middle-of-the-night feedings. The rewards and costs of a labor of
love. But was I ready for the pokes and jabs? Did I have the patience to
be the parent I wanted to be?

I arrived at Oscar and Kristin's place shortly after one o'clock, my
heart beating with excitement at the thought of sharing the news that
Jason and I were about to become parents at the same time as my old
friends. The entrance to the concrete and brick building was tucked
around the corner, hidden behind Bill's Baker Street Restaurant. I
passed a woman in hospital scrubs on my way into the flat, a nurse, I
presumed. After exchanging hugs, I asked, "Is everything okay?"

"Oh, yeah," Kristin said, cradling Harry in one arm and waving off
my concern with the other. She explained that although Harry was a
US citizen, born to two American parents, he was given a National
Health Service (NHS) number at the hospital, which meant that he
was entitled to the same free public health care services as any UK res-
ident. "The woman who visited was a midwife, a sort of an all-in-one
nurse and social worker," she continued. "She was here to give Harry a
checkup and make sure we're all settling in and doing okay."

"Wow," I said, thinking how different access to health care is in the
US. "That's pretty incredible. Does every new mom get this service?"

"I believe it's offered to anyone with an NHS number," she answered.

After all I had learned in foster parent training, I could see how
a universal child welfare program like this could be better poised

to respond to early risks and warning signs—from troubles with breastfeeding to postnatal depression to unemployment or economic insecurity—before they escalated into circumstances that might endanger a child. Kristin is a registered nurse by trade and Harry was her third child. She definitely knew what to expect. Maybe she didn't need this service, but *what if she had*?

I couldn't help but wonder about our future foster child. *What if they require serious medical care? God, I hope they don't. But if they do, I will advocate. I will find the experts. I will get the appointment even if it requires weeks of torturous hold music. But am I ready for the minute-to-minute realities of a sick child? Cleaning vomit, wiping boogers, and soothing nightmares when I'm exhausted myself?* Parenting is a lot more action than advocacy. I listened to Kristin, smiled and nodded, but inside my head a question was playing on repeat: *Am I ready for everything I just signed up for?*

We spent the next hour catching up and chatting about their adventures in Africa. Every time the older children spoke, Oscar smiled, a proud glint in his eyes. He was attentive, listening to them, valuing their contributions to the adult conversation. I wanted to be a dad just like him. As I sat on the green velvet couch in their living room, baby Harry swaddled tightly in a blue blanket asleep in my arms, I looked up and Oscar was smiling at me.

"Look at you, buddy," he said. "You're a natural." That's when I realized I had forgotten to share my news.

"Jason and I are expecting."

———

On the long flight home, I thought more about the midwife's visit and how her role was to detect the smoke before it turned into fire. She could prescribe interventions and services to help struggling families. How many children would be prevented from entering the system if a program like this existed in the States? In foster parent training we learned how to care for a child, but I wanted to know what holes in policy were allowing families to collapse and kids to fall into foster care. I tried to imagine how I would have felt at six years old, being ripped away from the sanctuary my mother provided. I could see myself, a little boy with a bowl cut and gap teeth, clutching my blanket and trembling as a social worker told me I'd be going to live with strangers. The powerlessness sent a jolt of fear through my veins before sadness for the children who actually experience this took over.

My mind raced and I couldn't escape the overarching question: When should kids stay with their birth parents, and when should they be removed? Throwing this question at Google, I quickly learned that foster care is governed at the federal and state level and often administered at a county or sometimes municipal level and that entire judicial systems had been created to ensure the rights of parents and children were protected. With all these layers of administration, there's little uniformity and no clear consensus as to when a child should be removed.

So much depends on whether we think about it as a child *protection* system or a child *welfare* system. If it's a child *protection* system, then there's a limited role for government to intervene—only when children's physical safety is compromised.

But even this is hard to determine. We can generally understand what constitutes physical abuse, yet there's no clear definition of neglect. It's subjective. What looks like neglect to one person—no adult at home all night while parents work second or third jobs on the swing shift—could look like devoted parenting while grappling with poverty to someone else.

And it's never just one adversity or challenge that determines whether or not a child enters care. It's cumulative. A constellation of risks. The baby was born with low birth weight—a risk factor because it may indicate there was substance use, or that the child is harder to care for. The mom is young. The family is low-income. There isn't a father's name listed on the birth certificate. And so on. Each additional social or economic risk factor makes it even more likely a family will come to the attention of the system, and more likely a child will end up in care. This is where a child *welfare* system comes into play.

Each risk factor signals an intervention point where an extra support or social service might have better shielded the child. Food stamps, Section 8 housing, addiction treatment, parenting support, child care, domestic violence services—with upstream interventions like these, we might ease the burdens on families that sometimes result in abuse and neglect.

Other countries handle the distinction between child welfare and child protection very differently. In Denmark there's a much lower threshold for involvement—but also a much higher rate of upstream intervention. Instead of waiting for an instance of abuse to trigger action, they offer a robust social safety net, monitoring risks and offering services early on, long before harm has occurred. For example, if a pregnant woman who is known to have struggled with substance use in the past shows up at a prenatal visit, she is immediately connected with services to help her recover during the pregnancy, and after the birth, she is visited *every day* for a month to make sure she's staying on track and not putting the infant in danger.

That kind of early intervention doesn't exist in the US. In California, hospital providers decide whether to refer substance-exposed infants to child protection.[2] But there's no hard-and-fast rule about how states across the US approach prenatal substance use. Similarly, there's not a universally accepted approach to newborn drug screening. Instead, hospitals are required to establish their own criteria, which often include maternal signs of withdrawal, the absence of prenatal care, or known drug history. This risk-based approach relies heavily on health care workers to identify signs and opens the door wide for potential bias. Many argue that lower-income or undocumented women without access to affordable health care could be unfairly targeted.

Some agencies invoke special legislation that allows them to bypass reunification services if a parent has had previous failed attempts to reunite with a substance-exposed newborn.[3] But typically, substance-exposed infants are only removed if it's expected the parent will continue to use substances after the baby goes home, or if the parent is unwilling or unable to care for the baby due to their substance use.[4]

The US model is construed as a child protection system, not a child welfare system. There's a very high threshold for agency involvement. In some ways, this is a good thing. Children aren't typically removed from their parents unless the abuse or neglect is confirmed and usually only if it is significant or chronic. But this also means we don't always intervene to help families where there's a *risk* of abuse, or where abuse is likely to escalate. I couldn't help but wonder, because we haven't supported parents early on, before a child's safety is on the line, do we lack the moral authority to intervene or detain a child later? Would simply removing a child from their birth parents guarantee their safety?

While many foster parents provide loving and nurturing environments for the children in their care, many children and youths experience continued maltreatment in foster care, which often goes undetected or leads to repeated and disruptive transitions from placement to placement. Evidence suggests unsafe foster homes affect Black and Indigenous children most severely.[5,6] How much of this could be prevented?

Missing opportunities for early support and intervention puts kids at risk; it also doesn't give families a fair chance to turn things around before removing a child becomes the best option.

I was beginning to come to terms with two uncomfortable truths. First, that for Jason and me to become parents, a child would have to experience extreme harm. Second, there was no clear consensus about when kids should stay with their birth parents and when they should be removed. The system meant to *protect* children from harm ironically required them to be harmed in order to intervene. It was baffling.

I was starting to see some of the flaws in the system. I didn't know how important the distinction between child welfare and protection would become.

Now I was asking myself if I could risk my whole heart in a situation where no matter what I did, I couldn't influence the outcome. I had started this journey wondering, what if we fall short?

By the end I was asking, what if we fall in love?

Chapter 5

Rainbow Baby Gate

It's not one baby." Jason sounded breathless, like he had just gotten back from a run. "It's two. Brothers. One is thirteen months old, the other three months. We have to decide an hour ago."

"How are two brothers ten months apart?" I was so shocked it was all I could think to ask.

"That's about how long it takes to make a baby, Mark," he said patiently, then added, "You're so pretty, babe."

"Shut up," I said, laughing nervously at his way of teasing me whenever I said something less than clever. I was confused. We'd only prepared for one kid. Why were they asking us to take two?

This day had played out in my mind countless times, but none of this was as I'd imagined. Jason and I were supposed to be together when we got the call from Cathy at Children's Bureau, or at the very least be in the same city. Instead I was hundreds of miles from home, standing in a stranger's office, being reminded of how little I knew about the reproductive process or the time it takes to make a baby.

A little over two weeks had passed since June 1, the date we had told the agency we'd be ready for a placement. Sixteen days during which we had roller-coastered from ecstatically thinking the call would come any minute to trying to just go about our lives and not think about it. According to the Facebook group shared by our training class, most of the other approved families had babies placed with them within forty-eight hours of their available dates, so we were surprised we hadn't heard already. Of course, the call came the one day that month that I had to travel for work.

A year earlier, I had committed to my friend Mie-Na that I would speak about building public awareness for social causes at a conference she was organizing for students at Stanford University. I'd also promised to sit in on some meetings with faculty in the afternoon. I had arrived in San Francisco early that morning and was booked on a flight back to LA later that night.

My phone never rang, but when we left the conference room after my first meeting of the afternoon my signal returned just strong enough to let me know I'd missed six calls from Jason and one from the Google phone number we'd set up on both our phones for baby-related calls—which I had saved in my contacts as "Bat Phone."

"Fuck," I said loud enough for Mie-Na to hear.

"Is everything okay?" she asked.

"Jason called," I said, staring at the flashing signal bars on the phone—one, none, one, none. "I think we may have a kid." Mie-Na's eyes grew big, a smile taking over her face. "Oh my god. Oh my god," she gasped.

"I can't get a signal to call him back." I was starting to panic.

"Shirley's office," she declared, grabbing my hand and leading me quickly down a long hallway to a corner office. "It's the only one with a signal."

I kept hitting send and finally heard ringing on the other end as Mie-Na opened the door without even knocking. I followed her into a narrow, windowless office where a petite woman with long, dark hair and glasses sat behind a desk on the opposite end. Jason picked up as Mie-Na explained to her colleague that I was her friend and needed to take an important call from her office. The woman looked over at me and nodded her approval.

Jason and I had prepared for this moment. My heart raced as I pulled up the checklist I'd created on my phone to guide our decision-making in what we knew would be an emotional moment. We didn't care about the child's race or gender, but other factors needed consideration.

Age? Would we get our baby?

Health? Did the baby require specialized care?

Drug exposure?

Has the child been in foster care before? If so, why did he or she leave that placement?

Do the biological parents have other kids? Any other kids that were placed in foster care or adopted? All of these questions could signal whether or not the parents were likely to reunify with the child. We wanted a slam-dunk case; a happy, healthy baby, ready for adoption on day one. I'd hoped these questions would help us weigh the odds.

Is there another family member who is interested in taking the kids? If so, we might just have the baby for a short time while they get their house in order to welcome the child.

What do we know about the family history and mental health of each biological parent? We wanted to see what we could find out early, to avoid surprises down the road.

———

"*Two* kids, Jay? Two kids under the age of two?"

"Remember when you told Boston Cathy we'd be open to siblings?" he said, a hint of nervous laughter in his voice. "Well, that's what she found us."

I remembered when she came to our home, when we first started the process, and asked if we were open to siblings. I'd said yes, but hadn't considered the possibility of a simultaneous placement. I assumed she meant if the mom got pregnant a few years later, could they call?

Jason put me on hold while he conferenced in Cathy to answer our questions.

"Oh my god," I muttered to myself before locking eyes with Shirley, the stranger whose office I had commandeered. "Sorry. My husband and I are having a baby—or two," I said, hoping my life unfolding in her office was at least more entertaining than the spreadsheet I was keeping her from reviewing.

She smiled at me and started to say something, but Jason returned to the line with the social worker, and I cut her off. Cathy told us the boys were in a county office now and were ready to be placed. I looked across the room. Shirley had stopped working and was hanging on my every word. I made a writing motion with my hand and she leapt from her chair, racing around the desk with a pen and pad of Post-its.

"The court sent them to live with their grandmother about a month ago," Cathy said. I heard the sound of papers ruffling in the background, like she was searching a cluttered desk for the notes she'd jotted down when the county called. "But it looks like she's no longer able to care for them and has asked the county to find them a foster home."

"Why? Why can't she care for them?" I asked.

"I don't know, Mahk." She still pronounced my name like family, but today her tone was serious and official, the friendly back-and-forth I remembered from her first visit displaced by the gravity of the decision Jason and I were about to make. "Two babies are a lot of work," she added, "and I don't know her situation."

I was only half-listening to Cathy's answers. A portrait of Jason and me with two boys had been painted in my mind and was stealing my attention. The initial shock of two kids had suddenly morphed into a feeling of exhilaration, like downhill skiing on a trail of fresh powder. Things were moving fast. An unexpected twist had steered us in a new direction, but I could get on board with it—an instant family.

"Maybe the grandmother is old or sick," I offered.

"I really don't know." She sounded genuinely at a loss. "When the county calls us about placing children, I ask a bunch of questions but most of the time they don't have a lot of answers. Let me tell you everything I know."

Cathy went on to tell us that the boys' mother had a child who had been adopted five or six years earlier by a relative, her brother, but he was unable or unwilling to care for them as well. We'd been told that parents who already lost one child to the system were less likely to reunify with their other children when they entered foster care. This time it wasn't just one child, it was two. It would be so much harder for her to reunify. Had Cathy served up the alley-oop? Was this our slam dunk?

"The mother has filed an appeal," she said. "That's pretty common, but it's more of a formality. The birth parents rarely ever win these appeals because judges don't like to overrule one another." We wanted to adopt, and Cathy had given all the right answers to our questions. The appeal sounded like it was nothing to worry about. But it still caused me some concern. Plus, two babies would be double the work. Fear of what I didn't know about the future, about parenting, was starting to take hold.

"The parents were granted three hours of supervised visits a week," she continued, "and they have to complete drug and alcohol rehabilitation."

"Do you know if the kids were exposed to drugs?" I asked.

"I don't," she said. "The caseworker said the children are in her office now and they are super cuddly."

"Aww. Well, what do we do?" I asked, throwing the question into the air like a jump ball, hoping someone would take the lead. All of the questions we'd prepared to keep our emotions out of the equation fell to the wayside. There were two children who were ready to come into our lives if we wanted them. If we were ready to open our lives and our hearts to them.

"They need a home," Jason said. "They need a home, and we want a family."

I could tell his mind was made up. He was excited and, as scared as

I felt, I was too. Excitement has the extraordinary ability to eclipse even the greatest of fears when a dream is within reach.

"We're doing this," I said, my voice rising. It was a question as much as a statement.

"We're doing this," Jason said firmly. "We're having a baby, two of them."

"Okay," Cathy's voice cut through. "I'll let the county know."

I pressed end and exhaled. I closed my eyes to take in the moment—shock, fear, and excitement all vying for my focus. I looked up and Shirley was standing next to me, still clutching the pen and Post-its. Our eyes met. A smile overtook both our faces.

"You're getting two babies," she shrieked, throwing her arms around my chest, her enthusiasm as contagious as it was adorable. We didn't have to say *yes*, but when the cards were laid out before us, it was a great hand. And we were all in.

———

Jason had received the placement call at one o'clock; by five o'clock, the children were at the house, and I was FaceTiming from a Lyft on the way to the airport, wishing I was home instead of catching my first glimpse of the boys who were now officially in our care from 360 miles away.

Jason had already figured out how we'd manage. Ethan, the one-year-old, would sleep in the crib in the nursery. Joe and Loyce, from next door, had offered us a bassinet—the same bassinet their children had slept in forty years ago, and had been passed down the street as other couples in the neighborhood had kids—for the infant, Logan. Jason had already set it up in our bedroom.

I leaned over my phone to get a better look.

Jason was holding Logan, who gurgled and smiled, moving his mouth around in that baby way, cracking himself up. Jason turned the phone so I could see Ethan, the thirteen-month-old, standing at the screen door. He was clutching a teething cookie and babbling to our one-hundred-pound Labrador, Brian, who was outside in the yard. Roxy, the thirteen-pound rat terrier I'd adopted twelve years earlier, followed Ethan's every step, holding a laserlike focus on the cookie.

"Say 'hi,'" Jason said, and Ethan, so big he could have easily passed for a four-year-old, stared at me with stunning blue eyes. He was a ginger like Jason, his hair longish, bangs jacked up as though he'd tried cutting them himself. He gave a happy, piercing yell and barreled off toward the living room.

"We miss you. We need you," Jason laughed. "Please come home now."

I hung out at the United Airlines counter for hours, trying to change my flight, but with the notorious Bay Area fog causing delays, they couldn't squeeze me onto an earlier plane. For most of the evening I was too caught up in the drama of getting home to freak out about what I'd find when I got there. I called my mom to share our news and the screenshots I'd grabbed from our FaceTime.

"Two? Two babies!" she shrieked into the phone so loud I had to hold it away from my ear. I could hear my dad questioning her in the background. "Paul, they got two babies. Brothers." They started talking over each other, and I couldn't understand what either of them was saying.

"Mom, I've never cared for an infant before," I said. "They don't come with an owner's manual."

I wanted to be home, to meet the boys, but the enormity of what lay ahead was starting to hit me.

"Don't worry about it, you'll be fine," she said. "When your brother was six months old, Daddy was in the navy and had to go away for a few weeks. I was so scared. I was twenty-one years old and had never slept in a house by myself, never mind with an infant, so I went to stay with Ma and Pa for two weeks."

Mom was twenty years old when she and Dad eloped. She had shared a bed in the projects of South Boston with her two younger sisters up until her wedding night. "I never thought about that." Ma and

Pa, Dad's parents, were empty nesters. They had room at their house and were excited to be grandparents.

"I wish you lived closer," I said.

"Oh, Mark. When can I come visit and meet the boys?" she asked.

"Jason's parents land tonight," I said, laughing. "Why don't you start shopping for flights?"

––––––

Finally on board the plane and on my way home, my mind was churning. What would it be like to hold babies who weren't my nieces or nephews or the children of my friends, but my foster sons, an infant and a toddler whose lives depended on my care? The ninety-minute flight felt like an eternity and the physical exhaustion of waking up at 4:00 a.m. was starting to take hold. Throughout taxi and takeoff, reaching our cruising altitude and then waiting for the captain to announce our final descent into Los Angeles, I tried to sleep, but adrenaline wasn't having any of that. I thought about holding the boys. Would they be afraid going to sleep in a strange house? Would they need some time to warm up to me? Did they miss their parents and grandmother? I thought about Jaime. The night sky was the only thing separating me from her dream of parenthood. Staring at the flashing lights on the wings, a peace began to wash over me. She had cried tears of joy when she passed along the message that I'd been accepted to study abroad at Oxford and I knew she'd be even more proud of me now.

Before long I was throwing open our wide red front door, dropping my bag inside the dimly lit living room, and being greeted by my cousin Christina, who was fifteen years younger than me and had just moved to Los Angeles. She had been staying with us for a few weeks and was supposed to have moved into her new apartment that morning. "Welcome home, Daddy," she joked, a giant smile radiating across her face. She wrapped her long, skinny arms around me, knocking my glasses with the brim of the Cubs hat holding back her blond hair.

"I thought you moved out already," I teased.

"I was about to head over to my new place when Jason got the call about the boys," she said, her smile broadening.

"I told her she wasn't allowed to leave until you got home," Jason interrupted from the dining room. He was standing in front of the hutch, holding the baby in his arms. I hadn't seen him open the swinging door that separates the kitchen from the rest of the house. "Come on," he said, motioning his head back toward the kitchen. "I was just making this guy a bottle. You can feed him." Christina and I raced behind him to the kitchen.

The center island was completely buried in bottles, nipples, tubs of formula, teething rings, swaddle blankets, baby monitors, ripped-up packaging. Logan was a point of calm at the center, gazing up at Jason and smiling, the most beautiful and perfect baby I'd ever seen.

"Where did all this stuff come from?" I asked Jason.

It looked like an entire Babies 'R' Us store had thrown up in our house. There was a high chair in the corner of the room that hadn't been there when I left this morning. It was a mess, covered in the remnants of a toddler's dinner.

"I was on the phone with my friend Lena when Cathy called," he explained. "She went to Target and spent a million dollars on all this stuff. The high chair belonged to her twins."

Jason gave me a tired, happy kiss and took me upstairs to the nursery, where Ethan was fast asleep in his crib, the mobile above his head playing a soft lullaby.

"Oh my god," I whispered, overcome.

Jason handed me the baby and Logan snuggled into me. I inhaled his fresh baby smell as I pulled him close. He opened his eyes and took me in. He didn't seem bothered at all to be in new arms. *Is this it?* I wondered. *Are these my kids? Will I watch them grow? Will theirs be the last faces I see at the end of my own life?* My heart broke wide.

It was close to 11:00 p.m. when the exhaustion hit. Jason sent me and the dogs off to bed. I placed Logan in the bassinet, brushed my teeth, and took one last look at him before climbing into my own bed.

Brian, the Lab, nestled himself underneath the bassinet, where he could keep a watchful eye. We were already in love.

I slept through two middle-of-the-night feedings and Jason's parents' arrival from the airport at 1:00 a.m.—months earlier we'd bought them tickets to see Steely Dan at the Hollywood Bowl, and by coincidence it was the same weekend the boys arrived. It was a lucky thing; Jason's dad, a nurse, and his mom, a teacher, were the ultimate grandparents, hands-on and loving. We were confident that with them in the house, we'd at least survive the first weekend of parenting.

I got up early with the baby, mixed my first bottle of formula, and sat in the living room holding Logan while he drank it. He was wrapped in a light blue swaddle blanket, his warm weight perfect in my arms. He studied my face, his gaze open and unbroken. For years I'd seen loved ones holding and feeding their children; now I was the one engaged in these universal actions of tenderness and care, so familiar and so profound.

When Ethan stirred through the monitor, Jason and I went into the nursery to get him. He was standing up in the crib in a white onesie, a pacifier in his mouth. He'd never seen me in person, and I'd expected that he'd need time to warm up, but as I lifted him, he smiled at me and grabbed my shoulders with his hands, instantly comfortable.

We were playing in the kitchen when Jason's mom came downstairs, fresh and put together even though she'd barely slept. Ethan was banging on Brian's food bowls when he saw her and stopped short. I wondered how he'd react to yet another new person in his sphere. He stood perfectly still, quietly staring, taking her in inch by inch, from her feet all the way to her bright blue eyes and curly blond hair. Then he threw his arms up in her direction and grunted, baby language for *pick me up*.

"Well played, pal," I said with a laugh, pointing at my beaming mother-in-law. "That's Nana. She's going to spoil you."

"He has no idea." She laughed playfully as she scooped Ethan up in her arms and began talking to him in baby voices. Watching Ethan squeal with joy as they formed an instant connection of warmth and love, I began to think about what yesterday was like for him or the day before. How different, even scary, it must have been to go to sleep in an unfamiliar crib, in a new house, with strangers. I felt so much sadness about the unknown, what he had gone through before he arrived, yet so much happiness that he was here, pouring his high-octane energy into our kitchen and our lives. And I couldn't believe how much he looked like my mother-in-law. Their eyes the same bold blue, and fair skin. It was as if she was holding her grandson. Jason's son.

The rest of the day was a blur of visitors. The foster agency had warned us about too many guests and too many presents. "You don't want the kids to feel overwhelmed or to set the expectation that every day is Christmas," Cindy had told us during training. But we couldn't keep our friends away. Peggy, who'd officiated our wedding, came with a mound of gifts. Trisha arrived and immediately put her hands out for the baby, joking, "Okay, I'm just going to take him now, thank you." Ethan didn't nap the entire day; he was delighted by the endless succession of fawning adults competing for the chance to chase him around the house, picking up all the things that his confident but clumsy thirty-six pounds knocked over.

Sometime in the afternoon it was my turn to fix Logan's bottle, but when I went into the kitchen, I couldn't find a single thing I needed. None of the bottles and lids seemed to match, and even the formula had disappeared.

"All right, people," I called. "Team meeting! Where are we keeping this stuff?" There had been barely enough time to gather the necessary supplies, much less establish any semblance of order or routine. The impossibility of preparing well struck me as hilarious. When you're pregnant, carrying a baby for the better part of a year, you have a lot of time to think about what you need. The biggest unknown is the baby's gender. However, when you tell an agency you'll take a child zero to three years old, there's a lot of mystery: Bottles or sippy cups? Formula or milk? What size diapers, bibs, onesies? Not only had I never heard of a Diaper Genie, but I sure didn't know where we were going to store one.

Trisha started laughing and once the two of us got going, we couldn't stop. I was wiping slap-happy tears off my face when my phone rang, the words "Bat Phone" flashing on the screen. Jason motioned me upstairs. I handed the baby to Peggy and followed him up to our bedroom, the sudden quiet disorienting.

"Hi, how are you?" a woman's soft voice greeted us. "I'm Kris, Ethan and Logan's grandmother."

My breath stopped for a second and Jason caught my eye, giving me his "keep calm" look.

"I just wanted to check on the boys," Kris said. "See how they're doing." Her voice sounded pained.

"Oh, hey!" Jason said, as though this were the most natural conversation in the world. "It's so great to hear from you." That was Jason to a T—pushing past his own discomfort, doing his best to make others feel safe. "We're so excited the boys are here," he went on. "They're wonderful kids. So adorable."

"It's been hard for me," Kris said, "because I wanted to make sure they were being well taken care of." The strain in her voice started to ease.

"Oh, don't worry," Jason said. "We're so happy they're here. We're crazy about them. Our dogs are crazy about them."

"They're both so cute," I added, and soon I was gushing. "I just can't get over Ethan's big bright blue eyes, and Logan is always smiling—"

Kris started to cry. "I'm sorry," she said. "I'm just so relieved. You know, you hear horror stories about foster care."

"We want the best for them, and for everyone," Jason said. "Please make sure their parents know that Ethan and Logan are safe." He paused. "And already loved."

Leaning against Jason, the voices of our nearest and dearest floating up the stairs, I felt for the first time the reality that our gain as parents was someone else's loss. The baby we'd been thinking about and planning for now had a name, or names, rather, and so did the loss. There was now a voice, an actual person, connected to that pain. Just as Kris's emotions revealed the unspoken, that she loved her grandsons and was distraught about handing them over, I hoped the warmth in our voices comforted her.

In the last twenty-four hours I'd thought constantly of the boys— but all we knew of their life before us was that Ethan was overweight and Logan was underweight, and that they'd come into placement with a few personal items—bundled into a green plastic milk crate and re- corded on a handwritten list:

> *1 Graco infant car seat—tan*
> *1 Graco toddler car seat—black*
> *1 infant pacifier—tan*
> *2 toddler pacifiers—multicolored*
> *1 Disney Cars blanket*
> *1 red blanket*
> *1 pair toddler striped shorts—size 4T*
> *1 green T-shirt—size 3T*
> *1 pair toddler shorts—size 4T*
> *3 onesies—size 0–3 months*
> *1 book*

I'd been so focused on babies in need—and how they filled our own need—that I hadn't let myself imagine parents in crisis. I'd seen chil- dren who were ready to be loved, but not the families who were missing them.

When we went back downstairs, Trisha had brought a huge package in from the porch, just delivered from my cousin Heather in Boston. We unwrapped a rainbow-colored plastic baby gate, a portable playpen with eight interlocking panels that could be adjusted to different sizes and set up indoors or outside. *Baby jail*, she jokingly called it in her card. I imagined nesting the boys inside the colorful border and keep- ing them there forever.

Chapter 6

Jagged Things

The rest of June was a crash course in caring for little ones. The first time Ethan had a full-on meltdown, I froze like a deer in headlights. He had found a remote control and was running around the living room with it hanging from his mouth like a cigar. He looked like Baby Boss with hair.

"Ethan, can I please have the remote?" I asked him politely.

He looked me dead in the eye, laughed, and kept running with the drool-soaked clicker still lodged between his lips. So, I reached over and took it from him.

Ethan paused for a second, which felt like a lifetime. His entire face turned red like a cartoon character right before steam shoots out both ears. He threw himself onto the ground and began wailing, rocking from side to side. His chubby little arms waved with wild abandon, bouncing off the rug and then the couch. Suddenly I was evil. Vladimir Putin had nothing on me. My heart heavy with guilt, the critical self-talk kicked in.

Why are you such a control freak? He just lost his parents, and you won't even let him destroy a remote? I realized the absurdity of these thoughts, but my rational mind, hijacked by guilt, was now desperate to comfort the flailing child at my feet.

"Ethan. Buddy. It's okay," I said softly, patting his back. Failing to get the response I wanted, I tried reasoning with the thirteen-month-old. "Remotes don't taste good. They'll hurt your belly and cut your gums." His sobbing intensified. Was this normal? Maybe something was really wrong with him?

Overhearing Ethan's meltdown and my ridiculous attempt to defuse the situation, Jason whisked into the room, grabbed the nearest toy, a singing Mickey Mouse doll, and began making it dance.

"Hot dog, hot dog, hot diggity dog," Mickey sang.

Ethan's tantrum stopped. He began breathing normally again. He looked up at the dancing toy and started laughing. Then he ran over to it, and just like that he was chattering and happy again.

"What kind of voodoo magic was that, Mary Poppins?" I asked Jason.

He looked at me with amusement. "Sometimes kids tantrum when they don't get their way or they're bored," he said. "Pick up a toy. Invite him to play with you. You just want to redirect his focus." I'd always known Jason would be an incredible father, but I had no idea I'd married a bona fide baby whisperer.

Ethan had a few more meltdowns, and every time I heard my Jedi Master's words echo in my ears: *Redirect his focus.* I got the hang of it once I realized managing a toddler's attention was similar to the redirection work I'd done for years as a press secretary. "*Senator Clinton voted against the bill because it would have increased gas prices for New Yorkers . . . but she has been a longtime supporter of ethanol and other alternative fuels.*"

What I didn't yet have the language for, what Jason was teaching me with his baby whispering, was how to establish the basis for emotional safety. Ethan had displayed big feelings and we didn't go away. We didn't react with big feelings of our own. We didn't meet his yelling with our yelling. At first I wanted to, but only because I was panicking and didn't know what else to do. Intellectually I knew this was normal behavior for any toddler, and I suspected extremely normal for any child going through trauma and significant change. But I learned during these tantrums that perhaps even more than my obligation to provide a physically safe space for these boys was my obligation to create an emotionally safe space. I wanted them to know they were loved. I wanted them to know they were safe and to feel every big feeling they had. I wanted them to know that Jason and I weren't going anywhere.

But in truth, I was the one not feeling emotionally safe, because I couldn't have the same assurance that they would never leave us.

————

It turned out tantrums were the easy part of parenting. Other aspects were harder to grasp. I kept worrying about the boys' health. Was Logan gaining enough weight? Had the kids been drug-exposed in utero and how might that impact their health now? Were there early signs of autism or learning delays that we were missing? Ethan had some tricky issues around food—wanting to eat all the time, self-soothing through food. No matter how recently we'd fed him, he'd walk around the house, calling, "Snack, snack, snack." I imagined there must have been times in his life when his family had food, and times when they didn't—times when he went hungry. I remembered one of my cousins who had been adopted from foster care at four years old would sit down to dinner and eat until every ounce of food on the table was gone. My aunt eventually started serving less food so he wouldn't overeat and get sick. It took a long time for him to feel secure, to accept the stability his new family provided and trust that each meal was not his last.

Logan also had a behavior that concerned me—sometimes he'd stretch his body long and completely rigid, his back arched, his face stern. He'd hold this uncomfortable-looking bridge position for a few minutes at a time, which to me felt like it carried on longer than a Kevin Costner film. The first time it happened I thought he was having a seizure.

It wasn't long before Jason grew tired of my questions, so I saved them for Patty, the social worker assigned to us from Children's Bureau. A perk of fostering with one of the county's nonprofit partners is that each foster family is supported by one of their social workers in addition to the one assigned to the case by the county. This allows for a little extra handholding if needed.

Patty quickly became a fixture in our house. She first visited the day after the boys arrived, then weekly for three months, and then every other week as part of the nonprofit's contracted services for the county. She held a smaller caseload than the county social worker and her job was to make sure we were doing our best to care for the boys and that they received any services they needed, such as therapists or other specialists. She had a grandmotherly presence, with jet-black hair and a warm smile; her soft perfume had a sweet, floral scent that made you want to be close to her. It was impossible to not love Patty. Ethan would sit on her lap when she was over and eventually nicknamed her "Patty-Cakes."

Patty had been adopted as a child, and empathy drove her work. She would listen to all of my questions and do her best to address my concerns, but often she didn't know the answers. I wanted to know what had happened to the boys. What should we plan for? How do I protect them? How do I shield my heart? She couldn't answer any of these questions, but she listened and she comforted me, while constantly reminding me, "We just don't know what's going to happen."

Patty was a fountain of knowledge on parenting and how certain behaviors may actually be the result of trauma. But the county hadn't shared the intricacies of the boys' case with her either. She knew as much as or less than we did about the kids' backstory, their parents' history, or progress toward getting their kids back. There had been so much talk about working as a team in our training that I'd expected the county to treat their nonprofit colleagues as peers, maybe having one-on-one meetings to discuss the case plan, or exchanging texts to address any concerns they had about the children. But county employees, I'd learn, were stretched too thin.

When Kendra, our county social worker, came for her first monthly visit I pummeled her with questions too. Impeccably dressed, with perfectly styled hair and nails so intricately painted her manicure must have taken a whole day, Kendra was a professional—open and direct with us, while also restrained with details.

I wanted to know everything I could about the boys' past, so we wouldn't overlook anything important in their care. I also wanted to know about their future. Were their parents taking the required steps so they could bring their babies home? What had the court told them they had to do? Would we be their dads for a short time, or forever? Kendra shared the important stuff—court dates and all the appointments we needed to arrange. She told us the county first took notice of them at the hospital when Logan was born, but she didn't say what occurred that brought them to the county's attention. She added that when they were detained, they were living with their parents at their great-grandmother's home in Lancaster, about seventy miles north of us.

"Was no one else at that house able to care for them?" I asked.

"That home wasn't approved by the county," she responded. Her vagueness appeared intentional, so I forced my follow-up questions to go unasked, simmering on the tip of my tongue.

"The court has ordered the parents to attend parenting classes and complete drug and alcohol rehabilitation," she added.

I kept fighting back the impulse to ask about their drug use, fidgeting in my seat like a second grader who waited too long to ask for a bathroom pass. Without ever admonishing me, Kendra set clear boundaries around what I could ask and what was off-limits, like an invisible third rail I quickly learned not to cross. What had happened to the parents, their experiences, their trauma, was none of my business. I wanted to learn more, out of curiosity and perhaps a bit of nosiness. There was so much mystery around them, and I thought knowing their past would help me calculate the odds of whether or not the boys would return to their parents. But Kendra had it right. The fact that we were caring for someone's children didn't mean we earned courtside seats to their life.

She had a plan for what the birth parents needed to do to get their kids back, and she was going to help them achieve it. And, as much as I already loved Ethan and Logan, I really didn't want their parents to fail, both for the boys' sake and for theirs. I couldn't imagine losing a child to foster care. Having to prove to a judge and strangers that you're fit to raise your own kids. But I had seen how terrifying and demoralizing it was to be faced with the possibility of having your child removed. Years earlier, a childhood friend called me in tears, after an investigator from Child Protective Services had shown up at her house to tell her she was looking into allegations of abuse.

"They stood at my front door and asked me if I beat my daughter," she sobbed, puffing deeply on a Newport. Kelly was a single mother with a six-year-old and had just taken in her four-year-old niece after finding out her sister was using heroin. "I have never hit my child." She was stunned but also afraid. The panic in her voice made her difficult to understand. "What if they take my baby away from me?"

"They are not going to take her away from you." I tried to sound confident, but I really didn't know what would happen.

"How do you prove you're a good parent?" Her question, floating through the phone, was something I'd never considered.

A few weeks later, Kelly got a letter from Child Protective Services informing her that the report of abuse was deemed "unfounded," and the investigation was closed, but the experience left her shaken. Eventually it came out that they were responding to an "anonymous" call her sister had made to the agency's hotline. Furious with Kelly for taking her daughter, she had exploited the very system meant to protect children.

I didn't know how common Kelly's situation was, but thirteen years later the memory was a colossal reminder of how important it is for investigators to sort what is real from what is bogus.

My gut was telling me the boys had experienced severe neglect, the kind I knew could impact them physically, mentally, and emotionally for the rest of their lives. But what if there wasn't anything? What if they were detained because the investigator didn't believe their parents? What if this was all a big misunderstanding?

I wanted to know more about child welfare investigations and how they worked. So I turned to the expert, Google. The search results were all over the place. I nosedived straight into the rabbit hole, devouring academic studies like candy. I began staying up later and later each night, ingesting reports on child abuse, parental substance use, children of incarcerated parents, and studies on allegations. I had an uncontrollable compulsion to just keep clicking and reading. I learned that US child welfare agencies receive almost ten thousand referrals each day.[1] But it's widely agreed that even more incidents of abuse and neglect go unreported.[2] I learned that 40 percent of the calls made to child protection hotlines are "screened out," meaning they're not considered to be valid or severe enough to initiate an investigation.[3] One study from Pennsylvania said that almost a quarter of two thousand sexual abuse allegations were screened out before investigation, considered unsubstantiated.[4]

When I thought of the hotline calls that are screened out and never pursued, I was reminded of Kelly's situation. Then I thought about her sister and how she had weaponized the system out of retaliation. How much time is spent sorting between vindictive allegations and legitimate concerns? Time that could be better served linking children and families to services like drug or alcohol treatment, anger management, or food and housing support.

Yet, despite Kelly's close call, I couldn't help but wonder, what happens when abuse really occurs and the child is left in the care of their abuser?

Why are so many reports of abuse passed over? In some cases, it appeared to be simple math: understaffed and underresourced agencies have to respond to a high volume of calls in a short amount of time. Screeners have only ten days—or, in the case of very severe allegations or those made on behalf of very young children, as few as two to twenty-four hours—to assess the child's level of risk.[5] A fast response isn't always an accurate response; crucial details can be overlooked or missed.

Ideally, a caseworker talks to everyone who might have information about the case, and collects all the public records—police reports, medical records—that shed light on the concern. Then they have to decide:

Did harm occur?

Is it likely to happen again?

What needs to be done to reduce that risk?

Most of the time, caseworkers make the judgment that harm hasn't occurred, and then they close the file. The more I read, the more I discovered that there are actually incentives for agencies *not* to intervene.

At the individual caseworker level, it requires a substantial amount of time, effort, and paperwork to remove a child from an unsafe home. And once a child enters foster care, the agency is responsible for what happens. Any negative outcome, a child being hurt or abused in a foster home, could result in a lawsuit. Even with the background checks and disclosure meetings foster parents are subjected to, more than 30 percent of youth in foster care have allegedly been a victim of maltreatment.[6] But if an investigator goes into a birth parent's home and says, "I don't see anything here," and then the child dies, the agency isn't responsible. They might get bad press, but historically there was no liability.

There was a chance, however, that was about to change.

The same month Ethan and Logan had been detained, two LA County social workers and their supervisors were brought up on felony charges of child abuse and falsifying public documents related to the horrific death of an eight-year-old boy three years earlier. Gabriel Fernandez was brutally beaten to death by his mother and her boyfriend. The boy's teacher had called the county's child abuse hotline and filed numerous complaints with the Department of Children and Family Services. Yet, despite the visible bruises and desperate pleas from his teacher, they never removed Gabriel from the home.

I first heard about the case while Jason and I were nearing the end of our foster parent training. It's the kind of story you don't forget; it haunts you, like Joanna's murder. In the months leading up to his death, Gabriel had been repeatedly beaten, sometimes with a wooden bat. He was shot in the face and groin with a BB gun, burned with cigarettes, and forced to eat cat feces. His siblings later testified that when he wasn't being tortured, their mother kept him locked in a cabinet in her bedroom (which the family called "the cubby"), a sock stuffed in his mouth, his hands bound with a shoelace, and handcuffs on his ankles.

In addition to the first-degree murder charges the mother and her boyfriend faced, LA County district attorney Jackie Lacey was attempting to hold the four social workers overseeing his case criminally liable, with charges that carried a prison sentence of up to eleven years. The case was being watched closely by everyone in child welfare. If Lacey succeeded in holding the workers accountable, it would dramatically change the role of child protection. (The charges against the social workers were dismissed in July 2020 after a ruling by a three-justice panel of California's Second District Court of Appeal.)

There were no physical indications Ethan or Logan had been harmed by their parents before they came into our care. They didn't arrive with any visible bruises, although they'd also been living with Kris, their grandmother, for a few weeks before they moved in with us. Kendra didn't mention anything about Logan testing positive for drugs at birth, so I didn't understand why rehab was included in the case plan. Maybe the parents had refused drug testing? From what I could tell, it was a typical foster care conundrum. If there's smoke, is there necessarily a fire? If gasoline is poured all over the floor and a box of matches is sitting nearby, but nothing is lit yet, is there reason to call "fire"? There was no evidence of harm, yet no guarantee that harm wouldn't occur.

Sitting at our dining room table, Kendra told us that as far as the county knew, the parents hadn't checked into rehab or complied with the court's guidelines for reunification. "I don't know what's going to happen," she said. Kendra was speaking candidly. As much as I wanted a wink and a nod, a vague hint to reassure me the boys were ours for good, she had no way of knowing what the future held.

Neither did we.

In foster care, reunification with birth parents is always plan A; if the parents are not able to care for the children, then a relative or close friend is the second choice. They call this kinship care. Adoption by foster parents is plan B. We'd been told in training that 55 percent of kids in foster care in California reunify with their birth families.[7] If reunification were possible for Ethan and Logan, if it served their best interests, of course that's what we wanted for them.

I accepted that, even though the uncertainty sat in my stomach like a bad oyster. If Ethan and Logan, whom it had taken all of one second for us to fall completely in love with, weren't going to be ours for life, I wanted to know. Was our job to watch them for a short while, or should we be saving for their education? I wouldn't love them any less or be any less devoted to their care. But if we knew, I thought, we could protect ourselves. We wouldn't allow ourselves to dream of our future life together, teaching Ethan to throw a baseball or sharing my love of skiing with Logan. Trying to accept that we had no knowledge of or control over the outcome was torture.

Also, it was hard to see clues from Ethan and Logan about their past without knowing if we were right, without being able to talk to them about it directly. We'd see Ethan throw himself at strangers, instantly attached, as though realizing the instability of caregivers and setting up his own safety net in case the current plan fell through. The boys didn't have the language to ask where their birth parents were or when they'd see them again. And even if they had, we didn't have any answers to share.

Kris, the boys' grandmother, continued to check in, and one morning we took the kids and met up with her at Pan Pacific Park on Beverly Boulevard. The place was a riot of activity, children of all ages flurrying past on bicycles, the giant playground teeming with families. We spread out a blanket under a shady tree and I held Logan while Jason and Kris took turns chasing Ethan around on the grass.

"It's so nice to meet you," Kris said. She was warm and friendly, but formal. She couldn't have been more than twelve or fifteen years older than me. She wore a flowy white linen shirt and shorts, her long blond hair pulled loosely to the side. The sky-blue crystal hanging around her neck brought out the color in her eyes. She reminded me of a character from a movie, a free spirit, who lived somewhere near Malibu, like Topanga Canyon, had an organic garden, and bottled her own jellies. Edging our pleasantries was the somber truth at the heart of our encounter—that we were caring for her grandchildren because her son and his wife could not. Because she could not.

Jason and I tried to avoid bringing up the boys' parents. Of course, we were dying for information, but we didn't want to pry. The point of the visit was to help maintain Ethan and Logan's connection with family and to let Kris see that they were safe and that we could be trusted. Slowly, details trickled out. Kris was divorced and had raised Zach, the boys' father, on her own. She lived alone and had a sister she didn't speak to. I sensed she was lonely—and disappointed, too, that her son was an addict. She told us that when the boys had been detained in May, she stepped in to care for them. Because she is family, she was considered a kinship caregiver. The court ran a quick background check, made sure her house was safe, and then allowed her to take in her grandsons. Had she kept Ethan and Logan, she would have had to go through the same training and certification process we went through. The courts almost always favor placing children with relatives because kinship care is recognized as the optimal way of maintaining familiarity, minimizing trauma, and keeping families together. Children who are placed with family are also less likely to be moved from one home to another.[8]

"I own a company," she explained. "I have employees, I'm single, I have no help at home, and I've had some health problems lately." Her situation didn't allow for an infant and a toddler. "Zach's father is remarried," she said. "I don't think he's even met Logan yet. I wanted to keep them, but I just couldn't do it," she said, fighting back tears. It was heartbreaking to watch someone being crushed under the weight of guilt and shame. I hoped that meeting us, seeing how Jason and I loved and cared for her grandsons, could ease some of her suffering, release some of the pressure.

Kris's circumstances had led her to the decision that handing her grandsons over to the county, with the hope of them finding good foster parents, was her best option. I couldn't imagine being in her situation, her fear, her pain. How was that her best option? How was there no other family member or friend who could step up or step in? Yet I believed her. As we listened to her relive the hardest decision of her life, I could see the mountain of agony she had been living under.

She told us that Amber, the boys' mother, had lost her own mother in a car accident when she was just two or three years old. "She was raised by her grandmother but that's not a good situation," she said. "She was abused and has some challenges developmentally. I tried so many times to help them, to teach them how to parent, but all they wanted from me was money."

"I'm so sorry for all that you're going through," I said, doing my best to comfort her.

"We will do everything we can to keep these guys safe and happy," Jason added, playfully hugging Ethan and trying to lighten the mood.

As we said our goodbyes and packed the boys into the car and turned on the kids' playlist (of mostly Beyoncé and Jimmy Buffett songs) for the drive home, I thought of our house full of friends and family, so many eager hands ready to hold the baby or mix the next bottle of formula or run to the store for more diapers. We had so many people rooting for us, showing up for us. And we had each other.

I checked to make sure the kids were asleep and turned to Jason. "My heart breaks so hard for Kris," I said.

"I know, right?" he replied. "Try to keep that feeling, no matter what happens."

I didn't know just how confusing my commitment to the boys and my empathy for their family would become.

———

A few weeks later, Kris, who was approved by the county to supervise visits between the boys and their biological parents, offered to host a visit at her home in the San Fernando Valley. The neighborhood had cul-de-sacs with sidewalks, kids riding bicycles, and ranch-style homes, with solar-panel-covered roofs and perfectly maintained, drought-resistant landscaping. Kris's house was no different.

Amber and Zach were already waiting inside. Zach was tall and blond, with acne scars and a few tattoos up and down his arms. He was built like a linebacker and wore black-rimmed glasses with thick lenses. Amber was wearing tattered yoga pants and a sweater, her tangled hair pulled up in a bun. She ran to the door and picked up Ethan, kissing him repeatedly. He squealed with pleasure but wanted to get down right away to inspect the toys Kris had laid out.

Amber turned to me. "Thank you so much for taking care of my babies," she said before giving me a hug.

"We are happy to do it," I said awkwardly. I couldn't take my eyes off her teeth. They were brown and jagged. I wondered if the damage was from meth use. I felt disgusted—and also disgusted with myself for having such a strong reaction. Later, we learned the damage to her teeth wasn't from drugs alone. She had braces when she was young and one night in a fit of anger, she ripped them off with pliers, breaking all of her teeth. What kind of pain would you have to be feeling to torture yourself like that? I thought meeting Amber and Zach might help us better understand the boys' needs, but now I realized how far apart our lives and experiences were. I felt the discomfort of peering into strangers' lives and the difficulty of bridging our differences.

Except we loved the same kids.

Both parents engaged with Ethan and steadily ignored Logan, who was snuggled into his car seat carrier. I lifted him out and handed him to Zach, but Amber didn't acknowledge the baby.

Jason and I stood uncomfortably in the entryway and then said goodbye. The two-hour visit had hardly begun and already it felt like an eternity to be away from the boys. We drove to a nearby mall and sat in the food court with sushi we didn't feel like eating.

"She didn't even look at Logan," I said, stirring wasabi into the meager puddle of soy sauce. "Do you think she was high?"

"It's not our job to know that," Jason said.

"I know, but do you think she was?" I asked again.

"I don't know," he said, in a tone that let me know he wasn't engaging in that conversation. Sometimes I wanted to stab his equanimity in the face.

But as soon as I stopped rushing to judgment, a new feeling took hold. A deep sadness. Maybe Amber couldn't look at her baby, not because she cared so little, but because she cared so much. Because she wanted to be able to care for him and couldn't. I wondered about her life, about the experiences and decisions that had landed her in this moment, about the things she could control and those she could not. No one's childhood is all rainbows and gummy bears. But some people carry a much heavier load. I remembered the *situational loss* exercise we'd done in our foster care training. How many situational losses did Amber have in her past? She'd now had three sons removed from her care. What experiences and family history had carried her to this juncture? What hardships had triggered more hardships? What parts of her story stemmed from loss or trauma, and what was just random, shitty luck?

I thought of my cousins Heather and Maureen. They were sisters. They had the same genes, they grew up in the same home, lost the same father, my dad's brother, to a drunk driver when they were young. But their lives had unspooled differently.

Maureen was a teenager when their dad was killed. She was young when she got pregnant and married the baby's father. But that didn't last. By the time she was twenty-five, she was divorced, a single mother to three boys. The older two were always punching and kicking and fighting. When her oldest was eight, he stabbed her with a knife. Not in a lethal way, but enough to scratch the surface and raise concern among the family. Heather was still in high school when she began stepping in to help her sister with child care. She would spend nights at Maureen's apartment to watch the boys so their mom could work or go out. She took them to doctor's appointments and attended teacher conferences when Maureen was not available.

Maureen was no monster. Quite the opposite. I'd always known her to be kind. I remembered spending a day on her couch when I was nine, too sick to go to school, too young to stay home all day alone. She brought me food, baby Ryan in her arms, her eyes warm but with something remote and unknowable at the corners, as if half her attention was in another room. She seemed glamorous to me, beautiful and yearning, like Pat Benatar.

———

I was still lost in my thoughts when the Bat Phone rang. It was Kris. Thirty minutes into the visit, Zach had started yelling at her, blaming her for putting the boys in foster care, badgering her for money. She was upset, her voice clearly rattled.

"I kicked them out," she said, "and almost called the police. Ethan and Logan are ready for you to take them home."

Chapter 7

All the Single Babies

The summer unfurled in a series of firsts. My mom's first visit to dote on the boys. Our first Fourth of July as a family at Peggy's annual block party in Redondo Beach—complete with egg tosses and bouncy houses. The first time Ethan called me Daddy, perched in his high chair, shoving tiny fistfuls of Cheerios in his mouth, I was so caught off guard, it took a few seconds to even realize he was talking to me. "Daddy" always felt like a title one has to earn, like doctor, senator, or Supreme Allied Commander. I certainly had nothing to do with bringing him into the world, but to him, I was filling this coveted role.

Hearing his squeaky, high-pitched voice call me Daddy sent a warm shot of joy through my veins. For the first time, I was somebody's *daddy*. In that life-changing instant, I mattered to another person in a way I never had before. Any hopes I'd had of keeping the lid on my dreams for his future, our future, were gone. I was his daddy now.

Our days took on new routines. Whenever I left my home office to take a break from work, Ethan would grab my hand and pull me toward the playroom. "Daddy, come sit," he'd say. "Daddy, come play." We'd have dance parties in the kitchen, Logan bouncing and laughing in his walker, Ethan running around and squealing. We'd blast Stevie Wonder and Beyoncé, singing, "All the single *babies*, all the single *babies*!" in a cacophony of pure joy.

We found someone to come over during the week to care for the boys while we worked. Josephine had raised three children of her own, and Jason had worked with her husband at a restaurant years earlier. When I'd freak out over a case of the sniffles, she would calm me down with the grace of a seasoned veteran. Between her and Jason I was getting a master class in parenting. On the days I finished work early, I would often find her rocking one of the boys and singing, "*A dormir, a dormir mi bebito.*" The first time I heard Ethan call out for *leche* my heart sang. He was soaking in Spanish like a sponge.

In early August, Patty hosted a "needs and services" meeting in her office with Kendra, the birth parents, and a psychiatrist—an opportunity to check in about all aspects of the boys' health and development. When we arrived, Amber raced to Ethan, the same way she had at Kris's house. Zach stood over Logan, who was still strapped into his car seat smiling up at his father, and asked, "Do you think he's going to be a slow kid?" The question came out of nowhere. I thought maybe he was referring to the effects of Amber's drug use, which I couldn't even confirm. But I also wondered if there was something else underlying his concern. Before I could unleash the barrage of questions his comment had just triggered in my mind, Jason said, "No," with a definitive tone that shut down any speculation.

Zach didn't bend over to pick up the baby. He just stood over Logan, looking down at his beautiful smile.

Patty greeted us in the foyer with her supervisor, Ramona, who she told us would be monitoring the meeting, and led us into a small visitation room. As we settled into the molded plastic chairs to begin, I took out a bottle and asked if either of the parents wanted to feed Logan. Neither did. Ramona caught my eye. This was the first time we had met but I knew she was picking up what I was sensing, that neither parent was concerned with Logan. Amber, who had barely looked at the baby since we arrived and didn't seem interested in acknowledging him, expressed outrage that the boys were taken from her.

"I'm a great mother. We shouldn't be in this situation," she declared, her voice rising and her hands shaking. "There is no reason I shouldn't have my kids," she continued, now yelling.

"Amber," Kendra calmly interrupted, "I don't have a negative drug test from you yet."

Amber immediately fell quiet, folded her hands, and looked down. Kendra's reprimand may have silenced Amber, but it had the opposite effect on Zach.

He jumped out of his chair and stood in front of Kendra, yelling and waving a finger in her face. "We're good parents. This is all bullshit. We shouldn't have to prove nothing to anyone." In that moment, Logan weighed a million pounds. The shock of the scene playing out in front of me left me momentarily trapped under his tiny frame. I couldn't move. That wasn't anger Zach displayed, it was rage. Kendra didn't flinch, but I was impacted by his outburst—astonished that he'd shown so much aggression toward Kendra, a woman.

And Kendra wasn't just *any woman*, she was *the woman* who would ultimately make a recommendation to the court about whether or not he should get his kids back. His voice carried an indisputable tone of desperation. I felt sorry for him. It must be demoralizing to lose your children and defeating to know that this time, simply saying, "Sorry, I'll do better," won't cut it. If he wanted his kids back, he'd have to prove it. Whatever my thoughts were about Zach's blowup, my greater fear was that someday the anger I'd just witnessed could be directed at Ethan or Logan. I imagined it had already been directed at Amber.

"Zach," Jason said, jumping up and putting a hand on his shoulder, "maybe you should take a walk to cool down." Zach followed Jason's advice and stepped out of the room.

I didn't know how to react, so I looked to Ramona, who moved just slightly in her chair.

Ramona was about my age, but she looked younger. Her poise

expressed both fierceness and grace. It was like, *I will cut you, then I'll walk the runway.* She didn't say much, but her presence was known. She didn't catch my gaze, and I joined her in watching Kendra redirect the conversation back to Amber and the checklist of actions she needed to perform.

Before we left, I asked the psychiatrist about the way Logan sometimes stiffened and arched his back. "He looks like he's trying to make himself uncomfortable."

"It's likely just a muscle spasm. That's fairly common in babies whose mothers used drugs while they were in utero," she responded, loud enough for everyone in the room to hear.

I tensed up and tried to maintain eye contact with her in order to avoid seeing Amber's reaction. It didn't matter. Amber was oblivious to our conversation. I was embarrassed for her, but desperately wanted her to tell us something. I felt overwhelmed by all the risks, known and unknown, that the boys had faced before they came to us. I was angry we were being left in the dark by the county, and that she wasn't sharing information that could help us care for them. I wanted to blurt out, "Hey, Amber, any chance you used meth or heroin while you were pregnant?" Obviously, I couldn't do that. That would be both extremely rude and highly insensitive. Not to mention, I couldn't risk angering Kendra or the other social workers. We were instructed, repeatedly, during our training that our role as foster parents was to support reunification at all cost until a judge says otherwise. We were plan B and we needed to wait patiently, showing up where they told us, when they told us, until our boarding group was called.

I was also troubled by the upcoming hearing. In a matter of months, a judge would sit before the facts and decide whether or not the boys would reunify. This would be the first court hearing Jason and I would attend. We had been told our presence was not required and that most foster parents do not attend, but there was no way we were going to skip a court date. We wanted the court to know the boys were being well cared for and looked after.

I needed a project to distract myself and woke up one Sunday morning determined to organize the closet in the nursery. We had stuffed the shelves with boxes of diapers and gifts of clothes that didn't fit yet and every time I opened the door it felt as disorderly as the emotions swirling inside me. I started pulling out clothes and hangers, baby shoes and toys. Ethan waddled into the room, saw the toys on the ground, and picked up two Matchbox cars, my favorite toys as a kid. He pushed them across the floor, howling with glee, as they crashed into the wall. I reached for the green milk crate that carried all their belongings when they arrived and had been tucked high up on a shelf. Ethan looked at me, his face going from pale to red. He burst into tears and threw himself on the ground.

At first, I thought he was hurt. Maybe he stepped on something? But then I realized it was the crate. The sight of me standing there holding it had triggered his meltdown. I threw the crate back into the closet and sat down next to him. Ethan crawled onto my lap, binkie popping in and out of his mouth. He wrapped both arms around one of mine and squeezed as tightly as he could, resting his face on my chest. I hugged him, repeating, "It's okay. I've got you, buddy." He began to calm down, his breath slowing, but my mind was just revving up. What did that crate mean to him? My imagination was painting possible scenarios of what could have upset him. Maybe he had fallen trying to climb onto it or into it? Or did he think he was leaving? Going to a new home?

I had to stop the free flow of what-ifs. What did I know for sure? I knew Ethan was here now and our court date was still a couple of months away.

I also knew that it was my job to make him feel safe in all the ways that mattered.

———

In late August, Kris asked for an overnight visit with Ethan. We thought it was nice that she was going to spend some time with her grandson. We dropped him off at her house on Saturday and arranged to meet up

with her after she and Ethan attended services the following morning at
Agape, the spiritual center founded by Rev. Dr. Michael Bernard Beck-
with. When we pulled up to the center, we were stunned to see Amber
standing beside Kris. Visits with the birth parents were supposed to be
arranged through Kendra and were restricted to three-hour windows,
three times a week. No one told us Amber would be there. Kris was au-
thorized to monitor visits; maybe she'd arranged this with Kendra and
forgot to tell us. But had Amber spent the night too? If she had, were
we obligated to tell Kendra?

Kris needed Jason's help grabbing our pack 'n' play and diaper bag
from her car, so Amber jumped into the front passenger seat of my car.
She was chatty and friendly, sipping a frozen coffee drink covered in
whipped cream, talking excitedly with her hands, and moving with the
energy of a five-year-old who had just chugged a Mountain Dew.

"I have something to ask you," she said, as I began the two-minute
drive to the other side of the parking lot. Without taking a breath she
said, "Do you and Jason want to be the boys' godparents?"

Before I could answer—or even process her surprising request—she
said, "I'm pregnant. The baby is due in February."

The voice in my head kept telling me to smile, just smile, keep smiling. But I kept thinking, *What the fuck? She's pregnant. Godparents? We
want to be the boys' parents, not their godparents. It was sweet of her to
want us in their lives. Was I being disingenuous wanting to parent them?
In February there will be three babies under the age of two. Holy shit.*

"Of course," I said, without breaking my smile. "Thank you. What
an honor. And wow, another baby, congratulations."

Amber seemed to be picturing a future where she and Zach parented
their three children, with Jason and me in the mix as family friends and
bonus caregivers. But I wasn't sure a judge would let Amber raise three
children when she was still struggling to take care of herself—as of a
few weeks ago, she hadn't produced a negative drug test and she had to
have been at least two months pregnant. If that were the case, the county
would try to keep siblings together, and when the next child was born,

Jason and I would be the likely choice for placement. If we were the boys' godparents, would our status go from foster parents to kinship? Would we say yes? How would we manage parenting three children? Yet we had the ability to say yes or no. Amber didn't have a choice. That baby was coming. Once the baby was born, a judge would decide Amber's fitness to parent. She couldn't control or predict the outcomes any more easily than Jason or I could. Of course, it was the kids who had the least choice of all. Their safety was on the line, and they couldn't say or do a single thing to influence what happened.

When Jason got into the car, I wasted no time. "Amber's pregnant, and she wants us to be the boys' godparents," I blurted out.

"You got all that in a two-minute car ride," he said, laughing.

"Yeah. She's due in February," I said. A third child wasn't out of the question for us, but it wasn't something we'd thought would happen anytime soon. This whole situation was beyond our control and every day it was growing in size and speed, like a tornado ripping through the Heartland. But unlike a tornado, we couldn't just duck into the basement and wait for it to blow over. "We're going to need a car with three rows."

"We are not getting a minivan," he declared.

Mom called later that day, and I told her about Amber asking us to be the boys' godparents and that she was having a baby. "Mom, if that baby ends up in foster care, they are going to ask us to take it. Who in their right mind signs up for three kids?" I joked.

"That's what Grandma Mary did," she said, reminding me that her stepmother had done just that for her and her siblings. Three years after their mother died, her dad remarried. Mary wasn't like most women of her era. She had a full-time job, wore business suits, and had served in Canada's military during World War II. She was beautiful, with blond hair that was coiffed at the salon once a week. Mary was a catch, yet somehow she had fallen for a widowed cop with three kids and a drinking problem.

"Okay," I said, at a loss for words, "fair point."

Mom didn't embrace Mary as a parental figure right away. Mary had stepped in and taken over many of the chores and responsibilities that had fallen onto Mom's young shoulders, but Mom had come to believe that caring for her siblings and even her father was *her* load to carry. Her siblings accepted this too. When Mary would tell Cheryl to get in the bathtub, my aunt would look to her older sister for assurance before following their stepmother's directions.

Over time, their initial tension waned and Mary's formidable presence provided a new layer of safety for Mom, Auntie Cheryl, Uncle Jimmy, and the two other children she had with my grandfather. For the first time since her mother's death, Mom was free from the obligations of her circumstances. She could play with kids her age, riding bikes in the park or skipping rocks on the shore. Of all the ways Mary rescued Mom's childhood, none was more impactful than the emotional safety she provided. Allowing Mom to be a kid, to feel and express pain, fear, jealousy, and love. The two of them grew very close, and while Mary could never fill the void left by her mother's passing, they created a strong and special relationship of their own. Mary passed away in Mom's care after a brief battle with cancer in 2014.

I was beginning to see many parallels between the boys and my mom. Losing her mother was a double-edged sword. On the one hand she lost that unconditional, first love of her mother. But on the other, she gained Mary. And Mary provided stability, support, and love of her own. Just like Mariah had talked about at our breakfast in North Carolina, she also grew up without her mother. If Jason and I adopted the boys, they, too, would grow up without their mother. Would we be able to fill the void of an absent mother? To provide the emotional safety my mother provided for me and Mary provided for her?

———

When Kendra arrived at her next regular visit, she did her spot check of the house and asked us the usual rundown of questions: How is everything going? Do you have any concerns? Have you heard from the birth parents? Are you keeping a communication log? Have there been any doctor's visits or medical issues? Then she let it slip that Zach and Amber had both entered rehab.

The air went out of the room. I struggled to catch my breath, to organize the questions and mixed feelings crashing through my head, to separate what I wanted to feel from what I actually felt.

I wanted to be relieved and happy for them. To root for them. To see this as good news for the boys I loved and the baby on the way.

But I didn't feel happy or relieved. For an entire season the arrows had kept pointing in one direction: Amber was unwilling or unable to comply with the court's requirements; until she did, the boys couldn't be surrendered to her care. I'd bought the three-row car. I'd embraced the idea that soon Jason and I would be parenting three.

Most of all, I'd fallen in love.

It was my choice to take that risk. I knew what the statistics said. The odds favored reunification. But we were all in.

There was no statistic, no number that could measure what it felt like when Ethan called me Daddy. What it felt like to hold their hands, kiss their cheeks, wipe their tears, make them laugh, see their curious eyes go soft with sleepiness, lift them into a warm bath, snuggle them into pajamas, and let them fall asleep against my chest. The visions I fought but couldn't escape, future Little League games and college visits, suddenly disappearing like the sun on the distant horizon.

A number couldn't hold the confusion and uncertainty I felt about Zach and Amber's ability to parent. Would they complete rehab, or drop out? Would they stay sober, or relapse? Would a negative drug test be enough to ensure the boys were safe in their care? Was it wrong for me to hope a little bit that they'd fail?

How was I supposed to protect the boys and protect my heart in such a confusing system? I couldn't stop loving them. But how could I keep loving them, being a family with them, when I knew we could lose them? Was I fighting or grieving?

Maybe this was how my uncle John had felt, bringing fresh blueberries to Auntie Cheryl every day all the months she lay dying. Loving her and losing her in the same breath, in the same instant. Was it hope that kept him fueling her with antioxidants long past the point when any doctor thought it possible for her to survive? Was it denial? Or was it just his heart doing what it knew how to do? An expression of a love so consuming and complete it didn't flinch at risk or grief and never stopped to calculate the odds.

Chapter 8

A Home for Little
Wanderers

It was 3:30 a.m. on a Wednesday. I had been pacing the nursery, rocking Logan back to sleep for the past hour. His eyes refused to close, small and blue staring up at mine, content in my embrace, unbothered by the passing of time. His tiny fingers softly pulled the hairs on my arm. I had a full day of meetings starting at 8:00 a.m. and my mind was sprinting in different directions.

Will Logan ever fall asleep? Will I even make sense in my meetings at work? I forgot to call Trisha back. My right arm is asleep. If I switch sides, will Lo see that as an invitation to play? Will I ever regain feeling in this arm? Do Amber and Zach know what they're missing? Do they even care?

I was exhausted. In the three months since the boys' arrival, I'd shown up at the office without my laptop twice. Sleep deprivation was real—I now understood why they used it as torture at Guantánamo Bay.

I slowly lowered myself into the armchair in the nursery and put my feet up on the ottoman, repositioning Logan half on my lap and half against my chest. I could feel the heat of his breath through my T-shirt as I inhaled his soft baby scent. I couldn't change what had happened to him or what was going to happen, but I was happy our fates had aligned to afford us this moment—to be his source of comfort this night. As my breaths grew longer and the beating of my heart slowed, he fell asleep.

I shut my eyes, hoping I could get a few hours of sleep in the chair because moving would risk waking him, and that was a gamble I was not willing to make. In Logan's sweet face, I saw only an innocent baby, one who had been dealt a bad hand. What would his future hold? Would this room be transformed from a nursery into a little boy's room—swapping out stuffed teddy bears for Batman and basketballs? Or would he return to Amber and Zach? Would their home be a safe place for him to grow? Could they get well and stay well enough to provide him and Ethan the childhood they deserved? And who would know if they weren't?

I hungered for certainty, a guarantee the boys would be safe, loved, and looked after. I wanted to be completely free to dream of our future together. Our family, with two dads, their sons, and possibly a third child—grilling burgers and watching movies, Wiffle ball games and ski trips. Yet if I looked beyond this moment, Logan's tiny belly rhythmically filling and emptying with air, if I set a vision of what could be, the hurt would be too great if it were to be abruptly yanked away.

Logan stretched his legs.

I wanted the one thing life cannot guarantee: tomorrow.

I had lost too many people I love to think you have any power over life's outcomes. I had fought the undercurrent of tragedy when it pulled at me and witnessed loved ones drowning in grief. I wanted to believe I could control what would happen. That I could keep them safe, that I could do something to prevent the universe from tearing us apart. But I couldn't.

Without any assurances or tea leaves I could trust, I needed to believe that the systems in place to protect and care for children worked. But I was skeptical. The effectiveness of the child protection system relies on its ability to assess and predict risk. To smell smoke and extinguish small fires before they have the oxygen to grow. But that is a difficult task.

A few nights earlier, I'd gone down a research rabbit hole. What began with one question—was there one singular risk factor that could forecast child abuse or neglect?—quickly budded into dozens more. If a parent had a drug addiction, was that the equivalent of drawing the Monopoly card reading *Go directly to foster care. Do not pass go. Do not collect $200*? My fingers typed queries as fast as they could move, while my elbow rested slightly on Roxy, who had cuddled in beside me on the sofa.

I quickly discovered a report, put out by the federal agency that oversees foster care, that included a list of the different bases for which children are removed from their caretakers and their prevalence. I began scrolling, reading the percentages assigned to each reason— neglect, 61 percent; parental drug abuse, 32 percent; abandonment, 5 percent; physical abuse, 13 percent; disability of a child, 2 percent; death of a parent, 1 percent. The list went on.[1] The percentages totaled 170, which meant they were not mutually exclusive. Neglect was often the by-product of a concomitant challenge. I wanted to know which struggles needed to be present in a home to make the environment ripe for abuse.

What role does mental health play in foster care detentions? What about social isolation? Homelessness? I waded into pages upon pages of academic studies. It was all so insightful, but none of it directly answered my initial question about whether or not there was a single factor whose presence could provide the clairvoyance to predict abuse or neglect, probably because there was no answer. As far as I could tell, there's no clear line of cause and effect, no one component that makes or breaks a parent's ability to protect their children. Risk is cumulative and uncertain. The more factors at play, the greater the probability, but risk alone is not an inevitability. The more I learned, the more I wanted to know about the ins and outs of foster care.

Taking away someone's child is a colossal decision, one that in practice has disproportionately impacted Black and Native American children, who, I learned, are overrepresented nationally in foster care at rates that are one and a half and two times their proportion of the general population, respectively.[2]

Our nation's unwillingness to engage in difficult conversations and put in the work needed to repair the damage caused by our shameful history of slavery and segregation has allowed structural, institutional, and systemic racism to go unchecked. The criminal justice system has been used to overpolice Black people. As a result, Black men account for 35 percent of those incarcerated, while representing just 13 percent of the overall male population.[3] How many Black women, earning just 63 cents for every dollar paid to white men,[4] are left to raise children alone because of this practice? Even more, discrimination in lending, the tax code, and employment has systematically denied generations of Black families access to wealth-building pathways, leaving them with a fraction of the financial safety net of the average white family.[5] Lack of access to quality health care and bias within the medical community are among the factors contributing to the horrific fact that Black women are three and a half times as likely to experience a pregnancy-related death than white women.[6] Pervasive systemic injustices, rooted squarely in racism, are contributing factors to the inflated numbers of Black children in foster care. The numbers are also inflated for Native American families. As recently as fifty years ago, three in ten Native American children had been removed from their homes and placed in adoptive homes, foster homes, or institutions.[7]

For over a century, Indigenous children were systematically separated from their families by the US government, the Catholic Church, and other religious organizations. Tens of thousands of children were sent to more than four hundred government-run or supported boarding schools, where physical, sexual, and emotional abuse ran rampant.[8] The schools were designed to force tribal children to assimilate to white culture, thereby decimating the future of tribes.[9]

Most of the children removed would never see their biological families again, never hear their Native languages spoken, never participate in another tribal ceremony. They lost all connections to their families, their culture, their traditions, and too many lost their lives. Indigenous children are still overrepresented in the foster system, accounting for less than 1 percent of the country's total population but 2 percent of its foster care population.[10]

Two peoples, one whose land was stolen, the other stolen and brought to this land, united by the unconscionable acts of the past, still echoing in the policies and systems surveilling families today. These communities share a bond of oppression and a well-justified distrust of government and the child welfare system. Many in these communities face challenges passed on to them like a torch handed from one generation to the next, the result of intergenerational trauma and society's limited understanding of the sustained impact of racism and cultural genocide.

Hispanic families face a different set of challenges. As of 2017, one in three children living in the United States was Hispanic.[11] On the surface this community is underrepresented in the foster care population nationally, accounting for 21 percent of all youth;[12] however, there are great disparities among states.[13] Hispanic children are overrepresented in foster care in a handful of states and significantly underrepresented in roughly seventeen states.[14] If a lack of cultural understanding and the inability to effectively communicate with Spanish-speaking families are seen as explanations for the overrepresentation of Latino youth in some states, the same challenges may also explain the underrepresentation in other states. Families with undocumented loved ones may shy away from public services because they don't believe they are eligible or they are concerned about potential repercussions resulting from their immigration status. While 94 percent of Latino children were born in the US, a quarter of them had a parent who lacked the required legal status to lawfully reside there. This puts the unimaginable stress of having a parent deported on an estimated four million Latino youth.[15]

One menacing characteristic that appeared time and time again in my search for answers was the oversized role of poverty in child welfare cases. One study found infants born in California's poorest neighborhoods were reported to Child Protective Services at seven times the rate of infants born in the wealthiest areas.[16] This does not suggest parents who struggle financially are incapable of caring for their children or keeping them safe. Rather, it demonstrates the stress of economic hardship felt by parents and the difficult decisions it forces them to make—groceries or rent, diapers or gas money. It also speaks to the way systems police poverty and how they determine what *good enough* parenting looks like. It seems that poverty, whether or not it's accompanied by maltreatment, is a lightning rod for intervention. And not always for the better.

There are so many ingredients that could be combined to cook up a foster care detention, but simply mixing them together does not guarantee a child will experience harm. Foretelling neglect or abuse is impossible.

If life were a sport, we could place bets on future success. Factors like poverty, in utero drug exposure, parents' education level, and marital status would all weigh into the over/under. The probability of graduating from high school or college, serving time in prison, or teenage pregnancy could be measured and predicted.

We begin life on an uneven playing field, like two NFL teams waiting for the coin toss on opening day. One team stacked with Pro Bowlers and the other trying to rebuild a franchise. But what happens if the star quarterback gets injured? A crushing blow sidelines him, possibly ending his career. The season in jeopardy, his replacement is young and untested, the 199th draft pick overall. A once-bright outlook, now dimming. Anxiety takes hold of morale, choking it in the locker room. The crowd thins, optimism wanes. One loss, one event, triggering a series. Suddenly the line shifts. The bettors who predicted a great season begin counting their losses before the next play is even called.

When the pillars bracing our lives begin crumbling upon us, are we prepared with the insight and the fortitude to look up? Do our feet move to prevent us from being flattened by the crashing beams? Can we dig through the debris to find something, anything, an iota of meaning, that makes perseverance worthwhile? In the chaos, do we lose what it means to be ourselves, or find the strength to emerge from the wreckage and begin again?

From an early age, the risk factors were stacked against Amber. Loss, trauma, and what I suspected was undiagnosed, or at the very least untreated, mental illness. In our training classes, Cindy had talked about physical age versus emotional age, and explained that children who experience abuse or neglect often become arrested in their emotional development as they mature into adulthood. Amber's emotional age seemed well below her physical age, which I found out from Facebook sleuthing was twenty-seven years old. That made me wonder if she had been stunted by the trauma of her childhood, emotionally trapped somewhere around middle school, her transition to maturity stymied by the unhealed wounds of her youth.

Kris told us Amber and Zach had moved to Las Vegas with the hopes of a fresh start shortly after Ethan was born. But Zach's addiction stood in the way of their dreams, anchoring any progress she'd hoped to see. Amber wanted a family like the ones she'd watched on TV, where love and forgiveness resolved all their problems by the end of each episode. She confronted Zach about his drug use, but he didn't stop. They weren't in Vegas long, a couple of months at most, before Zach started using again. That wasn't the life she wanted for Ethan or the baby growing inside her. In desperation, she reached out to Kris, who bought her and Ethan one-way bus tickets back to Los Angeles. She boarded the bus with no food, one diaper, and empty pockets. She moved back in with her grandmother, Rita, in the house where she was raised, but Zach followed shortly after. He told her he would change and begged her to take him back.

She did.

After the kids were detained, Rita kicked Amber and Zach out. With nowhere to go, they moved into the Prius they had leased. One by one, the pillars bracing their lives began to tip. Each falling beam ramming into the next. In a matter of months, they went from sharing a mattress in a living room with their sons to the reclining seats of a Toyota, catching shut-eye in the faintly lit parking lots of highway rest stops and state parks.

The boys' detention was a triggering event, the first domino to fall. Now they were homeless. Living in their car meant that Zach, who had been driving for Uber, was now unemployed. Repossession of the vehicle was imminent when Amber and Zach entered rehab and I couldn't help but wonder if their decision was a valiant move to heal and get their kids back or a sidestep to avoid living on the streets. Were they fighting to rebuild or merely trying to survive? What happened to make their lives unravel in a way that landed them in rehab and their kids in foster care? What could have gone differently? What, if any, intervention could have occurred that might have prevented them from arriving at this point? What if Amber had never been sent to live with her grandmother after her mother died? What if another family member had stepped in? Could she have been spared some of the trauma?

I saw a lot of similarities between Amber's childhood and my mom's. They both saw the safety of their worlds vanish the instant their mothers died. They both endured the unpredictability of a teetering and grieving caregiver. They both hungered for the belonging that slowly faded with the memories of their mothers.

The difference was that Mom had a stepmother, who fostered a sense of normalcy and stability. Amber wasn't as fortunate. Left to the care of a single, mourning grandmother who was struggling to make ends meet, the odds for Amber's future never returned to her favor. Maybe there were some spikes in her odds along the way, a caring teacher or the presence of a loving and overreaching relative. I didn't know enough to speculate, but ultimately any attempt to force a rebound had fallen short. Facing homelessness, kids taken away, pregnant, and entering rehab, she was at rock bottom.

Success was a long shot, failure a safer wager. But what would happen next? History is full of tales of those who overcame wounds and afflictions to rise to glory. The past cannot dictate the future. So, would she rise from the ashes or succumb to the pain? And why did that question cause me such agony?

I didn't want her to fail. But if her failing meant that her kids would be safe with us, I would embrace her loss. Only time would tell, and until that time was up, I'd keep weighing the odds.

In the absence of a crystal ball to warn and shield my heart from pain, I was left to wait, to ride out the storm of emotions raging inside me. Uncertainty is often the hardest thing to accept. I was now living at the mercy of a situation I couldn't control, with no inkling of what the future would hold.

Throughout our training, Cindy's answers to our questions often began, "It depends . . ."

"Every situation is different . . ."

"Every parent is different . . ."

"Every child is different . . ."

"Every social worker, judge, foster parent is different . . ."

There's no magic elixir that solves mental health issues, heals childhood trauma, or eradicates poverty with just a few swigs. We can't just unplug, wait thirty seconds, and reboot a parent to erase the bugs impacting their operating systems.

There are so many variables at play in each individual case within the child protection system, but just one constant in every situation: no child signs up for foster care. Hands aren't waving in the air, high-pitched voices squealing, "Pick me! Over here! I want to be ripped away from everything and everyone I know. Send me to a new school. I've been dying to say goodbye to my dog and my grandma."

Foster care is the recognition that something terrible has happened to a child.

For some, safe haven in a foster home is not a guarantee. Incidences of harm against children in foster care reported by states (0.3 percent in 2017)[17] seem implausibly low given that surveys of foster youth indicate rates as high as 30 percent.[18] It's more likely than not that many incidences don't get reported or are wrongfully discarded; some children are too young to voice their abuse and others may only be interviewed in the presence of their abusers. I understood now Kris's relief when she saw how much Jason and I cared for the boys.

———

Holding Logan, who had finally surrendered to sleep, in my arms, I thought again of the tragic death of my cousin's daughter. Was there a moment when the right intervention would have taken Ryan off the trajectory that left Joanna dead and put him in prison for life?

I'd only known him as an energetic little boy. But by the time Ryan was ten, he was acting out, telling his teachers to fuck off; once, he threw a cat. As he got older, Ryan's behavior got worse. The fighting, lying, and cursing were too much and he was sent to live at the Home for Little Wanderers, a group therapeutic facility in Plymouth, Massachusetts. I didn't know if Child Protective Services had ordered him there or if Maureen had voluntarily sent him away. Either way, Maureen and Ryan were both safer with him living there.

Heather visited Ryan twice a week. The facility had a beautiful pond, and Maureen had sent him a fishing rod, so Heather would bring worms and he'd fish while they talked. One day he told Heather he'd lit the barn—the facility's carpentry shop—on fire. He seemed proud of himself, as though defying her to love him any less. While he continued to insist on his mom's attachment to him, bragging about the fishing pole she'd sent and the unfulfilled promises he clung to, he started spending weekends with Heather and her husband, Jerry.

In 2004, when Ryan was seventeen, Heather and Jerry got foster certified and invited Ryan to move in with them and their young children—Joanna, three; Jeffrey, two.

Ryan was reluctant. "My mom's coming for me," he said. "She's going to bring me a PlayStation."

But she didn't come.

"We want to be with you," Heather insisted a few weeks later. "Come with us."

"On one condition," Jerry cautioned. "You can move in with us, but you're not going to lie."

For a while, Ryan thrived. He attended the neighborhood high school and was on track to graduate. Joanna and Jeffrey adored him. He was affectionate and playful. It was as though living with them had healed him, and taught him that he could count on being cared for.

He was seventeen now, but some nights he didn't want to sleep alone. He'd bring his blanket into Heather and Jerry's room and sleep curled up at the foot of their bed.

In 2005, he graduated from high school. He got a job working for one of Jerry's friends, sweeping floors and cleaning up his sheet metal shop. He seemed to be doing well.

After a while, he started to hang out with a new group of friends. He began skipping curfew and missing work. They caught him in some lies, the deal-breakers Jerry had warned him against. Then, one summer night, a local cop came to their house and asked Jerry, whose brothers were also Weymouth police officers, to step outside for a word.

"Look," he said, "the kid is trouble. He got in a fight the other day. He's going to keep getting into shit, and he lives in your house—you're going to be liable for anything he does."

"We're all he's got," Jerry said.

"I'm telling you, he's bad news. I've got my eye on him. The whole department does."

Ryan was eighteen now, an adult. He had aged out of foster care. Jerry and Heather had to think of their children, and Ryan said he was ready to try living on his own. So they bought him some furniture and helped him move into a nearby apartment. They worried about him, especially that he might be using drugs. But compared to his older brother, who had already done at least one stint in jail, Ryan seemed like he had his life together, that he was ready to test his independence.

He still had their support. Heather would check in on him daily and invite him over for dinner.

One afternoon he showed up at their house unannounced. The whole family was outside, Joanna and Jeffrey playing in the yard. Heather could tell right away that something was off—Ryan's eyes were glazed and darting, his body fidgety.

"You're not coming in today," Jerry said.

"No, man, you have to let me in," Ryan insisted. "I left something here. I need to get it."

"I don't think you did," Jerry said.

Ryan wouldn't let it go.

"Fine," Jerry said. "You need to come in? Come on in. I'll walk around with you, and you can show me what you left."

Jerry was the only stable, consistent father figure Ryan had known, and Ryan had never been disrespectful to him.

That day was different.

"Fuck you, Jerry," Ryan said, almost spitting the words. He slammed his car door and tore away from the curb, tires squealing.

Heather and Jerry didn't give up on Ryan. The next two years, there were still glimmers of the Ryan they knew, the warm, playful person who lit up the dinner table, wrestled with the little kids, and looked at them sometimes with a clear and uncomplicated gratitude for what they had become to one another. He'd been wounded, hurt, I imagined, in ways I couldn't understand. He tried to run from his pain, numbing with drugs and alcohol. But when finally his anger boiled over, he committed an unspeakable act of violence no one could have seen coming. His actions ended a precious life too soon and shattered a family. Yet, even after Joanna's death, Heather could never think of Ryan solely as the person who had murdered her daughter; he was a victim, too, a boy who'd been let down and sought safety in her home, curled up at the foot of her bed.

This was what made my feelings toward Amber so complicated. She was a victim too—of neglect and abuse, of poverty and grief. I felt for her predicament. I wanted her to feel better, to be well. But I couldn't let what she'd suffered become a cost or danger to Ethan and Logan, who had our hearts completely, whom we were bound to protect.

I'd once thought of trauma as a single incident, a stone that ripples the surface of the water for a time before it falls to the bottom and the disturbance subsides. Now trauma seemed more water than stone, a river that goes on and on, lives and generations swept up in its current.

Chapter 9

The Story of My Life

Two weeks into rehab, Amber dropped out.

It was a jarring disappointment.

And it was a huge relief.

I felt myself exhale a little. Technically, nothing had changed. We were still on Plan A, supporting reunification until a judge decided that was no longer the goal. We still didn't know how the story would end—and Jason kept reminding me how complicated the path to recovery could be. But in the confusing swirl of trying to predict and control outcomes, this was a clear fact: Amber had tried rehab and failed. It didn't tell us for sure what would happen next. But it was one known point in a moving sea of unanswered questions about Amber's capacity to parent, and potential risks for the boys.

Jason and my first year of marriage had blown by, a tornado of events. We hadn't anticipated a shotgun wedding, yet in just twelve months, we had become parents to two boys with potentially one more on the way. Never could we have predicted all of this when we walked hand in hand down the aisle of the Ebell a year earlier. When the quartet played "Crazy in Love," I saw the flash of lights from cameras and not the image of Amber on a bus from Vegas, with Ethan in her arms. I didn't know our paths would cross, or just how intertwined our futures would become.

I tried to let myself relax and enjoy the rituals of fall. We went to Mr. Bones Pumpkin Patch in Culver City, where Ethan chose the biggest, bumpiest pumpkin and rode a miniature horse, screaming like the first teen killed in a horror film. Our daily walks through the arcade of blooming jacarandas and trumpet trees lining the side streets of Larchmont Village, our neighborhood, provided a natural palette for Ethan to identify colors. On Sundays you could tell who dressed the boys by which team's jersey they were wearing; Steelers meant it was Jason and the Patriots was me.

We celebrated Halloween, Ethan dressed as a penguin with a black top hat, red bow tie, and bright yellow feet, a pacifier in his mouth. I took my favorite picture of Jason, Logan, and our terrier, Roxy, sleeping together, Jason spooning Lo, Lo's arm thrown up over his head, Roxy nestled into Jason's back—a perfect portrait of the blissful exhaustion of family life, of our all-in comfort and togetherness.

For the past few years, I had been consulting for FosterMore, a nonprofit working to reframe the conversation around foster care in America. The organization secures millions of dollars of donated television, streaming, and radio airtime for public service announcements each year and provides factual resources about foster care to writers, producers, and showrunners. Our deep ties within the entertainment industry allow us to consult for TV and film about foster care topics. I came up with the idea to combine my marketing background and personal passion to recruit foster parents through social media advertising. I'd been confronting the many forces—addiction, poverty, trauma—that work against birth parents. What about foster parents? Los Angeles County has roughly 21,000 youths in foster care, more than any other place in the country.[1] According to FosterMore, two-thirds of foster parents in

Los Angeles came from the lowest tax bracket. We took that to mean there were large swaths of the population who had yet to be reached by traditional recruiting methods, individuals and families who might be willing to foster a child.

The challenge facing Los Angeles wasn't unique. There were more children and teens in need of foster families than people willing to foster, and retention rates for foster parents were in the tank. Those who were opening their homes appeared to either know the young person they'd be caring for prior to signing up; were like Jason and me, looking to build a family; or were responding to a crisis in their community. Many lived on the same blocks as the youth entering care; sometimes it was a relative or a close friend's child. They recognized social workers making regular visits, coming and going throughout the week. Or they learned about the need from their church or other community group and wanted to be of service.

When a community runs out of foster homes, agencies may be forced to place adolescents and teens in a variety of settings, including group homes, emergency shelters, treatment facilities, and inpatient hospitals. There has been a decline in congregate care placements across the country, achieved in part by providing more up-front interventions, doubling down on efforts to find suitable homes for teenagers, and reserving the residential treatment beds for young people with the most complex behavioral and mental health needs.[2] But there are still too few available foster homes for the number of kids in waiting. I believed more people would be open to fostering if they could feel a connection to the youth and families, a sense of ownership for the county's challenge. We decided to focus our foster parent recruitment campaign on middle-income individuals and families, the largest population overlooked by existing efforts.

How could we generate an even broader base of support for foster youth? How could we get more people from diverse socioeconomic groups to work for the success and thriving of kids and families on the margins? How could we eradicate the myths and misperceptions about foster care in a culture that tends to paint foster parents in the extreme—as pious saints or financial opportunists or, worse, predators?

We needed to talk to some middle-income foster parents about their experiences and what made them decide to take this journey as well as some prospective foster parents, people who were likely to have never even thought about it before, to see what would make them consider fostering. From my experience in political campaigns, I knew polls tell you *what* people think, but focus groups tell you *why* they think it. I planned two back-to-back nights of focus groups in Los Angeles, to listen to foster parents and potential foster parents.

My research in advance of the focus groups revealed that 50 percent of licensed foster homes stop taking children in under a year, deeply widening the gap between foster home supply and demand.[3] The crisis-level shortage of homes across the country sometimes leaves well-meaning social workers asking well-intentioned foster parents to take on more youths than they can handle. Overburdened social workers and overloaded foster homes are a ticking time bomb. Homes with a half dozen foster children, all shouldering the heft of their own trauma, are a recipe for disaster. All signs point to the need for more capable and loving foster homes. If we had more people willing to share themselves with a child in need, social workers could actually match kids with families instead of available beds.

The foster parents who participated in my focus groups were happy to share their experiences. Some had adopted, some had cases ending in reunification, and some who survived reunifications had even signed up for a second round. I applaud their courage, but I'd rather volunteer for a second circumcision than a second round of foster-adopt purgatory. The focus groups quickly turned into a collective venting session, strangers commiserating over their shared experiences. They felt taken for granted, annoyed they were often told where and when to be somewhere, without any consideration of their time and schedule. They complained about overworked social workers who were too busy to answer their calls. They were frustrated they had no insights into their cases and that they had no say in the outcome. Much of what I heard was hitting very close to home. They had survived the uncertainty I was living and that gave me hope. Creating a new recruitment campaign was giving me hope too. If I could recruit more people like them, like Jason and me, to become foster parents, maybe we could solve the crisis.

When I returned home after the second night of focus groups—this time with potential foster parents—I excitedly told Jason, "Babe, I cracked the code."

"Great. Free Netflix!" he joked.

"Most of the people I interviewed said they cared and would like to be of service," I began, ignoring his joke, "but they'd never thought about fostering before."

I continued, "There was a common misperception of youth in foster care—that something *they* had done landed them in care, rather than something that was done to them."

"Like a bad kid in a bad situation, instead of a good kid in a bad situation," he responded.

"Exactly," I said, my passion and excitement building. "The people I interviewed tonight said that becoming a foster parent had never been presented to them as an option. When we showed videos depicting the positive impact being a foster or adoptive parent had on other people's lives, the participants in the focus group were able to see themselves in that role for the first time and a lot of them said they were now more likely to consider becoming one."

"You figured all that out just by talking to people for two nights?" he asked.

"Yeah. Well, actually, I get more from what they don't say," I added. "One lady told us an ad we tested wasn't believable because the child actor had braces and 'a kid in foster care wouldn't have braces.'"

"What did she mean by that?" he asked.

"What she was asking was, 'Who's paying for those?' But the deeper subtext I took away from her comment was that she didn't think any-one would be advocating hard enough for a child in foster care to get braces. It goes back to the point that people still believe kids enter foster care because they did something wrong, which is absolutely not true." Tackling this campaign was becoming a way of soothing my anxiety. It may not impact the outcome of Ethan and Logan's case, but maybe we could recruit enough people to help other kids in the future.

"Got it," he said, then, without missing a beat, he offered up an ingenious idea. "What if you got One Direction to give you the license to 'The Story of My Life' and you created a series of ads set to the song, which showcase the stories of real families, the experiences of real foster parents and foster kids?"

"That's fucking brilliant!" I kissed his scruffy face and fired off an email to a friend of mine who was involved with the boy pop wonders' management. By noon the next day, the band was in. They brought Sony Music in, too, and my colleague at FosterMore secured Ty Burrell of *Modern Family* to do the voice-overs for the new video campaign. (It proved the truth I'd always known deep inside—that despite whatever may have happened between him and Taylor Swift, Harry Styles was as bighearted as he was talented!)

In the first round of ads, we featured the story of Mary Lee, a young woman who entered foster care at twelve and was adopted by her social worker shortly before aging out, and the Smith-Knight family, an interracial gay couple with twin Latino sons who'd entered foster care when they were six months old.

"I remember when they moved in with us," one of the dads says, his voice breaking with emotion, "they walked into the house with their little bags and they ran right to their room. They knew it. It was *their room.*"

My heart grew fifteen sizes every time I watched the video. I felt the dads' love for their sons and their relief that the adoption was final; whatever uncertainty they'd experienced was a fading memory. I also felt the ache of wanting the same happy ending for my family, for our boys—who were our home, our family—I wanted them here to stay.

———

One Sunday night, a month after we learned Amber had dropped out of rehab, the Bat Phone rang. It was her. She'd checked herself back into a different rehab. We put her on speaker so the boys could hear her voice. Ethan squealed a few times, then promptly moved on to pressing buttons on the phone.

Amber sounded different, self-aware and accountable in ways I hadn't heard before. She wondered out loud where she'd made the wrong turn, which decision had landed her on this path. When she began smoking pot or messing around with other drugs? Was it the influence of friends? The lack of supervision at home? Or was it less a choice she'd made, and more something that had happened? Like her mom dying in a car crash when she was young, and the years she'd spent missing someone she barely had a chance to know? Or the inappropriate things adults did to her, the things no one was there to protect her from?

"I needed to get out of that house," she said. "Bad things happened to me there. I'm not going to let bad people near my kids." This was the first time I'd thought she sounded clearheaded.

"I have a lot of work to do. But I want to be the best mom I can be," she said with resolve. "I love my babies more than anything."

Jason tapped into his recovery wisdom. "All you can do is take it one day at a time," he said. "Focus on the moment." How he could forfeit his own worries and fears to support the only person whose actions could determine the outcome was astounding. I didn't have his experience with addiction to pull from, and even if I had, I'm not sure I would have. But I loved that he did.

"Yeah," Amber agreed.

She took a ragged breath and her voice unspooled in a string of stories and observations, what her days were like in rehab, what she remembered and thought about and hoped for. Jason leaned toward the phone as she spoke, offering mmm-hmms and words of encouragement. I was moved by the way he listened and supported, but I also felt like I was on the outside, able to empathize but somehow unable to connect. Fifteen years earlier, Jason had confronted his own alcohol addiction—sick and tired of being sick and tired, ready to make a change. He didn't share Amber's background of trauma and abuse—but if he hadn't worked on his recovery, he wouldn't have become the person, husband, or father I knew him to be. I felt a wave of appreciation for whatever grace had carried Jason to sobriety—and to our life—and a deep hope for Amber. A fear and sorrow for her too. A recognition of all she faced.

I ached for the boys. None of us could predict whether or not Amber could overcome all the obstacles she was up against, whether or not she could change and heal and become the parent they deserved and the mother she wanted to be.

When she'd asked us to be the boys' godparents, she seemed to have an idealized, old-timey black-and-white mental image of her and Zach raising the boys with us as the uncles and respite caregivers. In her mind's eye, we would be one big, happy family.

But I wasn't on board with this fantasy. In her picture, the important details were blurred, invisible to the naked eye. How would I know they were safe, spared from Zach's anger or the abuse of Amber's childhood, if I only got to see them at Sunday dinners?

"The other women here have been really supportive of me." Amber's voice on the other end of the phone snapped me out of my thought spiral. "I know Zach and I have a lot of work to do."

As soon as she said his name, it occurred to me that Zach was the wild card. If Amber got better, could she do this alone? I didn't think I could do it alone, and I had a lot more working in my favor—a good income, a house, and a doting community of family and friends, for starters. It wouldn't be easy. But if she could quit drugs, could she quit Zach?

Kris had told us that Zach had an on-again, off-again relationship with drugs and alcohol but that he'd recently checked into a rehab in El Segundo. Zach hadn't made any effort to call or see the boys, and I was so overwhelmed by everything going on with Amber that I hadn't even begun to think about his recovery. Now that Amber was working on herself, I worried about the impact he'd have on her sobriety.

For Amber, separating from Zach might be harder than giving up drugs.

After Jaime died, a therapist warned me that people who lose someone they love when they're not mature enough to process the loss often end up holding on to unhealthy relationships in the future. When a loved one dies or moves on, the feelings linger like the scent of a strong perfume. It's easy and common to ascribe the displaced feelings earned by the one we lost to someone who hasn't earned them, someone who hasn't put in the effort or the time. Amber had tried to leave Zach once before, when she boarded that Greyhound bus back to LA, but she took him back.

I kept returning to the idea that the safest scenario for the boys was that we adopt them and give Amber the time and space she needed to get well. She would be a part of their lives, visiting regularly, and Jason and I could mentor her on some of the big hurdles she was facing—finding a job, managing a budget, and staying on her feet. The boys would know her and be proud of the woman she became in the face of so much adversity. The way I saw it, Jason and I were already their day-to-day support, the parents who would clean their wounds, cook their meals, and be there for anything they may need.

It was impossible to know what would happen next. Ethan and Logan were defenseless, voiceless little beings who were going to endure whatever fate was cast upon them. And what I wanted most, what caused the pain in my gut, was an assurance they would be safe.

I stayed up most of that night researching, trying to find studies showing outcomes for kids who were adopted by foster parents and those who reunified with their birth families. This was never a case of "us versus them." Our intent was always to adopt a child who needed loving, caring, capable parents, never to take one from parents who had hit a rough patch and with the right supports could handle the responsibilities of parenting. But that night I struggled to reconcile what I knew was morally right with what my heart desired.

The best possible scenario was, of course, that parents like Amber and Zach be better supported in facing the challenges that could lead to neglect, namely poverty, addiction, and mental illness—that there be more of a social safety net, with better prevention services to show our commitment to children's safety and well-being. But on the couch that night, I just wanted to know, if the boys returned to Amber and Zach's care, what did the statistics predict their lives would be like? How would they fare in terms of education, health, safety? My search turned up thin.

In California, nearly one in five children who leave foster care re-enter the system within two years.[4] But how many children reentered after two years? I wanted longer-term studies. What happens down the road? Could the government hire the people who used to work for Blockbuster Video, the ones who relentlessly tracked us down over late fees, to check in on families to see how they are doing? To offer them help if they hit a bump in the road? From what I could tell, it appeared the system was conflating the terms "permanency" and "happily ever after." Happiness is often short-lived.

And what about the children like Ethan and Logan, who were in the system? How did we know if, post-reunification, they would be safe from the abuse or neglect that had necessitated their removal in the first place? Research showed infants were most likely to reenter the system, and in cases where parental drug and alcohol treatment was recommended, as it had been for Amber and Zach, were more than twice as likely to experience reentry.[5]

What kind of services and resources would be offered to Amber and Zach, to other families with chronic needs around substance use and mental health? What would they look like, how often would they be available to them, and how would they access them? There just wasn't good evidence, at least that I could find, on how to make a situation of abuse or neglect safe again.

I wondered if there was resistance in the field to delving too deeply into the realities of reunification, to exploring whether the outcomes are actually better or worse if a kid goes home. Was there a reluctance to pull back the curtain, to see what was really happening? Or was it just too hard to track information?

I thought about the nurse who visited Oscar and Kristin's flat in London after the birth of their son Harry. Was this service actually making a difference in the number of children entering foster care in the UK? They still have a foster care system. If this, and other impactful services, were offered universally to families in the US, could we prevent more kids from entering foster care? And even if we did offer these services, would distrust of government among oppressed and marginalized communities run too deep for families to accept the help of the interventions? Would the programs understand and respect the values, attitudes, and beliefs of all cultures? Would they offer services regardless of immigration status?

I don't know these answers. A midwife making home visits in the weeks after a child is born might be able to spot the warning signs of untreated substance use or mental illness. Expanding upstream interventions like free or subsidized child care could keep families from falling into poverty.[6] Predictive risk modeling might be a powerful tool in helping agencies do a better job of identifying and supporting those at risk and keeping families intact.[7] If nothing else, knowing we tried, that parents were given the opportunity to heal, to improve their situation, may give workers more peace of mind, a more solid moral standing, if they ultimately end up detaining a child.

Knowing I neither had the expertise nor the power to answer these questions, I closed my laptop and went upstairs. I peeked into Ethan's room and then stopped in the nursery to check on Logan, who was fast asleep in the warm glow of the nightlight. I didn't know what the future held, but I knew they were safe now. I adjusted his blanket, kissed his soft cheeks, and climbed into bed with my husband.

By all appearances we were winning—we were a family. But I couldn't escape the gut instinct gnawing at me, telling me that something was off and things were not going to turn out as we hoped.

Chapter 10

House on Fire

It was Tuesday, November 8, 2016. Election Day. A day that, for me, has always carried its own energy, a pulse that throughout the day beats faster and harder. The vibrations, ripples from the collision of hope and fear.

By midmorning, I had given up on getting any work done. To pass the time before the polls closed and ballots started getting counted, I spent the day catching up with some of my old campaign friends and calling Democrats in swing states to remind them to go vote. I was wholly unprepared for the results as they began coming in. The impact of the election was personal. In the years since we worked to have same-sex marriage legally recognized in Iowa, the pendulum had swung in our favor, but would that momentum hold? There were fifteen states with no laws prohibiting discrimination against sexual orientation or gender identity in adoption.[1] California felt safe. But what would that mean in this new administration for families like ours in other states and for the 400,000 kids in foster care, many of whom had no family and no place to call home? Same-sex couples are three times as likely to be raising an adopted child and more than twice as likely to be fostering a child as heterosexual couples.[2] How many of them would be deterred by fear or ignorance in their home states? How many states would outlaw gay adults from adopting altogether?

The hardest part for me was thinking about what this would mean for young gay kids, who make up a larger share of the foster care population than the general population.[3] LGBTQ+ youths often come out to loved ones and face rejection, hatred, or even violence. Some of them are thrown out of their homes or run away and end up in foster care. Knowing the shame I felt as a child, struggling to accept this part of myself, I couldn't imagine what it must be like for a gay child in foster care, who gets assigned to an agency that won't allow same-sex couples to foster. Children don't get to select their foster families. Government-run child welfare agencies place kids with organizations that recruit and train foster families. So, a child who has endured abuse or neglect because of their sexuality could end up exposed to further trauma by being forced into a family whose personal or religious beliefs are at extreme odds with the child's orientation or gender identity.

But it wasn't just those of us in the LGBTQ+ community I feared for. The anti-immigrant vitriol that had rallied the other side's base was just beginning a crescendo. When I thought about Josephine and her loved ones, my throat tightened, and it was hard to swallow. She arrived each morning when I was still in pajamas. She cared for the boys when Jason and I were at work and at the end of the day we'd all dance together in the kitchen to make the boys laugh. She was more than a caregiver; she had become family. I loved Josephine's soft smile and the way her shoulders sprang up and down when she laughed. I worried about her family. Would they be wrongfully profiled or detained because of their race?

At the end of the day, the loss I felt when I worked for Hillary Clinton in 2008 was easier to accept than this loss, to Donald Trump. A thick, choking cloud of dread washed over me. I feared what would happen next. What follows the defeat of compassion? When the greater good is overtaken by ignorance, would kindness survive, or would it be scorched like a California forest? I braced for the worst, paralyzed by all the unknowns that were beyond my control. Fearing at any moment, everything important to me could be taken away, one by one—my marriage, my children, my family.

A few days later, as I pulled the car up our narrow driveway and into our garage, Jason called. It was unlike him to call when he could have easily texted.

"Hey, babe," I answered, trying to sound chipper and not like my entire vision of our country's future was being held together by Scotch tape and bubble gum.

"You're not going to believe this shit," he started in. "I just got a call from someone at the county. They wanted to know if Lo was exhibiting any signs that he'd been shaken." I could hear the anger in his voice.

"What?" I said, in shock. "I don't understand."

"When the boys were first detained, Amber claimed that one night, a few weeks earlier, Logan was crying," he explained. "She told the social worker that Zach lost his temper and shook him."

"Oh my god." I felt instantly panicked. I wanted to run to Logan, to envelop him in my arms. "How would we even know?"

"They said he may have seizures or trouble staying awake," Jason explained.

"He doesn't have those," I said, adding, "He was doing that weird stretching thing, but the therapist said that was common in kids who've been drug exposed."

"It's not that. He's fine," he said. "He's got the best pediatrician in LA and she didn't see anything wrong with him. What I don't understand is, why the hell is the county just now asking us if he's okay? We've had the kids for six months." Jason was right. I hadn't even thought about that, but if the county had told us there was a possibility he was shaken, we could have been looking out for symptoms or taken him to a specialist.

"Did you ask them why they waited?"

"Yes," he said. "They told me they have a lot of cases to investigate and that they're short-staffed."

"That's bullshit," I said, opening my car door into our crammed garage, packed tightly with tools, pool rafts, and stacked boxes of holiday decorations that looked like the slightest seismic activity would send them crashing down on me. "Do you think that's why Zach asked if we thought he was going to be 'a slow kid'?"

"Well, Amber recanted and told them it never happened—that she'd made it up because the two of them were fighting."

"Of course she did," I said. "She probably changed her story when she realized he could go to jail. Why didn't she tell us? We could have gotten Logan checked out."

"Well, I'd like to give Amber and Zach the benefit of the doubt," Jason said. "But not the county. This investigation sat on someone's desk for six months. That's neglect."

My mind kept flashing back to the first time we met Amber and Zach, at Kris's house, when Amber didn't acknowledge Logan or even want to hold him. And then at Patty's office for the needs and services meeting, after Zach asked if we thought he was going to be a "slow kid," she smothered Ethan but wouldn't pay any attention to Logan. The writing was on the wall, but no one wanted to read it. If she was carrying the guilt of Lo's abuse, that she had failed to stop it, to keep her baby safe, then Zach must know he was to blame. I didn't want to believe any of it. How could I support reunification when my suspicions were this strong? How could I let Zach near the boys ever again? How could Amber stay with Zach after she had accused him of hurting her child? How could the system I wanted to trust be so flawed? And what if I was wrong? What if she *had* just made the whole thing up?

———

Over Christmas we took the boys on their first plane ride to visit our parents and extended families in Pittsburgh and then Brockton. The love and security of family buoyed me. There's a comfort that comes with being in the familiar circle of loved ones, but this time it was as a parent, watching Ethan and Logan pressed in hugs, held in laughter at our loud, happy gatherings. One night, my cousin Christopher, who'd been fostered and then adopted by my uncle Jimmy and aunt Sharon when he was five and I was seven, pulled me aside.

"Mark," he said, "I know why you chose to foster those boys." Choking up, he added, "You're the best man I know."

I knew it was a vulnerable thing for him to say, communicating both his appreciation for being a part of our family, and of my choice to extend that same invitation to children in the next generation. Yet his praise made me uncomfortable. I realized I'd never told him how much it had meant to me for him to join our family.

As close as we were growing up, swimming and catching dozens of frogs together in the summers at Lake Winnipesaukee during our family vacations in New Hampshire, he never talked about his birth parents or his life before he became my cousin. Growing up, as far as I knew, the day my aunt's station wagon pulled up in front of my house and Christopher emerged from the back seat in bright red Nikes and a Boston Bruins jersey was the first day of his life.

I gave him a hug and suddenly felt a pang of sorrow. Everyone else in the room had a seat at the family table for the rest of their lives. Not Ethan and Logan. No matter how much we all cherished them, no matter how much it felt like they belonged, we didn't know where they would be this time next year.

Mom saw me choking up and caught my eye. "It's going to be okay, honey," she said. "You'll see."

I didn't know if she was right or wrong, but it didn't matter. She was just doing what a parent does. Loving me. Supporting me. Reassuring me. Making me feel safe in treacherous waters.

I was learning just how complicated safety could be.

Another night during our visit, we gathered with Dad's side of the family. Divorces and in-laws made it a challenge to get everyone in the family together at the same time, so we always celebrated holidays in phases. That night Heather and a few other cousins and their kids came to my parents' house. My mom and sister laid out a spread of meatballs and other finger foods. Heather and I sat next to each other at the table. She was warm and chatty, her usual fun-to-be-around self. She could relate to the foster experience—the monthly social worker visits, the requirement to lock up knives and medicines. I didn't have a lot of people close to me who could relate to our experience, and I loved being able to share my journey with someone in my family.

I also wondered how much of Heather's attention was consumed by Joanna's absence. Joanna would have been fifteen. Did Heather picture her playing with the little kids? Lingering at the table after the meal, exploring her place in adult conversations? Did she always keep a chair at the table for the daughter who wasn't there?

I ached for Heather, for Kris, for every parent doing the best they can to protect a child. Some moments I longed to go back to the days when plan B meant a pharmacy visit with the girls before brunch—not the 55 percent chance my heart would be chewed up and spit out. But then I looked at my family—at Jason, Ethan, and Logan—and knew that this love, this warm shelter we had created, was worth the risk. I tried not to focus too much on how quickly it could all disappear.

———

The feelings of vulnerability and precariousness that had come over me before the holidays intensified a few weeks later. On Martin Luther King Jr. Day, Jason took the boys to the zoo, and I went into the empty office to catch up on paperwork while the place was quiet. We arrived home together, fed the kids dinner, and were just heading upstairs to give them baths when I said, "Jason, do you smell smoke?"

"No. I don't smell anything," he responded as Roxy, our ailing thirteen-year-old terrier, bounded up ahead of us and started doing cartwheels on the landing.

"What's up with Roxy?" I said, stepping out of the way so she wouldn't slam into me with her wild gymnastic flips. "Did she get her meds today, babe?"

"Yes," Jason said, tossing Ethan's diaper into the trash barrel.

Roxy stopped leaping and twisting, barked loudly, and gave me a long stare. Then she squatted down and lifted her leg slightly. She hadn't peed in the house since the night we brought Brian home as a puppy from a charity auction, and she'd done so out of spite—she had never asked for a sibling. I handed Logan to Jason, who was warming the water in the tub, and quickly scooped Roxy up, taking her downstairs and outside to the backyard. I had just closed the screen door behind me when she threw herself into it, slamming her body insistently against the wood.

"Babe, Roxy is going nuts," I called out, still watching her through the screen.

"I think I smell smoke now!" Jason shouted from upstairs. I turned around. I could see clouds of smoke in the hallway.

"Jason!" I yelled up the stairs. "Get the kids outside. Now!"

Smoke was now filling every room downstairs, but I couldn't see any flames. Jason ran down the stairs with the kids—both boys were naked, wrapped in one giant towel, with water dripping off their bodies.

"Call 9-1-1!" he shouted as he shut off the main power switch, grabbed diapers, and hustled the boys next door to Joe and Loyce. I followed his instructions.

"9-1-1 please hold," the voice on the other end of the phone said. I hung up and tried again. "9-1-1 please hold." I waited this time.

The HVAC system had been serviced that morning and I assumed that was the source of the fire. I stood at the door to the basement and touched the doorknob tentatively to see if it was hot. It wasn't. When I opened the door I couldn't see any flames from the top of the stairs, but I wasn't going to venture into the basement of a one-hundred-year-old house on fire.

Just then, I heard sirens. Best to let the cavalry handle this one. I held open the front door as firefighters ran up the steps wielding giant axes. I told them about the HVAC and waited in the front yard with a growing number of neighbors who had come over to observe the spectacle. I didn't know if the county would blame us for the fire and take the boys away or if they'd praise our quick action. Were we now guilty of "neglect"? Could it happen that quickly and easily? When we got the all clear, Jason suggested I take the boys and the dogs to a hotel while he stayed to talk to the firefighters and waited for the insurance rep.

"Keep sleep and routines consistent," I told myself as I drove our half-bathed, half-dressed children and dogs to a nearby hotel.

When Jason joined us around eleven o'clock, Ethan was still wide awake. The new space, the dogs barking at people coming off the elevator, and the noise outside on Wilshire Boulevard were too distracting for him to sleep. Jason had spoken to the insurance company and they said we'd need a new furnace, and that it'd likely be a month before we could return home.

The next day, Josephine met us to watch the boys at the house of our friend who was in New York for the week. I was physically in the office that day, but my head was preoccupied with figuring out where we were going to stay and making sure our lodging was acceptable to the county. We'd need outlet covers and baby gates, and to make sure all the cabinets had safety locks. Our insurance company kept trying to send us to a hotel with a single room near the airport and I kept saying *no*. If the crammed space didn't force me to go insane, the traffic to work would for sure. We held firm and were able to spend the next two nights at our friend's place. After two days of back-and-forth with the insurance agent, I finally said the words that changed everything: "Our foster children need their own room."

"Wait. What do you mean by that?" the agent asked.

"Jason and I are foster parents to two boys. Because we haven't adopted them yet, the county has to approve our living arrangement, and the biggest requirement is that we have at least two bedrooms. One for us and one for them to share."

"I didn't realize that," she responded. I was instantly annoyed. Jason had made this point abundantly clear, more than once. But that meant she also didn't understand the consequence of her getting this wrong.

"If you can stay at your friend's one more night, I promise I'll have this sorted out by morning," she assured me. The next day we checked into a two-bedroom town house at the AKA Hotel in Beverly Hills, and it began to rain.

———

As we settled into new, temporary routines, the gray that had overtaken the eternally blue SoCal sky charged even mundane moments with an extra sense of brittleness. One afternoon while I was at the office, Jason parked on the street in front of the hotel and Josephine helped him load the boys in to visit Amber in rehab. He was buckling Ethan in on the rear driver's side, and Josephine was on the sidewalk, getting Logan strapped into his seat, when an older man in a bright red Mercedes coupe drove by too fast and too close and swiped the open door of our car, missing Jason by inches. When the police arrived, the man's wife claimed Jason had opened his door into their car.

"That's impossible," Jason protested. "I would have had to have been sitting in my son's lap in his car seat."

He texted me to come home.

By the time I arrived, Jason was calm. He'd canceled the visit with Amber and reported the accident to our social workers. For him, the fight was over, but for me, it had just begun. Chest flaring with indignation, I ran to the office building across the street to see if they had security cameras that might have captured footage of the accident.

Jason shook his head at me. "You don't need to be a hero right now," he said. "Losing your cool is only going to hurt you."

The Mercedes driver conceded to his mistake while I was playing detective and so my meltdown felt justified—even purposeful.

Yet Jason was right. I could feel how stress and reactivity were becoming my default modes, how being powerless and out of control in the foster system was making me overly fixated on the things I felt I could control—like security cameras and men in Mercedes—especially as the kids' court date approached. It would be the first hearing since they'd entered our care. A judge would decide whether the kids would reunify with Amber and Zach or continue another six months in our home. It all seemed so impersonal, so mechanical. As though love were a car you leased on a six-month term, or a warranty you decided to let expire or renew—not a permanent fact of life, a force that humbled you again and again as it grew.

———

One day in early February, Logan stood, holding one arm out in front of him and one up in the air, and, smiling cheek to cheek, blue eyes beaming with pride, took his first steps in our hotel room. The funny position of his arms and the syncopated shuffle of his feet made it look like he was dancing the samba. Jason scrambled for his phone to take a video, and I held Brian to make sure the tail of his hundred-pound frame didn't accidentally shatter the moment.

It was exhilarating and mind-blowing to see this healthy baby, who eight months earlier had entered our lives skinny from malnourishment, lift himself up and take his first steps. How quickly he was learning the tools of life and survival. But as soon as I realized I was feeling joy, anxiety barged in, sideswiping my happiness and knocking it aside, like a bright red angry Mercedes. I had nowhere to be but in this moment, yet my mind couldn't stay put. I was sprinting on the treadmill of what-ifs. What if the judge sends them back to Amber and Zach? What if they get hurt? What if Zach uses drugs again or hurts one of them? I began to get frustrated. Goddammit, why couldn't I just let myself experience this moment? Why did I have to worry right now?

Two sides of my brain were at war with each other, one telling me to relax, to calm down, and the other telling me to prepare for the worst. A pattern of vulnerability intolerance had become stuck, like a broken record replaying over and over in my life. My subconscious wrestling to limit exposure to joy, to protect myself from disappointment and heartbreak when the other shoe drops. I had never let my heart be more vulnerable than it was now, watching Lo's sweet little face as his tiny legs scuttled across the floor.

That night as I was trying to fall asleep, my mind raced like never before. I couldn't escape my fear that the boys would be moved away from us and back to Amber and Zach. Suddenly it felt like a giant elephant was sitting on my chest. I tried to get air into my lungs, to swallow, but my body was frozen. I was wide awake, sitting up, panting for air. I had never had a panic attack before, yet I knew exactly what was happening.

Jason did too. He put a hand on my shoulder. "Where are your feet?" he said, trying to ground me to the present moment. "Where are your feet?"

I focused on the warm pressure of his hand against my skin and the sensation of my heels against the sheet. I took slow breaths, in for three, out for three, and slowly, like a curtain rising, the panic lifted, bringing me back to the present scene. I was aware of the bed, the room around me, the sound of our dogs breathing softly in the dark, Jason's soothing voice in my ear.

"I'm just so scared," I whispered when I was steady enough to speak.

"And what can you do in this very moment?" Jason asked.

"About the court date? Nothing."

"Right," Jason said. "Stay where your feet are. It's the only thing in your control."

It was such a hard reality to hold—that no amount of planning or preparation on our part could influence or even predict the outcome. *I don't know what's going to happen,* Kendra had told us from the start. All we had was the present. If I didn't stay in it, I was going to lose everything I had.

Chapter 11

Love Is Not All You Need

O n February 24, 2017, just three days before the court date, Jason brought the boys to a scheduled visit to see Amber at her rehab facility near Lancaster. Amber had recently given birth to her fourth child, a girl named Savannah. It seemed tough on the boys to spend two and a half hours in the car for a three-hour visit, but they hadn't seen their mom in months, and had never met their newborn sister.

Amber had confirmed the visit the night before, but when Jason and the boys arrived, she seemed flustered, and surprised to see them. Jason offered to hold Savannah so Amber could focus on the boys. She watched Logan show off his samba-walk and halfheartedly played with Ethan, but after forty-five minutes—less than a third of the time her visitation rights allowed—she asked Jason to leave.

"They're making me do a lot here," she said, and shrugged her shoulders.

He didn't know what to make of her behavior. She had her three children together for the first time, but her mind was somewhere else. She barely spoke during the entire visit and appeared annoyed by their presence. Was she just exhausted from caring for an infant while taking on the emotional work of recovery? Did she have postpartum depression—and if so, was she getting the help she needed? Or was she losing interest in her relationship with the boys? How would any of these factors impact what happened in court? And what about Zach? We never heard from him. He didn't call. He hadn't scheduled any visits with the boys. Did he even want them back? Was he working on himself? Would his kids even recognize him? Between Zach's disappearance and Amber's state of mind, I was even more afraid of what would happen to them if they returned home.

I wanted the judge to say they weren't doing enough to reunify with their sons. I was ashamed to tell anyone, even Jason, that I wanted the judge to say, there's no way they could care for three babies under the age of two. They weren't ready. Maybe they would be in six months, but not while still in rehab and not when they had barely spent any time with the boys. I knew I should be rooting for Amber and Zach's speedy recovery—for them to get better, to heal their family. But the boys needed more and deserved more than they could offer. Could they get better? Possibly, but they hadn't yet.

Jason noted the short duration of the visit in the parental visitation log we were required to keep, and we did our best to focus on having fun with the kids while we white-knuckled the remaining days till the hearing.

We had been told so many times that we must support reunification until that was no longer the plan—even if we didn't believe it was the right plan. Patty had told us a story of a case she'd worked on where the foster parents voiced so much concern about the biological parents' ability to care for the kids that the county worker moved the children to a different foster home. The way she described it, the worker had retaliated against the family for caring too much. In training we'd been warned that the concerns raised by foster parents are often pushed aside, written off as the biased statements of stakeholders trying to tank reunification efforts to serve their own interests. I didn't want to believe workers were vindictive or petty, but I wasn't going to ignore this advice and find out the hard way. It forced us into a difficult balancing act. We absolutely had to report any concerns we had, but what if they didn't believe us or thought we were posturing?

Not being heard was a new experience for me. I wasn't used to not having my opinion taken into consideration—it's one of the privileges I've never earned but has been afforded to me by the combination of my gender and race. But in this situation, who knew better than Jason or me how the boys were doing, what was happening at visits? We were the ones raising the boys and monitoring their visits with their parents. And it felt like Patty was the only one we could be truly open with, but the foster family agencies have as little a voice in the courts as we did. We danced on eggshells in our conversations with Kendra, trying to share Amber's indifference toward the boys and her detached behavior, afraid our observations would risk alienation. In my gut, I knew Kendra wanted what was best for the boys, but we'd been warned so many times, and I loved Ethan and Logan too much to take the risk. The few times I shared my fears with Kendra, letting it slip that Zach's display of anger toward her made me fear for the boys and that Amber's disinterest in Logan was alarming, she'd nod to let me know she was listening, but that was it. No words of validation or agreement. I was left staring into the flawless skin of her poker face.

One time, a month or so after the boys arrived, Ethan tripped on a step in the backyard and bumped his head. We were freaking out—not only were we new parents, but the toddler wasn't technically ours. Jason took him to the emergency room; we filed all the required incident reports and notified Kendra immediately. It took her three days to return our call. But when she did, she said, "I'm sorry for not getting back to you sooner. I've got about forty-five open cases right now and I was not at all concerned about you and Jason doing the right thing." Later she told me that when I had called, she had been dealing with a case involving an Amber alert, which helped me register that she's got a lot bigger problems going on than two scared, yet entirely capable, dads panicking over a stumbling toddler. I was, however, relieved to have her confidence.

Kendra had been doing this work for over a decade. She'd helped plenty of parents heal and get their kids back. She'd also helped kids who'd been subjected to unimaginable sexual and physical abuse. She knew the courts, and I wanted her to make a prediction, an educated guess. Are the boys going back to Zach and Amber or not? But I couldn't ask, and she couldn't tell me either way.

On the morning of the hearing, Josephine arrived early to watch the boys so we'd have plenty of time to cross Los Angeles and arrive at the courthouse in Monterey Park by 8:30 a.m. My stomach was tight with anxiety as Jason backed the car down the driveway. I feared the judge would send the boys home with Amber and Zach, ending the torment of my uncertainty, but creating new unease about their future safety. My hands were shaky. I didn't know if it was nerves or the two cups of coffee I'd downed on an empty stomach.

After a few turns, we exited our quiet tree-lined neighborhood and entered Koreatown, the joggers and dog owners out for their morning strolls quickly replaced by families waiting for buses to take them to school or work. I watched strangers going through the insignificant motions of their daily routines, a mother holding her young daughter's hand as they boarded a city bus, a teenager waving goodbye to his father on the sidewalk. I wanted what they had—certainty, predictability, family.

At a stoplight Jason turned to me and asked, "Are you all right?"

I looked at him, smiled, and fibbed, "Yeah." Trying my best to mask my concern: "You?"

"Yeah," he said, shooting a smile my way, and reminding me we were in this together.

We arrived at the Edmund D. Edelman Children's Court, paid six dollars—cash only—to park, went through security, checked in with the sheriff, and walked into the waiting area where hundreds of people hung around waiting for their case to be called. The waiting room was

L-shaped, a dozen or so courtrooms lining two sides with windows along the others. There were lots of kids, toddlers crying, coloring at little tables. Some groups carried balloons—clearly here for an adoption.

This was going to be the first time we'd seen Zach since learning he may or may not have shaken Logan. I felt uncomfortable about seeing him. I knew I wouldn't confront him about it, but I wasn't going to fake nice either. I just wanted to know what the future held and to move on. Timelines have been set by Congress for children under the age of three that say when a child has been in foster care for fifteen of twenty-two consecutive months, they should either reunify or parental rights should be terminated.[1] But in practice these guidelines are seen more as a suggestion than a mandate. Children often linger in the system for years, instability dragging on, making it harder and harder for them to be future oriented.[2] How do you dream of tomorrow, next year, or five years from now when you don't know what house you'll be living in next week?

Zach and Amber had already arrived with baby Savannah. They called to us and waved, gave us hugs, showed us the chairs they saved for us. Their warmth and friendliness soothed my discomfort about seeing them, but not my anxiety for the future. In a way, I was grateful for their enthusiasm—we were allies supporting the boys. I also found it a bit strange, like they didn't really understand the stakes. A judge could tell them today they were losing their boys for good. They wanted to reunite with their kids—but how was their family going to work when they were living in separate rehabs? How were they going to heal while caring for three very young children? Would Zach be able to control his temper when he was tired and the babies cried or broke something?

We waited for hours. Every fifteen minutes a sheriff would walk out of the courtroom doors and call a family name and room number. Jason went to the vending machines for snacks for Amber and Zach and talked with them about the boys and about recovery, but I couldn't concentrate on the conversation. I buried my head in work, writing and sending emails, proofreading documents on my phone, trying to give my brain something other than worry to chew on.

"Sorry I've been out of touch for a while," Zach said at one point, as though expressing regret to a friend, as though we were the ones he stood to disappoint. "It's just that I've been embarrassed. We are supposed to have our kids. I want to do right by them." There was something refreshing about his honesty. I felt relief knowing he cared about his sons and was aware of his absence in their lives. He certainly didn't owe us an apology, but his vulnerability felt sincere. And I wanted the boys to know their father loved them. He knew he'd messed up, but was he willing to put in the work to make it right?

As the hours wore on, I grew impatient. It was unfair to require people to arrive at 8:30 a.m. just to sit there all day. Jason and I both had the flexibility to miss a day's work, and losing time didn't affect our livelihood, but most people in that room were paying a steep cost. From the cash-only lot, to the all-day wait, to the impersonal "we'll-get-to-you-when-we-get-to-you" attitude, this didn't seem like a viable route to success for families trying to get their lives back together. The entire court experience felt like it was designed to cater to the professionals—the judges, lawyers, and staff—with no concern for the heartbroken parents working toward reunifying with the children they love.

At 1:30 p.m., the sheriff called our case: "Room four-twelve. Room four-twelve." Two attorneys, one representing Amber and one representing Zach, brought them into the courtroom first. Then the boys' attorney—called minors' counsel—came to get Jason and me. California guarantees children in child welfare cases their own lawyers to represent them, but fourteen states do not.[3] There are cases in those states where teenagers who have been abused, physically or sexually, are dragged into a courtroom, possibly even forced to face those who've victimized them, all without a lawyer.

The boys were represented by an attorney from the Children's Law Center, a nonprofit legal services organization.

"You didn't have to come," he said, his tone chastising, as he walked us into the hearing room, where the vibe was somehow both casual and tense. A fourth attorney was seated inside, this one representing the county.

"Actually, we feel that we need to be here," Jason replied, quickly and with resolve. Logan, now almost a year old, had been with his parents for only weeks of his life. We could best speak to the boys' current needs and development, and how could we sit at home while their future—and ours—was being decided?

The lawyer shrugged. "Suit yourself," he said, turning and walking away.

"That guy was so rude," I whispered to Jason. "Thank you for speaking up."

"We know the boys better than anyone, we should be here," Jason said.

Zach and Amber sat at the same table in front, flanked by their attorneys, like the defendants on *Judge Judy*. We took our seats on one of the wooden benches arranged in rows behind the counselors, each of their desktops heaped in papers and file folders. They thumbed quickly through the files, like an exam was about to start and they had failed to study.

"How do they keep track of which case they're on?" I whispered to Jason. We'd heard other foster parents tell us their cases had been postponed due to missing paperwork. It was easy to see how that could happen. We had completed an "optional" questionnaire about the boys' health and well-being for today's hearing. In order to ensure the judge received it, Jason had followed the instructions and dropped it off at the courthouse five days earlier, along with eight copies for the case files. It seemed so arcane and inefficient for a system this vital and extensive to be paper based. I didn't understand why Kendra couldn't just upload pdfs or scanned documents to some inexpensive software to be encrypted on a cloud. I didn't want to come in with a chip on my shoulder about a failed bureaucracy—yet it was hard to trust that good decisions would come from a system that was clearly so antiquated and overwhelmed. It just seemed so unfair, like the fate of families rested on so many moving parts, decided by an all-powerful judge, who wasn't possibly able to get a full picture of the situation from this arrangement.

The judge asked who was present for the hearing, and the bailiff told him the children's parents, minors' counsel, and the foster parents. The judge looked at us.

"Thank you for your service," she said, nodding in our direction.

Zach looked back at us and pumped his fist in the air, as though cheering us on.

"What was that about?" Jason mouthed.

"I have no idea," I whispered back, just as confused. "I think he was rooting for us?"

Amber bounced the baby in her arms. The lawyers shuffled papers and summarized the status of the case. The parents had entered rehab. They were short on visits with the kids.

"You need to make a better effort to be in communication with your sons, and spend more time with them," the county attorney told Amber and Zach.

"And who is this?" the judge asked, nodding her head toward the baby.

"This is Savannah," Amber said.

"Oh," the judge said. "Congratulations." It hadn't occurred to me that the judge wouldn't have known they had another child. It had been seven months since they appeared in court. But I assumed this development would have been in the case file. Maybe it was and the file hadn't been read.

After a few more minutes of paper shuffling and quiet conferring, the judge offered her decision. "The boys will remain with the foster parents. The birth parents will make a better effort to visit the children, and they'll keep up with rehab." She set the next court date for early August.

The judge had punted the case for six more months. I had hoped she would outline a set of milestones, a reunification rubric of sorts, that I could follow along with to predict what would happen in August. But she didn't. The ruling didn't give me the clarity I wanted, but the Band-Aid wasn't being ripped off either. I'd get more time with the boys. More time to know they were safe. More time to meet their emotional needs, and more time to fall in love.

Amber and Zach were happy and joking in the elevator on the way down. Amber smiled widely and I noticed her teeth had been fixed, her mouth full of clean, even crowns.

"Your teeth look amazing," I said.

"Thanks!" She laughed. "God, I can't even believe I went out in public before."

Out in the parking lot she told us, "We just can't tell you how much we appreciate this. You're taking such good care of the boys."

A sour feeling gathered in my gut. I was truly glad to see Amber happy and doing well. But how could I not also feel worried about what we could lose—was it even possible for me to see them clearly with so much at stake? And what about the boys? The decision just prolonged uncertainty in their lives.

Worse, there was no great outcome for them. Whatever happened, the boys got the short end of the stick. If they went back to their birth parents too soon, they ran the risk of instability and maltreatment. Yet the longer they stayed with us, the more likely it was that if they did re-unify one day, they'd be returning to parents they barely knew or would never get to know. The court proceeding had been more about buying time than building a stable, sustainable life for Ethan and Logan.

Just as I was trying to identify and ride these waves of ambivalence, Amber hit me with a tsunami. "You know, I've been reading up about becoming a surrogate. I think maybe when I get healthy again, and we get our kids back, I could be your surrogate."

I wondered for a second if she could be joking. But then Zach added, "Yeah, we make really cute kids."

I couldn't figure out what to say, or even how I felt. Was I being punked? Were they serious? Did he really believe that's how surrogacy worked? Thankfully, I didn't have to say anything because Jason responded for us: "That's so kind of you. But for now, you just focus on getting better."

Part of me was moved. She was so grateful to us for caring for her boys that she was ready to make the same sacrifice as the woman we'd met in the surrogacy office. I felt guilty for wanting to keep her sons, while she was thinking of ways she could help us become parents. She didn't seem to understand that her history of addiction and using while pregnant would make surrogacy impossible. Was she sincere? Or was she looking to make money? She deserved the benefit of the doubt, so I shut down any concern that she might be trying to manipulate us. Ultimately, the offer made me a little sad. They clearly didn't understand that Jason or I would be the biological father, not Zach, and that it wouldn't be her egg. It was another awkward moment that exposed how different we were, and at the same time, that we wanted the same thing—for the kids to thrive.

Until now they were following the court-ordered rehab plan, but other than that, they were putting very little effort into reunifying or maintaining a connection with the boys. We barely heard from them, and they cut short the few visits they'd had. During their time together they talked to us more than they engaged with the children. I wasn't sure Zach had even held Logan since he entered foster care. There was no question Amber and Zach loved the boys immensely. But love alone doesn't prepare you for parenthood. Love can't change a diaper, drive to the doctor, provide shelter. Love won't stop a toddler from choking, or fill a baby's belly with nourishment, or treat anxiety and attachment issues. Love alone wouldn't keep the boys I loved safe. It wouldn't soothe Logan's teething or comfort Ethan's nightmares or teach them to cross the street. Love is not all you need.

Jason saw sincerity in Amber's gratitude and wanted to help them. "If they follow through with rehab, we could connect them with Lift," Jason suggested as we walked back to the car. Lift was an exceptional nonprofit in LA that helps families rise out of poverty. Jason had produced some fundraising events for them.

"Yeah," I agreed.

"We could also give them a crib or a couch or some other furniture," he added. I nodded my head, and he began driving out of the parking structure. As we hit the 10 freeway, I began thinking about our role in this situation. We had signed up to foster and, ideally, adopt children. If the boys returned to Amber and Zach, we would need to set clear boundaries. I would help them with the boys and Savannah, too, babysitting or offering rides if needed. But I wasn't going to enable Amber and Zach. I voiced a new, fierce conviction.

"Jason," I said, "we're here to care for the boys. And that's it." I told Jason I loved his heart and his tenacity in helping people. "But it's not our role," I said. "Our job is to take care of their children during this difficult time, to give the boys love and support. It's not our job to save Amber and Zach."

I waited for Jason's reply. One of the most challenging things about being parents—and foster parents in particular—was that we were often flip-flopping between emotional states, but not at the same time. When I was upset, Jason would be in a state of acceptance; when he'd dip into worry, I'd be more assured. On the one hand, we balanced each other out. On the other, it sometimes felt like we were always missing each other, like we weren't in the same frame of mind, and therefore alone with whatever we were feeling most intensely.

But today Jason met me right where I was. "You're right," he said. "The system has other people whose job it is to connect them with these services, and . . . I guess it doesn't make sense. For us to get that involved."

I squeezed his hand, grateful beyond measure that whatever unknowns we'd eventually face, we'd face them together.

Chapter 12

Powerball

We were just three days into the purgatory of waiting for our next court date, and already it felt like a lifetime. I left Jason and the boys at home to fly to New York City with Jennifer Perry, FosterMore's co-founder, to attend the annual Social Good Awards breakfast, a media industry event highlighting the companies, programming, and campaigns using their platforms to inspire social change. We were there to accept an award for the Story of My Life ad featuring the adorable gay dads. The white linen cloths covering the tables at the Yale Club did nothing to conceal my feelings of anxiety and dread. My energy was entirely out of sync with the enthusiastic advertising executives and creatives networking their way around the ornate ballroom.

They aired our FosterMore video, and Jennifer took the stage to accept the award. As she spoke earnestly about the importance of stepping up to help children and families in need, I suddenly began to feel like an impostor. The uncertainty of our future with Ethan and Logan had been stewing inside me, keeping me up at night, distracting me from work and anything else that, less than a year ago, would have seemed so much more important. I thought about the 55 percent of children who reunify. How many of their foster parents were like me, unable to influence the outcome and petrified for the children's safety? How would I handle it if they were sent back to Amber and Zach? How would I say goodbye? What if Amber or Zach hurt one of them? I'd always wanted to think of myself as more of a *fighter* than a *flight-er*, but I didn't know if that was really true. Who would I blame? The system? Maybe I'd run for county supervisor so I could oversee the agency at fault? Or maybe I'd set my sights on the courts? Or an appointment from the governor to some powerful child-welfare-related board that may or may not even exist? My ruminations were creating an intense heat that was quickly working its way up my body. If something were to happen to either of the boys, I didn't know if I'd be a puddle of anguish or if it'd unleash my inner Kraken.

And what if nothing bad happened at all? What if they went back to Amber and Zach and they all lived happily ever after? Who could I fight when all that was at stake was my own broken heart? Intellectually I understood everything Jason and I were getting into when we agreed to foster, but I was unprepared for the emotional risk. The price of loving the boys and losing the boys was something I could never have comprehended in advance, not really, and I didn't know how I was ever going to pay it.

But here I was, sipping burnt coffee with marketing royalty and network executives being recognized for my role in luring others into this torment.

After Jennifer finished speaking, a man approached our table and asked to trade business cards with her. When the man walked away, Jennifer flashed his card, smiled at me, and said, "He's interested in fostering."

The ad worked, but why did that make me feel guilty?

———

A few weeks later, Jason and I were asked to appear in an advertising campaign for RaiseAChild, a nonprofit helping LGBTQ+ families navigate the foster care journey. As a part of their "Reimagine Foster

Parents" campaign, our images would be lining some of LA's major thoroughfares—La Brea, La Cienega, Beverly—crisscrossing the city on dozens of streetlight banners. Suddenly we were going to be poster foster parents.

The photo shoot took place on a Saturday morning in Los Feliz, a hillside neighborhood with an eclectic mix of hipsters and hippies in rented bungalows, multimillion-dollar homes of movie stars and Hollywood elites, and, like most LA enclaves, masses of unhoused people lining the sidewalks and alleys. As Jason and I stepped in front of the white screen, a makeup artist dusting powder across the bridge of my nose, I felt like I was about to crawl out of my skin—the irony of being so miserable in a neighborhood whose name in English means "the happy ones" was not lost on me. We were one of a dozen couples, mostly same-gender families and some famous adoptive parents like Jon Cryer and Lisa Joyner, all of whom, with the exception of Jason and me, had finalized their adoptions. The photographers staged the happy families in playful poses, celebrating their triumphant voyage across the turbulent and powerful waves of the foster system. We were the sole vessel still drifting at sea, praying for the tide to bring our family ashore and intact. The *happy* and the *unhappy*.

Then they sat us down on a black faux leather couch that looked like it had been borrowed from an orthodontist's waiting room, to film an interview about why fostering was important to us. "We need more people with the means to take care of children." Jason's response was quick and sincere. "There's still over four hundred thousand kids in foster care in the United States."

As he spoke, I felt the hot sting of tears welling up in my eyes. I wanted to look away, but we were on camera, so I just kept nodding. "These are good kids in search of an opportunity," I offered meekly, looking down and then back at Jason. "And I encourage anyone who's interested in doing it to seriously look into it." Once again, I was in-viting people to join me in the hell of uncertainty. Was I lying? *Yeah, it's hot, but it's a dry heat.* Not for one second did I regret fostering, exploring new terrain in my heart, or giving everything I had, so Ethan and Logan could feel loved and know they are safe. But none of this advocacy would have any bearing on the outcome for our boys.

———

Throughout that spring, the only predictable thing was unpredictability. We planned a first birthday party for Logan with our friends, and we met Zach and Amber at Olive Garden for a family celebration as well. The staff pushed a few tables together in a back corner. Lo sat between Amber and Jason, and across from me. Between Ethan's chatter and baby Savannah's demands, Amber seemed to have little bandwidth for Logan, yet on the whole I felt good about how we'd handled a first family celebration with both sets of parents.

But the next day, Amber and Zach didn't show up at Patty's office for the second needs and services meeting. It was a relief. After the way Zach had behaved at the last one, I was anxious about how he would interact with Kendra this time. Over the next few months, they missed almost all of their scheduled visits with Ethan and Logan and more and more entries in the required parental communication and visitation log stated: *Parents did not confirm or show up for visit.* When Amber did see the boys after a long absence, she'd make confusing statements. "I can't wait to get you home when we get our new apartment," she said once. Another time, when Jason stepped out of the room during a visit, Logan began crying inconsolably. Amber turned to Ethan and said, "This is how you were when they took you away from me."

———

Then I turned forty. Jason planned the celebration of my dreams, surrounded by our closest friends, in a large ranch-style home in the heart of California's wine country. He even arranged for his parents to fly out for the weekend to watch the boys.

But ever since Jaime died, my birthday had been colored by sadness.

For as long as I could remember, Jaime and I shared a birthday cake. We were born just three days apart, so our families always included a cake at the closest gathering to our birthdays. Whether that was an Easter brunch or a special Sunday dinner, someone, usually Auntie Cheryl, baked a white cake with whipped cream frosting and fresh strawberries. Jaime and I would blow out the candles in unison. We'd open gifts, cash from Grandma Mary, the new Billy Idol or Michael Jackson cassette from Auntie Mary, some rad Nikes from Auntie Sharon. A collection of faded Kodak pictures from each of these events sat in a shoe box in my closet, but the memories were so vivid I didn't need to look at them.

No kid ever wants to share their birthday, but as a grown-up, not being able to share it with Jaime felt like a part of me was missing. Like I woke up one day and my left arm was gone. I felt guilty for being the only one of us who got to turn twenty-five, thirty, and now forty. Nearly half of my life had passed without her. After she died, sometimes I'd see a woman about her height in a crowd, dark curls piled into an unruly bun, and I'd run up to her sort of hoping it was Jaime and then I'd get close and just smile awkwardly. What hurt the most was thinking of everything she had missed. The loving relationships with her nephews. Seeing Andrew play baseball, teasing and hugging Zachary, sharing tears of joy when Timothy married his high school sweetheart. She missed out on so many family celebrations and historic events. She never even got to hear Taylor Swift sing.

If my fortieth birthday had been anyone else's celebration, I would have been thrilled to be in such exquisite company, in the stunning home we'd rented in Sonoma with vineyards in the backyard, sharing amazing meals and memories and banter and laughter. But I just couldn't experience it.

The entire weekend was so thoughtfully planned. A private chef prepared a birthday dinner one night at the house. My friends toasted me with bottles of wine from some of the vineyards we'd visited that day. Jason had even put together a video with messages from dozens of relatives and friends who couldn't attend in person. In one clip, my uncle John jokingly admonished me for taking Jaime to get her nose pierced. I wondered, if she had lived, would she be in this room or on the video? Would we be celebrating our birthdays together, like we had for the first twenty-three? Would she have children of her own? Would they know she'd had her heart set on them ever since she was a little girl in a Wonder Woman bathing suit, puffing candy cigarettes in my parents' backyard? Would Ethan and Logan call her Auntie? Would Ethan still call me Daddy on my next birthday? Or will he have forgotten all about me by the time he enters kindergarten?

I started to feel sick, the familiar knot of grief tightening in my stomach.

Instead of relishing the joy of the weekend, my emotions were bouncing like the balls in a Powerball tank, all vying to be sucked up to the top spot. The kind words and hilarious memories in those birthday toasts were clouded by my longing for Jaime and anxiety about our future with the boys—leaving me wanting to crawl under the table and disappear. As Buffy offered up sidesplitting memories of the late nights and early mornings we had shared as roommates in Des Moines, I struggled to listen. It was as if my body were strapped to the chair and my closest friends were simultaneously torturing and eulogizing me. I was in so much pain and I didn't understand why. My heart was racing. I felt a stabbing in my stomach. I shifted in my seat with every breath I took.

Every person in that room knew what Jason and I were going through and every one of them would've understood if I just let my anger out. If I let my fear out. Had I stood up, slammed my hands on the table, and yelled for them to stop, they all would have understood. They would have seen my tears for what they were: fear, sadness, and anxiety. Emotions conjured up by love, by fully risking your heart when the future is unknown, by caring so deeply about two little beings who trust you to keep them safe and having no power to control their fate, by yearning for the familiar embrace of the past that you can no longer attain. I wanted to let out uncontrollable sobs like I'd imagined Auntie Cheryl and Heather had in the private moments after their daughters were taken from them. My friends would have forgiven me. They would have comforted me.

I looked down the table at Kim, who'd tossed the coin at our wedding to decide whether Jason or I would walk down the aisle first. She always had something witty to say, but that night she was biting her bottom lip. When our eyes met, I knew she could see my pain.

The next day, all nineteen of us loaded into the vans for more vineyard hopping, the vines intricately tied and perfectly spaced in rows lining the hills, waving as we passed through Sonoma's lush, green valley. There's a beauty in the art of farming that I first observed on the campaign trail in Iowa. Staring out the windows of speeding motorcades, I watched the seasons change, the snow melting, the stalks growing, and the corn being harvested, until the first snowfall brought about the beginning of a new cycle. All the while, the farmers nurturing their land, tending to its wounds, and helping it to grow.

At our second stop of the day, while everyone else was sipping chardonnay, listening to the vintner explain the hint of grapefruit they were tasting, I excused myself and stood alone on the lavender-lined walkway, taking in the perfectly manicured garden, thinking about Jaime, the boys, the impending court case.

"If you dump a few tons of pig shit this place would look just like the farm I grew up on," Kim joked as she walked up the path toward me. I laughed. I'd been to her family's farm in Wever, Iowa. There was no lavender and more pigs than I'd ever seen in my life.

"Are you okay?" she asked, lowering her voice. "I just wanted to check in with you because last night I got the sense something was bothering you." She spoke softly, but her words felt jarring, like sneakers squeaking across a polished floor. I felt my defenses, the walls we erect to protect our hearts from intruders, instinctively start to rise. But this was Kim. The friend I carried into the emergency room when her back went out. The partner I'd started a business with. It was safe to be honest with her.

I took a deep breath. "Thank you. This is all so hard." I exhaled, starting to laugh and cry at the same time, the kind of emotional release you can only have with a close friend. I didn't have to state the obvious, where my pain was coming from; she already knew. "I'm trying to be happy, but there's just so much going on." My voice was cracking through the tears. "What asshole wouldn't love to have all this as his birthday party?"

"Yeah," Kim agreed, meeting my laughter with her own. "This is my first one-percenters' pub crawl," she joked. "Wine is so much better when it doesn't come in a box."

Kim's humor helped to release a little bit of steam, but I still couldn't feel the joy of the weekend.

One hour and a few glasses of wine later, Jason approached me as I walked out of the men's room.

"Where do you want to go next?" he asked, flashing a smile at me.

"I don't care. What's everyone else thinking?"

"They're not thinking," he said, shaking his head. "Everyone is getting a little hungry and they want you to decide." Two grown-up responsibilities I absolutely despise are choosing an activity for a group to participate in and deciding what to have for dinner. I'd rather be stung by hornets or forced to attend a gender-reveal party than to do either of them.

"I don't care," I said, my voice reflecting my annoyance. "Can't we just order here? Don't they have food?" I could feel heat rising inside me, like a boiling pot of water, close to overflowing. I started to walk away, to return to the group.

"Mark," he called out, softly.

"What?" I shot back, my tone as nasty as the fertilizer lining the vineyard. He didn't say anything. He just stared at me. I knew I needed to shut my mouth, but I couldn't help myself. "Why do I have to decide? Can't you decide? Besides, I thought all this was planned already?

I hate making all the decisions. Let someone else decide." Even as I was lashing out at my sober husband, who had put tremendous effort into making this weekend in wine country an incredible celebration, I knew I was wrong. And he didn't try to stop me either. He let me have my tantrum, let me spew my emotions out onto him—even though he didn't deserve them. He didn't turn it into a big scene or storm off in a fit of his own. Instead, he let me simmer down, suggested our next stop, and then we joined our guests huddled around an oak-barrel tasting station.

When we returned to the house we'd rented, I followed Jason into the bedroom, feeling guilty about my outburst. He was sitting on the edge of the bed checking his phone. I sat down beside him and offered an apology.

"I'm sorry for what I said and the way I acted," I began, the tears I'd been holding back all weekend forming in my eyes. "You've done so much to make this an amazing trip. I'm just so tense. I can't handle this waiting to find out what's going to happen. I'm trying so hard to be present, to enjoy the moment, but it's so hard. And you're going through the same stuff. I'm sorry."

"It's okay," he said, placing his hand on the small of my back. "I understand."

"You deserve more. I am so lucky to have you and I hate that I took out my anxiety on you," I said.

"Yeah, well, don't do it again," he joked.

"I just keep worrying about what's going to happen with the boys. Are they going back to Amber and Zach? If they do, what will happen to them? I don't know if I can handle losing them."

"I feel the same way, but there's nothing we can do now to control what happens," he offered.

"You're right," I said, squeezing his hand, "and this party is more than I could have dreamed." But I knew there was more to the emotions I was feeling. "My birthdays are always difficult. I miss her so much and feel guilty that I even get to turn forty. She should be here. But she got robbed." The tears began to fall again. He put his arm around my shoulders and pulled me into him. He knew I was talking about Jaime. We lay in the bed, my head on his chest for a few minutes before I leaned up and kissed him.

"Thank you," I said. "I love you."

"You better."

I was grateful for his understanding and his willingness to accept my apology. We'd only been married a year and a half, and our young nuptials were already being dramatically tested. I had taken for granted the safety he provided, the compassion he offered. It felt safe to yell at him. He understood me and my childish reactions to stress.

But sometimes, more than his grace, I wanted his fury. It would have been easier if he threw hissy fits too. If he spoke my emotional language instead of just understanding it. But it wasn't his style. He was even and strong, never breaking down in immaturity. It left me feeling more ashamed of myself, childlike, and more distant from him.

As much as I didn't want to lose myself on this journey, I didn't want to lose Jason even more.

Chapter 13

Spineless

Mark, I just had the most bizarre conversation." Jason had called me at the office and, judging by the uncharacteristic edge in his voice, he was completely unnerved.

"The Bat Phone rang, so I picked it up," he continued, "the woman on the other end asked to speak with Zach. I told her, 'I think you have the wrong number,' and she corrected me. 'No. I have the right number,' and then introduced herself as Nadia, from the Department of Children and Family Services. Once I realized her mistake, I told her that I was Jason, the foster parent. I tried explaining that she must have called our number thinking she was contacting the birth parents, but she just kept asking me, 'What are you doing to get your kids back?'"

"What? Back from who? The nanny?" I joked.

"Mark, she just kept insisting she'd called the right number and talking to me like I was Zach. I told her four times, 'You're talking to the foster dad, not the bio dad.'"

"Oh man. What a hot mess," I said with a laugh.

"Well, she's *our* hot mess now. Apparently, Amber finished rehab in Lancaster and has moved temporarily to a sober living facility in Glendora. DCFS reassigned the boys' case from Kendra to Nadia, because she works out of the Glendora office."

"Because she moved, we get an entirely new county social worker?" I asked.

"Apparently."

Jason told me that after he finally made it clear to Nadia that she'd called us, the foster parents, instead of the birth parents, they scheduled her first visit to the house. "We've all made the mistake of dialing the wrong number, but there was something more. It was like she wasn't listening to anything I was saying," he said. His intuition was spot-on. This call was a sign of things to come.

One of the major flaws of the child protection system is that many of the professionals who enter the field for all the right reasons become so bogged down, overloaded with cases, paperwork, and bureaucracy, that they grow defeated. The result is that many good, frustrated workers leave the county's employment or become so jaded they lose the sense of purpose that inspired them to go into the field in the first place.

There are so many layers of bureaucracy, so many regulations from federal, state, and county governments, so many collaborating agencies all needing referrals, that it becomes a tedious endeavor just to file a report or get a child set up with a routine health assessment or connected to a therapist. Navigating the bare minimum of services requires an epic amount of time and, ultimately, the need to check a box to appease a bureaucrat often prevents kids in care from getting services they really need.

In most cases, foster parents are responsible for scheduling, transporting, and monitoring all of the court-ordered visitations with birth parents, which in our case was three hours, three times a week. That's nine hours—plus drive time. More than a fifth of a workweek every week. Then add two or three social worker visits per month, not to mention any services the child may need, like weekly therapy for trauma, physical rehabilitation, speech pathology, doctor or dental appointments. None of that includes time for the fun stuff—a dance class, soccer practice, or time at the playground. The result is a system that puts ex-treme time pressure on foster families. Visits with the birth parents and the social workers are mandatory, but therapy is optional, so for foster parents without the luxury of time, this critical service is often the one that gets skipped most frequently.

Amber and Zach made very few attempts to schedule visits with the boys, and when they did, they usually had some reason to end the visit early, if they showed up at all. However, if they had been working harder to spend time with their kids, the responsibility and stress of making sure it happened would've fallen squarely on us. Caseworkers are similarly pushed to the brink. Kendra had once told me she was working with forty-five families, but that it was usually more. In a typical month, she would need to visit one and a half houses per day in order to meet her monthly visitation requirements, in addition to filing the requisite, time-consuming paperwork for each case. It's no wonder the field experiences such high burnout. Social workers enter the field to do social work, not paperwork.

The morning of Nadia's first visit to our home, Patty arrived early. Nadia was forty-five minutes late. She wore a pale blue pantsuit and a warm smile. She was chatty, complimenting the neighborhood and our house. Ethan raced to the doorway to give her the inspection he be-stowed upon all visitors. She threw him a warm smile, bending down to his level and saying, "And you must be Ethan." He smiled and laughed, before toddling over to Josephine, who'd laid out some toy blocks on the floor and was sitting with Logan in her lap.

Nadia asked a lot of questions but remarkably never paused to let us answer a single one of them. She would say, "How is Ethan doing?" And as I started to speak, she'd cut me off: "He looks healthy. Yeah, big kid. He's a big boy." She was distracted and frenetic. It was like trying to have a conversation with a coked-out college student, minus the sweating and teeth licking.

Even though Amber had moved to Glendora, which in LA traffic is a solid hour-and-fifteen-minute drive from Kendra's office in Lancaster, I couldn't help thinking it was counterproductive for the county to transfer the case from Kendra, especially since this was a temporary move. She had invested so much time and knew the boys' history. It seemed like more of a hassle to catch someone else up on the case, which was now ten months old.

This meeting was the complete opposite of our first visit with Kendra, who was all business. I had printed a copy of the required "Parental Communication and Visitation Log" for Nadia. While most foster parents maintain a small notebook, Jason had designed a spreadsheet so intricate it would have been the envy of accountants everywhere. He included columns showing the date and time of each interaction with Amber and Zach, the total number of visitations they were allotted, and the actual amount of time they spent with their sons.

"The parents have had very few visits," I said. "The highlighted cell shows that they've used roughly six percent of the court-ordered visitation time and on the far right, you'll see the details of each interaction."

Jason had included the particulars of each call, text, or visit. He'd gone to painstaking lengths to ensure his entries were factual and free of opinion, so we wouldn't be perceived as not supporting reunification.

Nadia thumbed through the six-page log and then grabbed a stack of folders from her bag, reading the names on each file aloud: "Isabelle Valenzuela. Samuel Ortiz. Brendan Jackson." As Nadia casually violated the privacy of the other families she was working with, I glanced over at Patty, whose face carried a look of horror. "Oops, looks like I forgot your file. I'll just add this to it when I get back to my office," Nadia said, stuffing the document into her already packed bag.

Before Nadia left, we compared calendars for her next visit and told her what days worked best for us to supervise visits with Amber and Zach as well. Patty, who'd stuck around to have us sign our expense reports, closed the door behind Nadia, turned to me, and sighed. "That was exhausting."

A few weeks later, we emailed Nadia to confirm the next visit. No reply. The date came, Jason stayed home to greet her, and Patty came by, but Nadia never showed. The following week, she called at four o'clock on Thursday afternoon. "I'm going to be at your place tomorrow at ten a.m.," she informed me.

"Well, you'll be the only one there," I said, laughing, trying to make light of the situation. "I'm sorry, Nadia, but Jason's out of town on a business trip, and I'll be at work."

"But that's the last day of the month, and I have to see the children once a month," she insisted.

I paused for a moment, so I didn't let my anger get the best of me. There was so much I wanted to say. *Well, you should've thought of that sooner. Sucks to be you. I emailed you over a week ago to remind you about the meeting you scheduled.* But, however disorganized or forgetful she was, she wielded too much power over our lives for me to say how I really felt.

I took a deep breath and swallowed my frustration. "I can move my ten a.m. meeting tomorrow, but I'll have to be done by noon. Does that work?"

"Yes. I'll see you then." She hung up abruptly.

"No problem. Happy to oblige . . . *AHHH*," I screamed into the void on the other end of the phone.

The next morning, I sat in the living room with my feet up on the coffee table and laptop resting on my thighs. I sent emails and edited some documents, the minutes passing by on the upper right-hand corner of the screen. 10:02 . . . 10:17 . . . 10:43 . . . 11:10 . . . Finally, at 11:30 a.m., Nadia arrived at the door—ninety minutes late. No apology. No blaming LA traffic or recounting a horrific accident on the 101 freeway.

"Hi*ii*," she said, dragging out the greeting like we were old friends, excited to catch up after a long time apart.

"Hi," I said sharply, giving her the fake smile I usually reserve for people who talk incessantly about CrossFit. We sat down and I reminded her that I had to leave for work at noon, so we now only had thirty minutes. As she began firing off questions that she seemed perfectly happy to answer herself, I zoned out.

At our first meeting, Nadia mentioned she'd been working for the county for close to two decades. She was likely making a decent salary, receiving incredible health insurance benefits, and would retire with a taxpayer-backed pension—but she wouldn't have lasted a month in a private sector job. It was a stark contrast to Kendra's professionalism and laid bare the reality that we were navigating a system where accountability is overpowered by a bureaucracy that puts so many cooks in the kitchen, no one has ownership of the outcome; where people are often promoted to supervisory positions because of seniority, rather than merit; and where dedicated caseworkers and newer talent can easily become so disillusioned and overburdened, they ultimately leave.

There are things county agencies are supposed to do—but just don't. Like notify foster parents in writing about court hearings. We never received notifications. We were learning firsthand that when an agency fails to do what it's supposed to do, there's often no one noticing or recording the violation, and no penalty or consequence. Foster parents most often don't know how things are supposed to work. The timelines we were taught in training get stretched by court backlogs and delays. We're told there's no need for us to attend court dates, and even if we did, it's not like we'd get a sidebar with the judge to say, "This is how things are really going down." I could suddenly relate to the foster parents from the FosterMore focus groups, who told us they felt taken for granted and ultimately stopped fostering after their initial placement.

As Nadia droned on, asking and answering her own questions—"Have you heard much from the birth parents since the boys moved in with you? No, they don't call regularly. Are you worried about any health issues with the boys? No, they look healthy"—I couldn't stop thinking. This person was responsible for making recommendations to the court, yet she inspired as much confidence as the Texas power grid.

I would've given anything to have Kendra back.

––––––––

The following Monday morning, on my drive to the office I was still fuming about the meeting with Nadia. She'd asked the same questions she'd asked at the previous visit—if only she'd let me answer them, instead of answering herself, she would have actually known what was going on with the boys. It felt like I was learning to play baseball and she was the drunk Little League coach, showing up late, barking incoherent orders, and then passing out in the dugout. Her forgetful and disorganized approach seemed frighteningly reflective of the broader child welfare system.

State governments, courts, child welfare agencies, foster parents, and all the other parties relevant to children's care don't operate like a family, working together, jumping in to help each other out. When an agency drops the ball, if there's any acknowledgment at all, at best it's a shrug and a "We'll do better next time." The only parties who get held accountable are the birth parents, who face losing their children, and foster parents, who could lose their certification.

I pulled up to a stoplight on Beverly Boulevard. The early morning sun hadn't yet pierced the marine layer. I looked up, and through the misty haze I saw Jason's and my giant faces smiling down from a streetlight banner, like big gay superheroes watching over the Grove. I'd completely forgotten the RaiseAChild campaign had just launched. Our enormous Irish heads were on one side of the pole, while the talented Cleo King, from *Mike & Molly*, and her beautiful family graced the other side. Was I being duplicitous? At the exact same moment I was carping about a disorganized social worker to anyone who'd listen, I was also smiling down at pedestrians sipping twenty-dollar smoothies, inviting them to share in the torture of the foster system. It seemed disingenuous, like the *thoughts and prayers* of a Republican senator. Our images, hanging above a parked Prius, enticed passersby to "Reimagine Foster Care," but as I was learning, it was going to take a lot more than imagination to fix the cracks in this busted system.

In the weeks that followed, I noticed Nadia began cc'ing a colleague on all of her emails. I didn't trust her, so at the following month's visit, I asked, "Who's Brian Soften? The person you copy on all your emails?"

"He's my supervisor. He wants to be kept in the loop on all my cases," she responded quickly, almost as if she'd anticipated my question.

I was caught completely off guard by her answer. I was shocked and slightly relieved. *Was Nadia on probation? Was she being monitored? Please, God, tell me someone has already complained about her.*

"How many cases do you have?" I asked, trying to sound casual.

"Right now, thirteen," she answered, looking down at her notebook.

It required every ounce of restraint I could muster to keep from reacting. My mind was sprinting like Usain Bolt in the 100-meter. *Thirteen?! Holy shit. Kendra's caseload had topped out at forty-five. Nadia does suck at her job! And we aren't the only ones who see it.* But as hard and fast as this realization hit me, so did the reality that we, along with a dozen other families, were stuck with her.

A few weeks later, Ethan turned two. Jason dropped the boys with Kris, who took them to celebrate at the sober living facility with Amber, Zach, and Rita. The visit was scheduled for four hours, but Zach called and asked us to pick the boys up an hour early. Jason had barely been home for twenty minutes before we had to get right back in the car and head back to Glendora. When we got there, Rita mentioned that her ride home hadn't even left Lancaster yet.

This was the first time we'd met Rita. The image I'd conjured up of the woman whose house the county had deemed unsafe for the boys was nothing like the reality. She wore a knee-length slate blue dress, accented with a floral brooch and loudly colored belt. Her gray hair was cut in a shoulder-length bob, bangs falling sharply into the wire-frame glasses resting on the bridge of her nose. She looked more like a librarian or kindergarten teacher than the hardened grandma I'd imagined.

"We have to take the 210 West. We could drop you somewhere in Pasadena so they don't have to come all this way?" Jason offered.

"That would be wonderful," she said.

We had the boys on a predictable napping and feeding schedule, and visits always threw a curveball at their routine. Logan was having an especially rough time, so Jason sat in back with the boys and Rita rode shotgun. "My son's girlfriend is coming to get me, but she's just leaving home now so this ride will save me from waiting. Thank you," she said, as we started our drive.

"No worries. Do they live near you?" I asked.

"Yes. Actually, they live with me," she said.

"Sounds like you have a full house."

"It's me, the two of them, my grandson, who is raising Amber's first child. He's seven now."

"I bet there's never a dull moment at your house," I said, trying to keep the conversation light.

"No. There certainly is not," she said with a laugh.

"It must've been crazy when the boys and Amber and Zach were there, too," I said.

"We had no space," she said. "The four of them shared an air mattress in the living room. They would just lay around in bed all day, watching TV and eating. Everyone would have to walk around them."

"Finally, the boys are both asleep," Jason piped in with relief from the back seat.

"Logan's teething. Poor guy is especially miserable," I said. "Amber's teeth look great, by the way."

"They sure do," she said, sitting up in her seat. "After my daughter died, Amber and her brother moved in with me. They didn't have anyone else. Their father doesn't live nearby and he wasn't around a lot. But when she was a teen, he paid for her to get braces. I think the braces meant a lot to her because he had bought them. But one night, she must have been fourteen or fifteen, she was upset with him, I don't remember what about, and she pulled them off using a pair of plyers. She ended up breaking all her teeth."

"Oh my god, that must've hurt so bad," I said, cringing at the thought.

"When they fixed them, Amber was in rehab so they wouldn't give her any pain meds."

"I can't imagine how painful that must have been. I'd need a Vicodin just for a paper cut," I joked, trying to lighten the conversation. What could Amber's father possibly have done to cause her to inflict so much harm, so much pain on herself? Did he yell at her? Pick on her? Did he break a promise to visit? Or not call when he said he would? I felt a crushing sense of sadness for Amber, whose childhood had been so full of heartache.

We didn't talk much the rest of the ride. As the boys napped peacefully in the back seat, I kept wondering what I'd have to be feeling to deliberately subject myself to that much pain. I'd experienced normal stuff growing up, disappointment over not getting a toy I wanted, embarrassment when I would get hurt and cry in public or did something less masculine than expected of a boy in the 1980s. I'd encountered a few bullies and been picked on from time to time, but I always found love and safety at home. My life would have been so different if I, like Amber, had been raised by someone other than my mother. I had been so focused on how unfit she was to care for her sons that I hadn't given much thought as to *why*. Her childhood was a battle for survival. She hid from abuse while I only hid from myself. She must have dreamed of the day she'd finally be free from Rita's house and the painful reminders of her past. And then to have her family snatched away—to be told she wasn't capable of caring for her own kids—must have been fresh slashes to the scars of her youth.

The next weekend, we hosted a birthday party of our own. Tons of friends and family turned out to celebrate Ethan. I was running around making sure the pretzel bowls were full when I saw a friend jog past with Ethan on his shoulders, laughing crazily, and it hit me: every single person in our incredible village had welcomed the boys with open arms. They were loved and supported, and we were so blessed. I wondered what Amber was doing. Was she dreaming of a moment like this? More than fifty people she'd never met had shown up to celebrate her son. Did that many people ever show up for her? To one of her birthdays? When she married Zach? After all, only Kris had stood up to take in the boys when she needed it most.

When we brought out the blue vanilla-frosted confetti cake and sang "Happy Birthday," Ethan beamed like a tiny sun. For an afternoon, love felt as simple as that—showing up together for a child who is the absolute center of our world.

As spring rolled into summer—marking the one-year anniversary of the boys' arrival—the situation with Amber and Zach continued to deteriorate. Amber left the sober living facility in Glendora and moved to a new one near Lancaster. My hopes that the case would be transferred back to Kendra were quickly quashed.

Amber and Zach continued to miss visits with the boys and Nadia told us she'd given them a stern warning that skipping visits would reflect poorly when they got to court in August. Her lecture worked and they requested a three-hour visit with less than two days' notice. Patty knew Jason and I needed more time to rearrange our work schedules and she graciously offered to monitor the visit in her office at Children's Bureau. Jason dropped the boys off with Patty, leaving a diaper bag fully stocked with toys and snacks, before heading to a meeting.

I was planning to pick them up in three hours, but Jason called after dropping the boys off. "Zach and Amber have an appointment. They have to leave in an hour," he said. "Can you pick the kids up early?"

"No. What the fuck? I have two meetings." I wasn't even trying to suppress my frustration.

"I know. I'm sorry, babe."

"Did they just now learn about this appointment? They couldn't have told us sooner?" I knew I was preaching to the choir, but as always, Jason let me vent. The truth was, he had more flexibility in his schedule, so he had shouldered most of the responsibilities of doctors' appointments and visitations.

"I'll figure it out," I said, defeated.

"Sorry, babe."

"It's not your fault."

When I arrived at Children's Bureau, Amber and Zach were seated next to each other, with Patty on the opposite side of the same small room we'd been in for the initial needs and services meeting a year earlier, the one where Zach yelled at Kendra. Amber looked pissed off, scowling with her arms folded across her chest. Both of the boys ran over to me for hugs, Ethan elbowing Logan for my sole attention. Not even Patty's sweet perfume could cover the stink coming from Ethan's diaper. "Oh," I said, wincing at the smell. "Did Jason leave the diaper bag?" I asked, already knowing the answer but hinting for one of them to change him. "We've got a situation going on over here."

"Yeah. It's on the chair," Amber said, pointing to the bag in the corner. I moved slowly toward it in case either of them would offer to change him. They didn't, and I wasn't surprised. I got the supplies out of the bag, knelt down on the carpet, spread out the changing pad, and began removing Ethan's dirty diaper. Amber and Zach just sat there, watching me clean up another mess that happened on their watch.

"His jeans are too tight," Amber remarked, with a bite in her tone.

"Okay," I said, stopping myself from saying what I was really thinking, that they were designer skinny jeans and he looked adorable. But maybe she had a point; the boys were constantly outgrowing their clothes and shoes. This was a good thing—a sign of health, especially for Logan, who'd come to us underweight.

But Amber wouldn't let it go. Looking down at me, on my knees changing her son's nasty diaper she had ignored, she continued, "He can barely walk. They're too tight." My anger was building and I could see my hands start to shake as I pressed the tape of Ethan's new diaper down to seal it around his waist. I wanted to unload all of my frustrations onto her, telling her how entitled she was acting and how I had just left an important meeting because she was too inconsiderate to let us know ahead of time that she had to leave early. Instead, I took a deep breath, exhaled, and looked up at her over my glasses. I didn't smile. I just nodded.

"We're big people," Zach offered, trying to lighten the mood. "Ethan's like us." He smiled at me.

I nodded again, gathering up the toys and snacks and water bottles and diaper bag items.

"They're too tight," she said again.

"Got it," I snapped, stopping myself from saying anything else.

Amber and Zach left while I was loading the boys into the stroller. Patty, who'd excused herself when I arrived, returned to check on me.

"I'm sorry you had to leave work early," she said. "This process can be very frustrating."

Just then the dam burst, and my anger came flowing out. "They are so incredibly selfish. They expect everyone to just drop everything for them. Aren't we doing enough already? They didn't know about this appointment ahead of time? They couldn't have told us sooner? I skipped an important meeting to be here, and then she bitches to me about his skinny jeans being too tight, fuck her."

Patty winced, and I realized I'd raised my voice and cursed.

"I'm sorry, Patty," I said. "I'm at my wits' end with them and this whole system."

When Jason got home that night, the boys were asleep upstairs and I was on the couch in the family room, working on my laptop. He sat in the chair opposite me, and I realized I was still fuming.

"How can anyone with a job be a foster parent?" I wondered. "If I didn't own my company, I'd never be able to be this flexible. The way this system is structured makes fostering almost impossible for working families."

I couldn't help feeling the cumulative frustration that we were always expected to drop everything for Amber and Zach—yet no one was taking our needs as foster parents into account. The court didn't want our opinions, despite the fact that we had spent more time with Ethan and Logan than anyone, including their birth parents.

"We're just supposed to shut up, show up, and be at their beck and call. And if we complain, if we say anything, then we aren't supporting reunification," I vented.

Any other day, Jason would have been the cool air to my steam. But tonight, he'd had it. "Why is everybody in the system so fucking spineless?" he asked, pointedly. "Why is everyone so afraid to say what's really going on? Too scared of upsetting Amber and Zach or the judge." Leaning forward in the chair and pointing with his finger, he continued: "Everyone is so afraid of doing something that will get them in trouble, so they just don't do anything. And the only ones who suffer are the kids."

There'd been plenty of days when I didn't voice my grief or uncertainty, afraid it might lead to a fight. Sometimes I'd felt alone in my anxiety and rage. Tonight his anger was sweet, sweet music to my ears—like a surprise Beyoncé album. We were perfectly aligned.

Hearing the fight in his voice made me want to fight harder too.

That night, we wrote to Patty and cc'd Ramona, her supervisor, expressing everything we'd been keeping pent up: our concern over Zach and Amber's missed visits and inappropriate comments; our frustration over the increasingly poor communication with them; our worry about what would be decided at the August hearing; our fears about Nadia. Then we decided to wait until morning to hit send.

The morning air didn't cool our heads. We hit send.

All day we waited for a response. What if they saw things differently? What if they thought we weren't supporting reunification and wanted to have the boys moved to a new home? What if they agreed with us?

By the next evening, we had our response:

We spent the day conferring with our colleagues and we agree
with you, 100 percent. Let's make sure these kids don't fall

through the cracks. If they reunify, let's make sure they are going to be properly cared for.

It was the validation we needed. We weren't being selfish, wanting someone else's babies. We were fighting to protect the boys from the cycle of abuse and pain that had dogged Amber. At last we didn't feel so alone.

Chapter 14

Bullet-Riddled Nissan

Ethan snatched an unguarded cell phone from the coffee table, which began a heated pursuit, passing through the family room and on into the dining room before coming to an abrupt ending in the kitchen, where my size advantage allowed me to retrieve the stolen property. Ethan looked angry, but instead of having a tantrum, he shot me a fiery look, dropped to his diaper-clad butt, and began taking brisk, short breaths, in and out, in and out. He was sucking in air and blowing it out loudly, with enough force to extinguish a house fire. Jason had taught him how to use breathing techniques as a way to manage his anger or sadness, but this was the first time I'd witnessed his baby breath work in action.

I sensed that his attempt at self-regulation, while valiant, was not likely to lead to sustained inner peace. "Great job using your breathing to manage your anger, buddy," I said, praising his ability to recognize the sensation of his emotions, and then grabbed a nearby red Matchbox car with yellow flames painted on the side and rolled it over to him.

Ethan looked at the spinning wheels and then up at me. The loud exhales stopped, he smiled, and those adorable cavernous dimples appeared on his cheeks. He grabbed the toy, and just like that we were patched.

I had been skeptical at first, but the technique started to come in handy as Ethan was begrudgingly learning to share with his now very active younger brother. When Logan took a toy or attention Ethan wanted, instead of charging him with the determination of a defensive lineman, sometimes he would fall to the ground and meditate. He was only two years old and he was able to identify anger and respond to the emotion better than I could at forty. And seeing him progress from the baby who pointed and shrieked for things to a toddler taming his fury made me forget the frustration of being a foster parent—at least for the moment. The consistency and predictability Jason and I provided to Ethan and Logan was paying off and we knew we needed a plan to prevent any surprises at the next court hearing, just three months away.

As much as I don't like uncertainty, I dislike surprises even more. I moved to Los Angeles because it's predictable. Every hour is rush hour; expect delays. Every day is sunny with a light breeze—except, of course, during *May gray* and *June gloom* when the air rising off the Pacific collides with the warmer air above, resulting in a frigid marine layer (and creating an unexpected market for Uggs in Southern California). We needed a plan for August, a strategy, so that whatever the outcome of the judge's decision, we trusted the boys were going to be safe. If this were an electoral campaign, our war room would've been laser-focused on one message: *It's their safety, stupid.* James Carville would've been proud.

One of the biggest challenges we were facing was that, besides the two of us, only Patty had ever witnessed the way Amber and Zach interacted with the boys. We needed a new presence at the parental visits, someone well versed in the system who could observe and report back to the county. Everyone involved in the case knew we wanted to adopt, so we feared our word would be perceived as biased. The boys needed a credible, neutral observer to advocate for their welfare. Our concerns about Amber and Zach's capacity to parent three children under the age of two were legitimate, but someone other than us had to express those concerns as well.

We had learned in our training that we were entitled to request a human services aide (HSA), a person from the Department of Children and Family Services (DCFS) who would both monitor and provide transportation to and from parental visits. But when Ethan and Logan came into our lives, we balked at the idea of requesting one. They'd had enough transitions and adults coming in and out of their lives. Why would we trust a stranger to do something in our sphere of care? We felt differently now. Advocating for safety required the objectivity of a third party.

We sent an email to Nadia making our request, and she assured us it would happen "soon." Yet, week after week, each time we followed up it was as if we were making the request for the first time. We began copying Brian Soften, her supervisor, on the requests, but he never replied. And we continued as we had the previous year, waiting at the ready to drive the boys long distances, at unpredictable intervals, to supervise visits ourselves—that is, of course, if Amber and Zach actually made themselves available.

Patty and her colleagues, now digging in to support us, got Nadia to agree that the parents had to confirm twenty-four hours in advance with Patty or else the visit would not take place. In June, Amber and Zach didn't stick to a single one of the six scheduled visits. The night before each, we'd get an email from Patty letting us know they'd failed to confirm and we could go to back to our regularly scheduled lives. As much as it was a relief for us to know in advance if Amber and Zach were bailing on a visit, I felt bad for the boys. Ethan and Logan were still too young to know from day to day whether or not a visit was planned, or that their birth parents had skipped out on another opportunity to spend time with them, but it crushed me to think Amber and Zach would not move mountains to be with the boys they had birthed and were fighting to keep, the two little humans who ruled our lives.

In contrast, Kris had been a constant presence in the boys' life. In the year we'd known her, she'd sold her home, which led to a series of unfortunate moves—first, a town house with "loud neighbors," then an apartment where "the landlord wouldn't fix anything." Her company, which marketed candles to gift shops, had lost a few big accounts and she was still struggling with respiratory and foot issues. Yet, no matter what was going on in her life, Kris regularly made time to call, Face-Time, or text to check in on her grandsons.

Toward the end of June, Jason took the boys to visit with her in a park near her new apartment in Thousand Oaks, an upscale LA sub-urb on the opposite side of the Santa Monica Mountains from Malibu. "Kris seems to be doing really well," Jason said, helping me put away the groceries I'd grabbed on my way home from the gym. "She's got the boot off her foot and she says her pulmonary issues are under control."

"That's great. She must be so relieved," I said, carefully trying to force a carton of milk into our overstuffed refrigerator without pushing any other items from the crowded shelf onto the floor.

"And she seems much more settled in her new place," he added, folding the grocery bags.

"Thank God. She was miserable in the last one."

"She brought a bunch of salads from Whole Foods and we had a picnic. The boys climbed all over her and she sent me home with a bag full of aromatherapy candles for us," he said, pointing to a stack of three candles hidden behind the grocery bags.

"That's so sweet," I said, picking one up for a sniff.

"That one's supposed to calm you down," he added. "We'll put it in your office."

"Ha. No joke."

"She asked if it would be okay if she took the boys for an overnight visit right after the Fourth of July," he said, leaning against the kitchen's center island. "Her birthday's coming up and she's thinking of renting an Airbnb in the desert or possibly near the beach. She just wants to spoil her grandsons."

"I don't see why not."

"I asked if she'd take us away, too," he added, with a smile.

"Kris was approved by the county to care for both of them before they moved in with us, right?" Jason nodded. "So, an overnight isn't really our decision, but I appreciate that she asked for our blessing."

The last time Kris had taken Ethan overnight was just about one year earlier. I remembered Amber, all hyped up on caffeine and sugar, hopping into my car in the Agape parking lot. During the two-minute drive to Kris's car, she'd told me she was pregnant and asked if Jason and I would be the boys' godparents. In that moment, I thought her image of us as one big happy family seemed naive, and given everything that had happened in the past year, I couldn't imagine she still held that vision.

"I told her I'd reach out to Nadia to let her know about the overnight with the boys and that she should probably stay in LA County, so she doesn't need to get a judge to approve the out-of-county travel."

Jason sent off an email to Nadia that night. When a few days went by with no reply we figured that was the end of it. Over FaceTime that Sunday evening, Kris told us she'd gone forward with booking a place in Santa Monica. "It's a few blocks from the ocean and Zach and Amber can visit if they want," she said, beaming with excitement.

"You'll have so much fun," I said. "We take the boys to the beach all the time. My cousin Dave and his wife live in Hermosa with their son, Sully, who's the same age as Logan. Sully and Logan love to dig in the sand, and wait until you see Ethan chase seagulls, he's like a clumsy baby panda."

"I just can't wait," she said, her crystal blue eyes smiling through the phone's tiny screen.

The next morning, we received a lengthy email from Nadia, laying out a schedule for upcoming visits with Amber and Zach, as well as her monthly check-in at our place. Immediately, I noticed she had scheduled the next home visit with the boys on the same date and time that she'd scheduled a visit with their parents ten miles away. Her disorganization had become so commonplace that we had begun to anticipate some mistake in every communication.

Her email went on to say she was preparing her report and recommendations for the early August court date and "wanted our thoughts on reunification with the bio parents."

"I thought we weren't allowed to offer our opinion," I said to Jason, puzzled.

"Nadia's not like other social workers," he said. "I think we've already established that."

"Do you want to draft the reply or should I?"

"Go for it," he offered. "I know how you love to write."

I was so taken aback that Nadia had asked for our perspective on reunification I nearly missed that buried at the end of her email was a one-sentence reply to Kris's request: "The case notes don't mention overnights with the grandmother, so I'll have to walk that onto the court."

"Kris is going to be pissed," I commented to Jason. "With the holiday coming up, there's no way they can get her request in front of a judge before her trip, and she's already paid for the rental."

"That sucks. She was really looking forward to it."

I spent the better part of the morning carefully constructing our reply to Nadia. I didn't trust she'd read it carefully, so I made sure not to bury the lede. "Over the past two months, the parents have spent less than three hours with the boys," I wrote. "We do not feel reunification at this time will result in positive outcomes for Ethan and Logan." I provided specific examples of Amber's indifference to Logan during the visits and then addressed Kris's overnight request. "It has always been our understanding that she could have overnight visits with the boys. She remains the only member of their family who has shown up for them with a healthy level of consistency and she has proven to be a loving and wonderful grandmother." Jason and I went back and forth on the draft a few times before finally hitting send.

In less than two hours we got a reply.

Nadia's greeting, "Hello Team," followed by "The case code is Family Reunification," felt smug, like she was schooling us for responding to her question. Had she forgotten she'd asked for our opinion? Was she reprimanding us for speaking our truth? For being honest? Was she angry? The email went on, "There is NO overnight Court Approval for Kris and the children." And there was something else: she'd copied Kris on her reply. I'm sure she wanted us all on the same page, but it also meant that Kris could see our full email to Nadia and how we'd said the boys shouldn't reunify in August. My heart sank. I felt like I'd swallowed a brick. I called Jason.

"Do you think Kris will hate us for saying the boys shouldn't reunify?"

"I don't know," he said. "But it's the truth."

"Yeah, but we basically said her son is an unfit parent."

"True."

"I guess . . . at least we said nice things about her."

"She's done right by her grandkids."

We didn't have to wait long to see Kris's reaction. While we were still on the phone, her name appeared in our inboxes. One reply, then another and another. In the first email Kris said she'd invited Amber and Zach to join her at the overnight and that she'd already rented an Airbnb. In the second email she accused Nadia of blocking her overnight visits. In the third, with her anger on full display, she said she was lodging a complaint with the department against Nadia.

"I guess she wasn't too upset about our recommendation," Jason joked.

"No shit," I said. "I feel bad for her."

I thought about my mom and Jason's mother, both of whom had spent more time with the boys than any member of their biological family. How would they feel if they were suddenly told they couldn't take their grandkids overnight? My mother lived for her grandchildren and while she'd never admit it, I'm pretty sure my mother-in-law retired early to spend more time with hers.

"Kris's birthday is next week. What if we had her over for dinner?" Jason offered. "It might be nice if she could see the boys at home."

I liked the idea, but was also a little hesitant. We had been warned not to share our address with the bio parents, but Kris wasn't Amber or Zach. She truly wanted what was best for them.

Patty and Ramona approved of the idea, so we extended the invitation, and Kris immediately accepted. The following week, she arrived with flowers for us and toys for the boys—whose bedrooms and playroom were looking increasingly like a toy store. Ethan ran to her when she stepped through the doorway, wrapping his arms around her legs. It reminded me of when my grandma Mary would visit. My siblings and I would stampede over each other to greet her at the door, throwing our arms around her before she could even take off her coat or put down the box of Dunkin' Donuts she always arrived carrying. Watching Kris react to Ethan's outpouring of love would have softened the hardest of hearts. Her eyes filled with tears and her voice cracked as she said, "Oh Ethan, Grandma is so happy to see you." Kneeling down to return his embrace and kiss his cheeks, she said, "I love you so much."

The five of us sat in the dining room, a high chair on either end of the oval table. I served my go-to dish, a roast chicken with vegetables I lifted from an Ina Garten cookbook. It's pretty easy to make and feels healthy, but most importantly it makes your guests think you spent the entire day in the kitchen. Jason placed a plate in front of Ethan, steam rising from the food. Ethan pointed at the dish and began singing, "Too hot, baby. Too hot, baby." We all burst out laughing.

"He's a big Kool and the Gang fan," I joked.

"How does he know that song?" Kris asked, through fits of laughter.

"We do a lot of singing around here," Jason added. "Mostly Stevie Wonder and Beyoncé with some Jimmy Buffett thrown in from time to time."

"Logan and I like Taylor Swift. Don't we, Lo?" I piped in, looking at the baby and singing, "Shake it off. Shake it off." He smiled brightly and rocked side to side in his high chair, raising one arm above his head and putting a fistful of tiny pieces of chicken into his mouth with the other.

We laughed throughout dinner, entertained by the boys' reactions to the food, the messes on their hands and faces. We shared stories of fun times and teachable parenting moments, like the time I'd confused the sign language words for *milk* and *more*, and how angry Ethan had gotten when I kept giving him Cheerios instead of refilling his sippy cup. After about five minutes, he yelled "leche" and I burst out laughing. He didn't think it was funny at all.

I thought back to our first meeting at Pan Pacific Park, right after the boys had moved in and Kris had made that impossible decision to hand them over to the county. It was hard to believe how much things had shifted in the past year. I remembered feeling sad for Kris that day. She was lonely and sick. She was single, her son and his wife were in a bad place, and she didn't speak to her only sister. She didn't have much of a support network to lean on. Her stress was inconceivable. But tonight was different. She was different. She seemed lighter and healthier, secure in the knowledge that her grandsons were happy, loved, and very well cared for, all because she had made that difficult decision. She seemed right at home sitting at our table, with the boys alternating in and out of her lap, Logan tangling himself in her long necklace as we sang "Happy Birthday" and indulged in the overpriced birthday cake Jason had picked up from Milk Bar. She shared stories of parenting Zach as a single mother, how he was such an active toddler, always bumping into things and hurting himself. We laughed like old friends catching up after a long time apart. As she read the boys their good-night stories and helped us put them to bed, I could imagine her fitting in seamlessly with our family and friends at future holidays, birthdays, and other celebrations.

After the boys were down, the three of us sat in the living room, sipping tea. She thanked us repeatedly for dinner and making her birthday so special.

"My relationship with Zach is really strained right now," she said, opening up about her son for the first time. "He was diagnosed with some serious mental health issues when he was a teenager. He's fine when he's on his meds, but if he's not taking his pills or if he's using drugs, he's a different person."

"I'm sorry," I offered. "This all must be really hard for you."

"Thank you. It is," she confided. "The boys are doing great, thanks to you guys."

"We are so lucky to have them," Jason said.

"You know, Ethan was briefly in foster care once before," she said slowly, as if she'd been weighing whether or not to reveal this piece of information.

"Really? I didn't know that," I said.

"He got sick when he was just a few months old and they took him to a hospital in Orange County," she said. "Amber was really nervous and upset. She was freaking out and the nurses thought she was on drugs, so they kept him. They called Child Protective Services and she had to go to court to get him back a few days later."

"They thought she was high?" I asked, trying to understand how a mother's concern could be so misconstrued.

"Amber has trouble communicating, especially when she's emotional," Kris said, pausing to consider her words. "I don't know if she's on the spectrum or if she's got developmental issues or what, but she's delayed." I caught myself nodding; I'd sensed this, too, but had never voiced my thoughts. "She's told me she was abused as a child—that no one was there for her growing up the way kids need. It's almost like she's stunted."

"That's so sad," I said.

"She's had to deal with so much," Jason added. I could see the sadness and depth of understanding in his eyes. His mom had worked with women who were victims of domestic violence and he had shared some of the horrific stories she'd passed along to him. Every time he talked about the torment these women endured, the fear dominating their lives, I was reminded of his immense capacity for empathy. I put my hand on his and looked to Kris.

"So, this isn't Ethan's first time in care?" I asked, wondering if Nadia even knew. There's no way the child welfare agencies in Orange and Los Angeles counties share files, I thought, LA can't even arrange a driver to pick up our kids for a visitation.

"He was taken from Amber and Zach, and I wasn't even called. I don't know if he went to an emergency shelter or a foster home, but the judge gave him back when she went to court a few days later. I think that's why they decided to move to Las Vegas."

"How long did they live in Vegas?" Jason asked.

"They weren't there very long. They wanted a fresh start but a few weeks in, Zach was off his meds and using again. Amber called me. She was hysterical. I didn't know what to do, so I bought her and Ethan, who couldn't have been more than five or six months old, bus tickets back to California. They rode for six hours without any food or diapers. She kept calling me asking, 'What do I do? Ethan won't stop crying.' At one point I told her to ask the driver to buy him food and I'd pay him back when I picked her up."

"That's awful. She must've been pregnant with Logan, too," Jason chimed in.

"Yes. She had to be four or five months along at the time," Kris answered.

"I can't imagine what that must have been like for them," I said, picturing a pregnant Amber, alone and scared, riding on a bus in the desert heat, with Ethan, a tired, hungry, diaper-soaked baby, on her lap. "She's lucky she had you to call," I offered, thinking about all the people in my life I could have called—my parents, my brother or sister, any number of close friends, all of whom would have stepped up to help without a moment of hesitation.

"She has no one else," Kris responded quickly. "It's sad. But I wish she didn't just call when she needs something. Money or a ride somewhere." I could tell Kris really cared for Amber and had hoped they would be close. "Her family is a mess. Rita is a nice lady, but her house is overrun by family and their partners. The place is so filthy, I won't even go inside. I can't imagine the boys ever going back there."

That night, as Jason and I lay in bed, his arm wrapped around me, I teetered back and forth between empathy for young Amber, the victim, the motherless child, who was dealt a shit hand and abused; and adult

Amber, the mother and perpetrator of whatever cause led a judge to decide she was not fit to care for her children. She had spent her life barely treading water in a sea of trauma, and I was terrified the boys would be swept away with her.

––––––

After all of June's missed visits, Nadia told us she'd issued another strong warning to Amber and Zach that if they wanted the boys back, they needed to follow through on visits. She sent us an email with a bunch of dates and times that worked for Amber and Zach, much like she had the month before and the month before that. We agreed to the dates, just like we had before, with little expectation of them actually making good on their promises to visit.

Then, on a one-hundred-degree day in early July, Amber and Zach met us at a park in Paramount, a city just east of Compton. The park was beautifully cared for, with tall trees offering shade, freshly cut grass, giant lavender plants that reminded me of the hydrangeas back home in Massachusetts, and a playground complete with all the fixings—plastic slides, monkey bars, and a variety of swings. Amber and Zach were sitting on a cement bench in the parking lot when we arrived, the smoke from their cigarettes wafting over the head of baby Savannah, asleep in a stroller beside them. They leapt up when they saw us, extinguishing their smokes and charging toward the boys.

Patty had instructed Jason and me to stand down during visits, to let Amber and Zach parent, change diapers, handle tantrums, comfort falls. We found a shaded picnic table to set up and I sat there holding Savannah, who'd just woken up in my lap, as Zach and Amber started running around the playground with the boys. Jason couldn't sit still. He stood along the edge of the playground watching the boys and their oversized playmates dash from slide to slide. Logan welcomed Zach's attention, but every few seconds he'd stop what he was doing to make sure Jason was close by.

Within ten minutes, Zach and Amber were winded and flushed. At lightning speed, they went from super-playmates with tons of energy to sweaty, exhausted twenty-somethings. I invited them to sit down and passed around some water bottles and snacks Jason had packed. The boys were as content at the table in the shade as they were on the slides, but it wasn't long before they, too, were growing uncomfortable and agitated in the heat. Jason and I entertained the three kids while Amber and Zach sat in the grass, arguing.

"Let's cut this one short," Zach told Amber, speaking loud enough for us all to hear.

"No!" Amber hissed. "We're never going to get the kids back if we walk out on visits."

I wanted to believe Amber knew they had messed up and was now trying to turn things around, that she was motivated by the force of her desire to reunite with her kids—but the way she said it made me uncomfortable, like she was acknowledging the calculation behind her behavior.

A few minutes passed and Ethan, whose rosy cheeks were now covered in applesauce, began to whine. Amber took that as her opening. "Hey, guys, I think the kids are getting hot, we should get going."

"It is really hot," I agreed.

"There's a Denny's around the corner if you'd rather go grab a bite in the air-conditioning?" Jason suggested, trying to give them a way to extend the visit.

"No. I think we should just get going," Zach said.

They kissed Ethan and Logan, and we all began walking toward the parking lot. I thought, *Where are they going? How did they even get here?* The Prius we'd last seen them drive had been repossessed months ago.

So I asked, "How'd you guys get here?"

"I got a car," Zach said with excitement. "My dad helped me get it. He's helping us find an apartment too."

"That's great. Congratulations," I said instinctively, although I wasn't sure if I was really happy about this progress.

"Thirty-seven minutes," I said to Jason, checking the time on my phone as we rode out of the parking lot. "That's all the visit lasted. Make sure you capture that in the visitation log."

"I don't know why they didn't suggest an indoor location," he said.

———

After she learned Amber and Zach blamed the excessive heat for the premature ending to their last visit in the park, Nadia arranged the next two visits, the following Friday and Saturday, at indoor locations. Friday's visit was supposed to take place at Patty's office, but they didn't confirm the day before, so Patty told us not to bother bringing the boys. On Friday afternoon Amber called Patty to confirm the 9:00 a.m. visit the following morning at a McDonald's with an indoor playground. Since Jason had been shouldering the bulk of the responsibility for these visits, I offered to take the boys alone so he could have the morning to himself to work out or catch up on sleep. He happily accepted my offer.

I allowed myself extra time to get the boys ready. The location wasn't too far away, but it was in the heart of South LA and I wasn't very familiar with the area. Waze told me there was no traffic and the boys entertained me the entire ride, babbling back and forth. I could see the golden arches reaching up into the morning sky, a few blocks before arriving at the building. As I took the left turn onto the side street leading into the lot, I saw a black Nissan parked on the sidewalk faced in the opposite direction of traffic. The windows were smashed, and the doors were riddled with bullet holes. It was as if we'd driven onto the set of a crime drama.

I ordered some pancakes for the boys, and we sat down to eat. I watched the hands on the clock intently as I poured maple syrup over their food. Patty had said, if they don't call you to tell you they're running late, you only have to stay fifteen minutes. I waited close to thirty minutes, trying to be generous before texting Jason, *They aren't here. We're coming home.* This was their seventeenth missed or canceled visit since the end of February.

Five days later, Nadia emailed us to let us know Amber and Zach had "earned"—her word—unmonitored visits with the kids. What exactly had they done to "earn" unmonitored visits? They had missed visit after visit. Of the few they did show up for, none had lasted the fully allotted time and they spent more time arguing with one another than watching or interacting with their children. I was apoplectic.

Our request for an HSA to monitor visits, which still hadn't been approved, no longer mattered. All future visits would be unmonitored. Yet every time we brought it up with Nadia, she'd say, "I'm still waiting on approval," or "Oh, right. I need to set that up," which ultimately confirmed our suspicions that she'd never requested one in the first place. On the other hand, Amber and Zach, who'd been unreliable at best, were granted every possible accommodation. I could not understand how they'd "earned" unsupervised visits. It felt like Jason and I were being restrained, forced to watch Ethan and Logan, the babies we loved, being blindly led on a collision course by the very people tasked with looking out for them. This wasn't what we signed up for. It was as if they were being rewarded for phoning it in, and that wasn't good enough. Not for Ethan and Logan or for any child. Why was no one listening to us? It was infuriating.

"Some things don't ever make sense," my cousin Heather had told me when she'd called to ask for my help writing speeches for two summer events—one a motorcycle run fundraiser held on what would have been Joanna's sixteenth birthday, another to accept a Citizen of the Year award from the Weymouth Rotary Club. "There's no doubt losing a child is the most difficult thing you can ever face," she said, pausing, perhaps evaluating how much more she should say. We came from a family where it was unusual to express emotion. I was four when Heather's dad died; she was eight. "Your father's gone," she was told that day. The funeral occurred and she, her mother, and her siblings were expected to accept it and adjust. Therapy for five kids and a working widow wasn't an option in 1981 and vulnerability only made others uncomfortable.

"It's also true that tragedy brings you face-to-face with what life's actually about," she continued, "the people who show up for you, the choice you have to criticize or feel sorry for yourself, or to be there for your family and community."

My sense of loss was so different from Heather's. Hers had been sudden, violent, final. Her loss had been the result of betrayal from someone she loved. Mine was a fear, playing out in stages, the risks anticipated, not absolute. If the boys left our lives and returned to an uncertain state where their safety wasn't guaranteed, how would I meet that pain, that void? Heather had another baby, Jayne, born the June after Joanna died. She started a nonprofit called Joanna's Place, serving grieving children and families. Her posts on Facebook made me laugh till I cried. *When I send Jeffrey to school in his pajamas—the day* before *Pajama Day.* Or: *When the dog has a healthier breakfast than Jayne.*

Would Jason and I survive our loss with even a fraction of her grace?

Chapter 15

No Blood, No Foul

Ethan and Logan's first unmonitored visit with their birth parents was held just three days later. We met Amber and Zach in a Starbucks parking lot, and they loaded the boys into the back seat of the used Volvo Zach's dad had purchased for them. They took our car seats and somehow managed to wedge them on either side of Savannah's. I forced a smile, fighting back tears as they drove away, Logan screaming out for Jason and me.

"Hearing him cry like that rips my heart out," I said to Jason as we made our way out of the lot.

"I know," he said. "I know . . ."

The visit lasted three hours and they were in the lot waiting for us when we arrived. The boys were tired and cranky, having missed a nap. Their cheeks were pink and flushed, tiny beads of sweat dotted their foreheads.

Logan cried the entire ride home. It wasn't the same separation tears he'd shed when we left him with his parents. These were tears of exhaustion. Like he was relieved the stress was finally over but voicing his frustration for having had to live through it. Their diapers were filthy, with a putrid, green-colored diarrhea, like they'd drunk a 7-Eleven

Slurpee or had overdone it on Hostess treats. Ethan was acting out too. He was angry, storming around the house like a miniature warden, banging things just because he could, Roxy and Brian scattering to get out of his way. Then he bit Jason out of the blue. A month ago he was meditating and now he was Mike Tyson.

After the second unsupervised visit a week later, Ethan seemed to regress even further, barking out orders with sounds again, like he'd done when he first moved in. "Ehh," he'd groan, pointing at things he wanted instead of using the words we'd taught him.

Patty reassured us lots of children regress. "When a child who has changed returns to an environment that is unchanged, it's only natural for them to fall back into their old behaviors. And for those of us who love them, it's really hard to watch." Ethan was a cheerful, vibrant little boy who'd call out, "Daddy, come play. Daddy, come sit." Jason, Josephine, and I had worked so hard to make him feel safe, to know he was loved, and truly worthy of love. It was heartbreaking to watch him slipping back into behaviors he'd outgrown.

I was devastated knowing my happy little boy was so unhappy and angry after these visits.

On the morning of August 6, we returned to court holding our breath. Jason had already delivered our JV-290, the same "optional" questionnaire we'd submitted back in February. Only this time we checked the box saying we had additional information to share and attached Jason's intricate spreadsheet showing all communication and visits with Amber and Zach since the last court date in February. In five months, they had used only 8 percent of the time they were allowed to spend with their children. Kris had also prepared a JV-285—a similar form to the one we completed, only for relatives. Both forms had to arrive at the courthouse, along with eight copies, a week prior to the hearing, a requirement burdensome enough that most people don't bother to complete it. Kris asked if we'd file her form when we dropped off ours and we happily obliged.

Through the series of narrow, targeted questions on the document, Kris made the case that she feared for the boys' safety if they returned to Amber and Zach. She included a list of reasons why her son and his wife weren't ready to care for the boys. She shared that Amber had often left Logan alone, crying in a car seat when he was an infant, and that when Ethan was hungry she'd insist, "Tell me you love me," before she would give him any food. But what upset me most was a story she shared about Logan. When he was just one month old, Zach had dropped him in the middle of the night and left him crying on the floor until Rita heard him and came in to pick him up. As soon as I read Kris's report, I knew this was why Zach had asked if we thought Logan was going to be a "slow kid" and why the county had called to see if the baby showed any signs of having been shaken. I saw Kris's report as a hand grenade to Amber and Zach's case, and if they were to read it, that report might also destroy her relationship with them. She must have known the risk and chosen to ignore it, putting her grandsons' safety ahead of her own needs.

Ramona also sent an official letter to the attorney representing Ethan and Logan in advance of the hearing. In her letter Ramona noted that Amber and Zach had made some progress since the last court hearing six months earlier, but that they were struggling to be compliant with visitations, not taking advantage of the time awarded to them, and terminating visits prematurely. She reminded him that not utilizing the court-ordered time to spend with the children could have a negative impact on the success of reunification. She also wrote about Patty's observation of Zach swearing at and belittling Amber in front of the boys just a few weeks earlier.

Jason and I entered the courtroom with a clear conscience. We'd done everything in our power to keep the boys safe.

"Tell me they're staying forever . . . or rip off the Band-Aid," I whispered to Jason as we entered the courtroom. As much as I didn't want to lose them, this limbo was unbearable. I wasn't sure how much more I could stand. Sitting on the wooden bench in the back of the courtroom reminded me of Sunday morning mass as a child, feeling small and powerless, while a man in a robe sits on an altar. It had been a long time since I'd set foot in a church, but prayer felt like a good choice in that moment.

Waiting for the judge's ruling, I prayed that the boys, who in my heart were now my children, would not be taken away from me.

I prayed that my family would not be torn apart.

But mostly, I prayed for closure.

When the judge granted another six-month extension, the relief didn't feel like relief. Some of the pressure was released, but the uncertainty was still simmering.

"A lot can happen in six months," my mother said when I called to relay the news. She was trying to comfort me, to calm my anxiety.

"They still have a lot to prove," I said into the phone. "Can they get a place to live? Find a way to provide for their kids?"

"It's not over yet," she said.

The six-month extension felt like a shift in the odds for reunification. Suddenly it was becoming more likely than not. It hurt too much to think about what could happen to the boys if they returned to Amber and Zach, what fate awaited them. I wasn't confident the boys' biological parents, the ones who brought them into this world, were capable of rising to the occasion. I also began thinking about what this could mean for me and Jason. We loved being parents and we were good at it. We'd spent more than a year pouring everything we had into loving Ethan and Logan, nurturing them, while rolling the dice with our hearts. How would we survive losing them? I was forty years old. Could I do this again? What if we tried to foster a second time? Would we ever be able to love another child like we loved these two? What if we lost again?

Or what if the boys were detained again? Next time, detention would include Savannah. Of course we'd take her, but could we handle three children? If we decided we wanted to parent again, how long should we wait for them to come back into care before we accepted

another placement? Should we reconsider surrogacy? The judge's decision prolonged the torture of uncertainty.

I didn't know that in a matter of days, I'd be longing for limbo.

––––––––

Two days after the court hearing, I retrieved my phone from the
locker after a Spin class to find a missed call from Jason and a text
message reading, *Call me!* I changed my shoes and called him as I
walked to the car.

"Amber won her appeal," he said as he answered the phone.

"What? What are you talking about?"

When we first became Ethan and Logan's foster parents, Jason had
discovered and signed up for an online service through the court's website that sends email notifications about the legal movement of specific
cases. We knew Amber had appealed the boys' detention, but we had
been told that all birth parents appeal, but they rarely ever win. "Judges
don't like to overrule one another in these types of cases," Cathy had
told us, when she called about the two boys at the county office waiting
to be placed. Because of this advice, I hadn't given much thought to her
appeal.

"I got an email from the court, evidently a hearing was held last
week, and the appellate court ruled in her favor." I didn't want to believe
him. But Jason would never joke about this.

"I thought 'no one ever wins their appeal,'" I said, with obvious
confusion. "What does this mean?" I knew what it meant, but I wanted
him to tell me he'd figured out a solution.

"I don't know. I have a call in to Ramona to find out."

"Okay. I'll be right home." This was worse than my worst fear.

"I'll forward you the email."

"Thanks. I love you." Overturning the boys' detention meant it was
all a big mistake. The investigator got it wrong, the county was wrong,
the judge was wrong. My foreboding was the only thing right.

"I love you too."

———

In the parking lot of Flywheel on Larchmont Boulevard, an indoor cycling gym where I'd gone almost daily to distract myself and sweat out my anxiety, I pulled out my phone and clicked the link Jason shared. My perspiration-soaked shirt sticking to my chest as I stood next to the car squinting at the phone's screen, I began reading the seventeen-page document. Halfway down, on page two, was this statement: "We agree the evidence did not support the juvenile court's jurisdictional findings and order, and therefore reverse."

What does this mean? Are the boys going back to Amber and Zach? If so, when? How can this be happening?

I got home a few minutes later and retreated to my office to take a deep dive into the court's ruling. The document gave us a lot of new information about the circumstances surrounding the boys' initial detention, stuff I wanted Kendra to tell us early on, but she had been too professional to divulge.

The appellate court judges unanimously decided Amber's untreated bipolar disorder and history of drug use weren't grounds for detention because, at least on paper, abuse hadn't happened yet. This I interpreted to mean: no blood, no foul.

It didn't make sense. I learned in the court decision that Amber received disability payments for bipolar disorder. So I researched the qualification requirements for disability due to her mental illness and learned you must prove that the condition impairs you in at least two of three ways: that it severely limits daily activity; results in an inability to interact with others in a normal way; and/or leads to recurring and extended episodes of decompensation—times when treatment fails to relieve symptoms.[1] I just couldn't see how Amber, who had no family or community support and was refusing to take her prescribed medication, would be able to care for three young children.

Also, there were studies showing that even without the added challenge of mental illness, the outcomes for children in care who reunified weren't great. Up to 32 percent of reunified children have been found to reenter foster care, especially those who were first removed as infants.[2] Children who reunify were shown in some cases to have worse developmental outcomes compared to those who remained in care.[3] It made me physically ill to imagine a future in which Ethan and Logan were harmed.

Even more upsetting than the risks of reunification was the ruling that the boys should never have been detained in the first place. This meant that if the boys should come back into foster care, it would be treated as a first-time placement, because the past fifteen months were being expunged, wiped clean from their records. A clean slate might work on paper, but it wouldn't reset their memories. They couldn't simply reboot their attachments to us, the life we'd built, and the love we shared. I grew more and more upset with each passing minute and spent the day anxiously waiting to hear back from Ramona and Patty, and researching foster care outcomes.

A study of all children born in California from 1999 to 2006 rang the alarm bells for me. It found that children who'd been the subject of a maltreatment allegation, whether substantiated or not, died from intentional injuries (those inflicted on them) at a rate five and a half times that of nonreported children. They died from unintentional (or accidental) injuries at twice the rate of nonreported children.[4] As soon as I read this finding, my heart rate started to accelerate. Memories began flashing in my mind like a strobe light. First, I was in my car, in the garage, Jason's voice on the phone saying, "They want to know if Logan shows signs he's been shaken." I blinked and suddenly Zach was looking down at his son, asking, "Do you think Logan's going to be a slow kid?" Then the words Kris wrote to the court on her JV-285 staring back up at me from the page: "Zach dropped Logan and left him screaming on the floor."

I could feel my chest contracting, my shoulders caving in. My breathing had morphed to panting. The signs of a panic attack were now all too familiar.

I closed my eyes and rested my hands in my lap. Putting my feet solidly on the floor, I did my best to sit up straight. *Where are your feet?* I asked myself, repeating the question Jason had asked during my first panic attack. Forcing deep breaths, *inhale-three-two-one, hold-three-two-one, exhale-three-two-one, hold-three-two-one, and inhale* . . . I repeated this over and over. After a few minutes, my body began to loosen. The pain slowly melted from my chest and my shoulders unlocked. I opened my eyes and went back to reading the appellate court's ruling.

Logan was born in a hospital in Los Angeles County, and now I learned that two days later, a child protection investigator had gone to Rita's house to check on him because Amber had tested positive for marijuana on a hospital toxicology screen. There was nothing random about her selection for drug screening. This was a maternity ward, not TSA. Her actions must have set off alarm bells in the delivery room like they had when Ethan was first detained in Orange County.

The appellate court's decision to overrule the boys' detention cited a report from the social worker that described Rita's house as *cluttered with a very repugnant smell permeating throughout,* adding that dog feces were visible on the floor. The worker took Ethan and Logan away with her that day.

In March of 2016, three days after the boys were initially detained, there was a hearing at the Edmund D. Edelman Children's Court. A judge reviewed the following facts to decide whether or not the boys could go home:

- Amber said she had smoked marijuana during her pregnancy because it helped with her nausea and anxiety but that she didn't use it before or while caring for the boys.
- When Logan was born five days earlier, she told the hospital social worker she was "extremely bipolar" but hadn't taken those prescriptions in years, not since she was pregnant with her first son, now seven years old.

- Amber did not work and both she and Zach had been declared "disabled" based on their mental health diagnoses and were receiving Social Security Disability Insurance benefits.
- In the seventy-two hours since the boys' detention, both she and Zach had gone to a mental health urgent care center, where she was again diagnosed with bipolar disorder, was given new prescriptions, and received a referral to a psychiatrist.
- Lastly, Amber's first child came to the county's attention at birth, when he tested positive for amphetamine and cocaine. He was placed in a legal guardianship situation with her brother and she explained that she didn't seek to reunify with him because she was not prepared to parent at that time and felt her brother could offer him a better life.

The judge had decided to release Ethan and Logan to Amber and Zach, with the direction that they both submit to drug testing and take their prescribed medications for mental health conditions. He told Amber not to breastfeed and that he would see them back in court in two months, at the end of May.

In April, one month later, a social worker made a planned visit to the Lancaster home and found the children *safe, clean, fed, and cared for*. She gave Amber and Zach contact information for several family shelters and housing assistance programs. In advance of the May hearing, the county interviewed Amber for the report they'd have to share with the judge. During the interview, Amber shared that she began smoking marijuana at the age of twelve and by fourteen was using crack cocaine and methamphetamine. She also shared that she had a few psychiatric hospitalizations growing up because she had failed to cooperate when her family sought help for her mental health issues.

A couple of weeks before the court date, the county social worker made an unannounced visit to Rita's house and found the children to be "free of visible marks or bruises." She noted that Amber and Zach were making breakfast, Zach was holding one child, feeding him a bottle of milk. The living space was messy, and "there was evidence of dog feces that were not picked up." The worker reported observing tension between Amber and her grandmother, who had threatened to kick them out.

At the end of the month, Amber and Zach returned to court for a second hearing. They had both tested positive for marijuana four times since their last court date in March. The judge noted they hadn't followed up with the referrals to the shelters or housing programs, and that Amber hadn't filled her prescriptions for bipolar disorder, or received a doctor's referral for medical marijuana. The county reported it was "unknown if the parents are caring for the children while they are under the influence."

The judge reviewed the case and found Amber's history of substance use, including methamphetamine, amphetamine, cocaine, and marijuana; her current use of marijuana; her failure to take prescribed bipolar medication and resume psychiatric care; combined with the requirements of constant care and supervision needed for children of such young ages rendered her incapable of caring for her sons. He ordered the boys' removal, stating that Amber's "substance abuse and untreated mental health issues endanger the children's physical health and safety, create a detrimental home environment and place the children at risk of serious physical harm, damage and danger."

The services offered to Amber and Zach included those designed to preserve and enhance their family, like parenting classes, as well as full drug and alcohol treatment with aftercare. Amber was ordered to take all prescribed psychotropic medications and granted monitored three-hour visits, three times a week with her sons.

Any judge who orders that a child be removed from their home knows the gravity of that decision, the trauma that ruling will bring forth onto the child. I couldn't imagine they don't lose sleep second-guessing some decisions, wondering, if they had made the right call or if they had ruled differently, could there have been a different outcome? The alternative to foster care is leaving a child in a home potentially subjected to continued abuse and neglect. Which is worse, keeping a child in a traumatizing home or the trauma of foster care? I guess *it depends*. Like Cindy told us, every case, every set of circumstances, is different. Judges don't universally agree on what merits a detention and what issues could be solved with services. Difficult decisions need to be made.

The appeals process is necessary to ensure balance to these critical decisions. Not all parents are capable of keeping their children safe. Yet the judgments of the children's court carry life-altering implications. They should be reviewed and questioned because they are far too impactful to be left up to the discretion of a single person.

Jason found the attorney representing Amber on LinkedIn, and it turned out Amber had been appointed a resourceful and adept Harvard Law School grad to lay out her appeal. Her counsel used prior appellate court decisions to push back against the findings and conclusions of the dependency court that allowed for the boys to be removed from Amber and Zach. The young attorney's brief argued that Amber's history of substance use, long-term untreated mental health issues, and self-medication through marijuana instead of taking prescribed medicines shouldn't have been a concern because prior appellate court cases concluded these challenges did not pose a significant risk to the children in those cases. Also, the county's counsel must have been under the same assumption we were, that *no one ever wins their appeal*, because it appeared they were embarrassingly outgunned in court.

Yet there was so much the appellate judges had no way of knowing. How Logan cried when he was left in his parents' care and then came home to us with diarrhea and diaper rash that would last a full week. How Ethan was regressing—coming back angry, biting and hitting—two things he never did before. How Amber still barely acknowledged Logan's existence. That she now had a third child. Regardless of the trauma she'd endured or how badly she wanted to see the boys, she hadn't yet done the work to be ready to care for them. The decision on the appeal didn't take into account the numerous missed or canceled visits. The judges simply found, in reviewing events from over a year ago, that there was insufficient evidence of neglect or abuse for the boys to have been removed from their mother's care in the house with dog shit. Judges who had never met the parents in the courtroom were able to overturn the decision of a judge who had.

Ramona called and confirmed our fears. It was every bit as bad as we had imagined. This was the first time she or any of her colleagues at Children's Bureau could recall a detention being overturned. She reached out to the boys' attorney, the same man who'd told Jason and me "we didn't have to show up" in court at the February hearing. He emailed her back to say, "The appellate court was very clear in their belief that no allegations should have been sustained against the mother and the children shouldn't have been detained." He explained there would be a hearing in a month or so and following that hearing, the kids would "most likely" be returned to their mother. I couldn't accept this outcome.

"How can this be happening?" I said to Jason, crossing my arms and slumping against the kitchen sink in defeat.

"What did he mean by 'most likely'?" he said as he reviewed Ramona's email again on his phone. "Do we still have a fighting chance?"

"I hope so. Do you think we should call an attorney?" I asked him. We'd been given the name of a dependency law practitioner a few months earlier.

"Yes," he said slowly and with resolve. "Now is definitely the time to lawyer up." It was exactly what I wanted to hear. "Even if it's just to let us know what our options are, then we can decide what to do next."

To the outside world, Jason appears laid-back, gifted with an ability to clear the tension in a room with wit and compassion. But his true superpower is his commitment to fighting for justice. He wasn't going to accept this decision any easier than I was, and if I was going into the trenches, the best man had my six.

"I'm going to set up an appointment now. I love you," I said, walking over to give him a kiss.

"I love you, too, babe."

Nadia arrived, late as usual, for her scheduled visit the next day. Jason and I met her at the door, still shaken by the news of the appeal, and bursting with questions about the reunification process. Could it be stopped, and if not, how should we prepare the boys and ourselves? Patty and Ramona joined us for the visit.

"What do you mean?" Nadia asked. "What appeal?"

Jason handed her the pages we'd printed the day before.

"No," she said, shaking her head and setting the documents down on the coffee table. "I don't know anything about that."

I picked up the pages and handed them back to her. "Nadia, this says Amber won her appeal and the boys are to be returned to her. Can you please take a look at it?"

"This isn't anything." She dismissed me with a wave of her hand, without so much as glancing at the pages. I was asking her to read paperwork that someone in her position had seen hundreds of times and she was acting as if I'd asked her to teach Common Core math. I was furious.

Ramona stepped in. "Nadia, I have spoken to minors' counsel," she began with a deliberate calm, a tone of solemn authority, commanding the attention of everyone in the room. "He informed me that the appellate court has made it very clear. They believe the boys should never have been taken from their mother and that, after another hearing, they should be returned to her."

Nadia, who hadn't fully listened to anything anyone had said since taking over this case, sat in silence, processing Ramona's words. Seeing her finally absorb the enormity of what was happening allowed me to exhale and begin to cool down.

"Children's Bureau believes the county should appeal this decision and we hope that you and county counsel agree," Ramona continued. Nadia remained silent, dumbstruck by the gravity of Ramona's words. Hearing Ramona say her agency was supporting us felt good. Our army of resistance was growing. We weren't fighting alone, and their support also affirmed we weren't just reacting poorly to things not going our way. She was validating our experience as the foster parents and our concerns for the boys' safety going forward.

Since she first arrived at our door five months earlier Nadia had moved like a hummingbird, chattering incessantly. It was satisfying to finally see her idle.

"Both Patty and I have observed Amber and Zach interact with the boys and what we've witnessed gives us serious concern for their safety if they are to reunify," Ramona added.

"I'll share your concerns with my supervisor," Nadia responded. She stood abruptly and gathered her bag. "I'll do some research on my end and report back," she said as she raced to the door.

She left, and we sat with Ramona and Patty. This was Nadia's shortest visit yet.

"Thank you," I said, looking at the two women, who were speaking up for Ethan and Logan's safety.

"Thank you both so much," Jason added. "It means everything to know you're standing beside us."

"It's the right side to be on," Patty said.

"I'm not confident Nadia's going to do anything, so I'll reach out to her supervisor directly," Ramona added. I wasn't sure what clout Ramona or Children's Bureau carried, but other than Jason and myself, they were the only ones who had observed Amber and Zach during visits with the boys. Patty had cautioned them about arguing in front of the children and witnessed Amber's behavior toward Logan firsthand. They both were present when Zach got in Kendra's face, before Jason encouraged him to take a walk and cool down. And they were professionals, social workers, not just foster parents protecting their own hearts from the pain of loss.

After Patty and Ramona left, I followed Jason upstairs and into our bedroom. He was standing at the foot of the bed with his back to me when I walked into the room. "They're really going to leave," I said, my voice strained, a lump in my throat. He turned to face me, biting his lower lip with his teeth.

"I don't know what else we can do," he said slowly, lowering his head. I took a seat on the bed, kicking my legs up onto the mattress and lying back against the pillows. I was almost too exhausted, too overwhelmed to cry or to feel any emotion. I gave my heavy eyes a break, sinking my head into the thick pillow.

"There's nothing else we can do," I said, stretching to soothe the aching in my calves and legs. He lay down next to me, grabbing my hand in his.

"I can't believe this is happening," I said.

"I know."

"I feel so defeated," I said.

Jason rolled over, taking me in his arms. "Me too."

———

That night, I called my mom, my throat tight with grief.

"When they go—" I said, but she cut me off.

"I don't see how they could be leaving," she insisted.

I could feel her clinging to a fantasy version of a life where the boys stayed with us forever, where she could spare us all the terrible loss. Grief had visited Mom too often. She'd suffered more than most. Perhaps it was because of her own agony that she wanted so badly to protect me. But she couldn't. Not this time. It was out of her control. In that moment, I wanted to protect her. Burying her head in the sand was only going to make it hurt even more.

"Mom, you have to stop saying it's not happening," I said. "It's not helping me, and it's not helping you. We all love the boys . . ." My voice broke as the grief came. "But they're going back."

In one of the most excruciating conversations of my life, I told my mother not to do the thing she wanted most of all—to keep her child and grandchildren safe.

Chapter 16

The Short Straw

When we arrived at Mona Leung's office for a consultation, I didn't know what to expect. Jason and I wanted a lawyer to explain the situation to us, to let us know what, if anything, we could do. As foster parents, we were not a party to the case. We didn't have anyone standing up in court arguing on our behalf, but if we could change that, I wanted to know how. I had told Patty I wanted the Olivia Pope of child welfare lawyers.

"We want advice from a lawyer who glides into the courtroom on gale-force winds, firing off motions like lightning bolts," I said. "We want someone who knows everything about the legal process to explain our options." Ethan and Logan deserved nothing less.

"Then you'd better call Mona," she said.

Her office building was just a few blocks from our home, and I had passed it thousands of times, paying it little mind except for when Jason would criticize its dated brick facade. "They've got uninterrupted views of the Hollywood sign and they put in tiny windows. What did they think they were building, a storage unit?"

The building required a code to enter, so Mona greeted us in the lobby and instructed us to follow her down a short hallway, lined with what I suspected from the wear was original carpeting. We took an elevator to the third floor and she made little attempt at small talk, despite Jason's best effort. "Have you been in this office a long time?"

"Not really."

"We live just around the corner."

"Nice," she said.

"We could've walked but we were running late," I added, a subtle jab at Jason's ongoing feud with punctuality.

She unlocked her suite and led us through an empty reception area, flipping on lights as she walked. "Forgive the mess. I don't come to the office much," she said as we entered a private office. "I'm mostly at court." The space was dark and dank, atypical for a law office, or an LA office in general, which usually boast big windows that pour in natural light. There was no secretary or team of associates reading and drafting briefs. Her field of law attracts people who are passionate about helping children and families, not getting rich. Mona Leung was a one-woman child-protecting machine. She'd been practicing dependency law for more than thirty years and had a stellar reputation. We were grateful she squeezed us into her packed schedule with just two days' notice.

"I looked over the court documents you sent." Mona dove in, taking a seat behind an antique partners desk and motioning for us to sit in the two leather-backed chairs opposite the desk. She wasted no time, a quality I appreciated. "The best outcome is for the Department of Children and Family Services to appeal the appellate court's decision. Do you know if they plan on doing that?"

"No. We don't know yet," Jason said.

"Well, in my opinion, it looks like county counsel may have just phoned it in on this one," she said, raising her bottom lip into a frown. It was the first bit of emotion she'd displayed since we arrived at her office.

"Before detaining a child," she continued, "the county has to build a case. The investigating social worker needs hard evidence to show a child has been harmed or that harm is imminent before the county's counsel can argue for detention." She removed her glasses and placed them on the yellow notepad in front of her. "Removing children from their parents shouldn't be an easy thing to do."

"Of course," I said, Jason and I both nodding in agreement.

"Look, the first thing you need to do is figure out if the county is going to appeal the decision and see what minors' counsel is planning to do as well," she said.

"The boys' attorney is terrible," Jason said.

"Can you go above him?"

I knew exactly what she meant. Children in the county's care are represented in court by the Children's Law Center, a nonprofit law firm.

"That's a good idea." I nodded, already flipping through my mental Rolodex for who we knew who could get us connected with their leadership. "I think we know some folks who could get us in there."

"Good," she said. "Now, I just want to level with you, winning an appeal, like Amber has done in your case, is not something that happens frequently. Her lawyer must've been really convincing. Either that, or the county's attorney really dropped the ball."

Mona explained that the appellate decision cited precedent, or previously settled case law, to chip away at the reasons the county had detained the boys—Amber's untreated mental health issues, her use of marijuana during and after pregnancy, her history of other drug use, losing parental rights over her oldest son, an unsanitary and unstable housing situation.

"There are two fundamental problems I see with this decision. First, it cites cases involving older children, who require significantly less care and attention than the babies you took in. Second, the judges never even considered the combined weight of all of the issues Amber faced stacked upon each other. As far as I can tell, the appellate court looked at each of the reasons cited for detention in isolation, rather than as a collection of compounding evidence that warranted the boys' removal from their parents' care." She paused to make sure we were following, putting her glasses back on. I nodded, jotting notes on my notepad. "For each issue Amber faced, they found a previous decision.

History of drug use, check. Losing parental rights over her oldest child, check, and so on," she said, waving a finger in the air like she was ticking off boxes.

The juvenile court, which had detained the boys, found Amber's situation to be a recipe for disaster—one just waiting to happen. The appellate court, however, disagreed and used settled cases to show how a parent in a different case was able to care for their child while dealing with one of the challenges Amber faced. What they didn't do was find a case where a parent faced *all* of the same challenges as Amber.

"Would you consider this a precedent-setting case?" I asked Mona, tapping into the knowledge I'd acquired from countless hours bingeing courtroom dramas.

"Absolutely," she said emphatically. "If this case gets published, I'm going to use it in several of my birth parent cases."

"What do you mean by 'if it gets published'?" Jason asked.

"Cases are either published or unpublished. Only published opinions can be cited as precedent in future cases. The Court of Appeal or sometimes the California Supreme Court gets to decide which ones get published. In some cases, the county may specifically argue for a case not to be published."

"Why would they care either way?" I asked.

"Well, it depends," Mona said, using her index finger to push her Warby Parkers farther up the bridge of her nose. "When they aren't happy with the result of a case, they may want to keep it hidden."

I leaned forward in my chair. "So, the social worker gathers all the evidence during their investigation and then the court decides whether or not the evidence is strong enough to support detaining a child, based on precedent? And the judge gets to decide?" I asked.

"In theory, yes. That's how it's supposed to work. However, sometimes the county may lose a case they should have won, and they don't want it used against them in the future."

"I don't understand," Jason said.

"Let's look at your case, for example. The ruling talks about reports filed by a social worker who made both planned and unplanned visits to the house. We obviously don't have access to those, so we have no way of knowing what other details were included in those reports that may have been glossed over by county counsel or ignored by the judges. Several things could have happened . . ."

I was scribbling notes, listening with the intensity I normally reserve for an Oprah podcast.

"One scenario is that the worker provided loads of details and county counsel, who was overloaded with cases, only took a cursory look at the reports before making the case to the judge. Given that the attorney would have likely appeared before this judge in dozens of detention hearings, she probably knew which factors were most likely to impact his decision and just pulled those facts from the report."

I appreciated her effort to humanize the process, but the possibility that Ethan and Logan were casualties of a dysfunctional bureaucracy was outrageous and unacceptable. I thought about our first visit to court, and the stacks of file folders I'd observed on the county counsel's table. It reeked of disorganization.

"Another scenario is that the social worker was simply overworked and undersupported. The county responded in person to more than sixty-five thousand emergency response referrals last year, and the report could have been rushed, with few details, forcing the lawyer to have to stretch to make a case for detention.

"Regardless of what happened at the county level, when the case rose to the appellate court, the judges reversed the decision. Above all else . . ." She paused briefly, and I looked up from my notebook, waiting for her to continue. ". . . this case demonstrates how strain on county workers harms the well-being of the very children they're charged to protect." Each word, a new puncture to my already wounded heart. The system was defective, and we were hostages to its incompetence.

"Now, if the decision gets published, it can be used by lawyers like me to argue on behalf of birth parents."

"Why wouldn't the county just appeal the decision?" Jason asked.

"Hopefully, they will. But appealing an appellate court decision is a lot of work. Whether they decide to appeal or not, my best guess is they'll try to keep it from being published."

"So their mistake is not broadcast," Jason said.

"To cover their asses," I interjected.

"That's one way of saying it."

"So if they don't appeal, the boys just go back to Amber and Zach?" I asked.

"Yes," she said, nodding slowly.

I could feel the breath escaping my lungs as soon as the word crossed her lips. We all sat in silence. I could tell by Jason's tightly clasped hands that he was feeling the same unease. The heart doesn't typically break in one quick snap; it splinters under the pressure of a thousand tiny jabs, until finally giving out. I didn't notice the tears falling down from my cheeks until they splashed onto my notepad. Jason placed his hand on my knee and I wiped my eyes.

"I'll follow up with Ramona, the supervisor at our foster family agency, to see if she heard back from county counsel," Jason said to Mona, leaning closer and softly squeezing my leg. "She's trying to find out if they intend to appeal."

"Great," she said.

"I'll find a way to connect with someone on the board at Children's Law Center," I added.

"Good," she said. "Please let me know if I can do anything."

———

Jason and I rode the few blocks home without speaking, still feeling the aftershock of the news Mona had delivered.

"I'm going to reach out to Jill," I said, breaking the silence. "Her foundation donates a lot of money to the Children's Law Center. Maybe she can ask them to support an appeal."

"Good," Jason said as we pulled up to our house. "I'll ask Ramona to follow up with county counsel. We need them to appeal."

"We really do."

The moment we stepped through the front door we heard the boys' laughter coming from the kitchen. Jason squeezed my hand, and we traded our somber faces for forced smiles. We acted like everything was right in the world, kissing Ethan and Logan's sticky cheeks as they sat in their high chairs chewing on the Nutri-Grain bars Josephine had given them. The pair reminded me of dueling pianists at a New Orleans nightclub, laughing and hollering, loudly competing for attention and playing off each other. Their joy was infectious. Not even the heaviness of what might lie ahead could prevent me from sharing in the delight they found in one another.

Later that afternoon, I ducked into my office upstairs to send an email to Jill. I asked her to grab coffee, so I could get her advice about the boys' case. She quickly accepted.

We met the next morning at Groundwork, a café on Larchmont Boulevard just a few doors down from her yoga class. We had only ever had a few one-on-one conversations, most of which occurred while refilling our water glasses at one of the FosterMore funders meetings. I knew how hard it was to get on her calendar, so it meant a lot that she made time to meet so quickly.

We found a table outside and she tucked her yoga mat underneath as we took our seats. "What's going on with your little ones?" Jill asked, the curls of her chestnut hair bouncing in harmony as she tilted her head to the side.

"They are so awesome," I said. "But their case has taken an unexpected turn and we may need some help."

We sat for over an hour, and I explained what Mona had shared with us, how the appellate court had siloed each of Amber's challenges, considering them individually instead of as one rapidly growing, downhill-tumbling snowball. How our best hope was for the county to appeal and that we weren't happy with the boys' attorney.

"If you send me something, I'm happy to forward it to Children's Law Center," she offered.

"Thank you so much. I'll get you something to send right away," I said before we hugged our goodbyes.

When I got back home, I began reading all of the cases cited in the appellate court's ruling, highlighting the discrepancies between Amber's case and the ones used as precedent. I needed the letter Jill would send to the higher-ups at Children's Law Center to be an irrefutable argument as to the absurdity of this ruling. I wanted them to force or shame the county into appealing.

The question in every appeal of a child detention is whether or not the juvenile dependency court was presented with enough evidence to detain someone's child. The evidence had to demonstrate either that the child suffered serious physical harm, or that a substantial risk of physical harm or illness existed as a result of the parents' inability to supervise or protect the child. In Amber's case there was no clear evidence, no cuts or bruises, indicating the boys had been harmed. The decision to detain Ethan and Logan was based on the probability that harm would occur given the multiple obstacles Amber faced.

The juvenile dependency court saw the issues facing Amber as the ingredients of the perfect storm, while the Court of Appeal disagreed. As I read through the cases, it was just as Mona had told us: the judges found one case after another to check the individual box for each of Amber's questionable circumstances. In many instances, the precedent cited was a complete misfit for the combination of circumstances swirling about Amber. The more I read, the more upset I became.

None of these cases addressed Amber's refusal to treat her mental health issues, and what stung the most was a ruling I stumbled upon, released just five days prior to Amber's ruling. In that case, three different judges of the exact same court found that a father's refusal to take prescribed medication for his depression and bipolar disorder was reason enough to infer his issues were unresolved, and therefore impaired his ability to provide regular care to his young son, resulting in a substantial risk of physical harm to the child. Once again, Ethan and Logan had been dealt the short straw.

Being placed on the docket of these particular three judges was a fortuity with life-altering implications. It was shit luck for sure, but was it destiny? Was the power that had awarded Amber a top-tier law school graduate as her counsel the same force that paired the boys with an attorney who was indifferent, one who questioned why foster parents would even show up to court? Was it misfortune that transferred their case from Kendra to Nadia? Was it fate that our paths would intersect only briefly before careening off in different directions? Was our time together really nearing an end?

I finished an email for Jill to pass along to the Children's Law Center and attached four pages of notes on the cases cited in the decision. I hit send on the email and took a deep breath. This, like so many events of the past fifteen months, was completely out of my control.

We didn't know if the Department of Children and Family Services was planning to appeal yet, but if Nadia's actions were any indicator, they were preparing for the boys to reunify with Amber and Zach. She called Jason a couple of days after the Court of Appeal's decision was released to let him know the agency was planning to increase visits to six hours, twice a week. Just one week earlier at the court hearing, the county, along with minors' counsel, had opposed expanding the duration of visits because Amber and Zach had skipped so many previous visits. The judge had agreed but gave the county authority to extend the visits if they saw progress from Amber and Zach. The only shift that had occurred in the past seven days was the appellate court ruling. So why else would the county suddenly reverse its position?

Over email, Nadia pushed for visits to occur on both Saturdays and Sundays, saying Zach had gotten a job driving a tow truck Monday through Friday and weekend visits would allow him to help Amber care for the boys and Savannah. Ramona pushed back immediately. "If the boys reunify, Amber will be alone with all three children five days a week. She's going to have to get used to it," she replied, suggesting visits occur on Fridays and Saturdays. Nadia's supervisor agreed with Ramona's recommendation and the longer visits were set to begin immediately.

We were still waiting for an approved HSA to transport the boys and had no idea if Nadia had even submitted our request, so that weekend Jason drove the boys to Amber and Zach's new apartment in the Glassell Park neighborhood. Amber told him the apartment was owned by a friend of Zach's father, who had waived the traditional credit checks and security deposit.

"The building is nice," Jason told me over the phone after dropping off the boys. "The neighborhood has a lot of older buildings with lots of charm and character. It's a one-bedroom on the first floor, with a big living room and a good-sized kitchen. They don't have a lot of furniture or anything on the walls, but they just moved in."

"Yeah? I can go with you to pick them up," I said. "I really want to see it for myself. Did she mention anything about the appeal?"

"No. I bet she doesn't even know about it yet."

When Jason and I pulled up in front of the yellow-painted brick building six hours later, the boys were playing in the large grassy area out front. Logan was sweeping an oversized rake on the ground and Ethan was being pushed on a faded *Paw Patrol* ride-on toy by a little boy who appeared to be about four years old. Amber stood cross-armed in the doorway, smoking a cigarette.

When Logan saw us get out of the car, he dropped the rake and ran to me, arms stretched wide. Ethan leapt off the toy and sprinted over to Jason, pointing to the car and saying, "We go ride. We go ride in car now." There was an older boy riding a bike on the sidewalk and a woman I assumed was their mother, with braids pulled into a tight bun, sitting in a lawn chair holding a baby girl in her arms.

"Oh, they are excited to see you two," she exclaimed, her bright smile exuding warmth.

"We're excited to see them, too," I said, scooping up Logan and pulling him in close.

"And to meet all their friends," Jason added, as he turned to her son, who was reclaiming his *Paw Patrol* toy Ethan had abandoned. "What's up, buddy?"

"I like *Paw Patrol*," the boy who had been pushing Ethan said, his big smile showing the adorable gap in his front baby teeth.

"Me too. Chase is my favorite," Jason said. "Who's your favorite?"

"Chase."

"All right," Jason cheered, offering him a high-five. The boy's mother smiled. In the time since I'd become a parent, I'd learned quickly that I immediately like people who are good to my kids.

"Jason," Amber called out, dropping her Newport and stubbing it out in the grass under her flip-flop. "Sorry I was so out of it when you got here this morning. Nadia told me you were coming tomorrow. So I wasn't expecting you all today."

"I didn't notice anything, Amber," Jason assured her.

"Nadia is really bad at scheduling stuff," she said, and Jason and I laughed.

"That's an understatement," he said.

"She couldn't organize a two-car parade," I chimed in.

"Every time she calls about a visit, she changes the date and time. Last week she gave me an address to get drug tested and when I got there, it was a 7-Eleven. I'm like, *Lady, I'm trying to get my kids back.*" She laughed. "*Why are you making this so difficult?*"

"I'm sorry," Jason said.

"She's a nightmare," I added. Through all of our frustration with Nadia, I had never stopped to contemplate what it must be like for Amber and Zach. Nadia was scattered, forgetful, and disorganized. But to Amber, she was the linchpin on which getting her kids back depended. Maybe Amber was trying harder than I realized? But would her best effort be enough? Could she protect three babies from getting hurt, running into the street, or choking on a small toy? Would she know how to soothe Ethan when he's tired and whining? Or redirect Logan when he's having a tantrum?

The boys were already asleep in their car seats by the time we turned onto Eagle Rock Boulevard, just a few blocks from Amber and Zach's new home. I assumed they hadn't napped, and judging from the grass stains on their knees they'd played hard. "I like that there's kids in their building to play with," I said to Jason, who nodded in agreement. "Is it bad that I want to give the neighbor lady our number in case she sees anything?"

"You're not doing that," he said, like he was giving an order.

"I know. But I just want her to know there's someone to call if she's worried about them."

"I know," he said.

I looked at my phone and saw a reply from Jill.

"Babe, Jill emailed me back. She says, 'I'm sorry to tell you this, I spoke with the executive director of the Children's Law Center and she agrees with the appellate court's decision.'" My heart sank. "They're not going to do anything."

"Oh my god," he said. "Who are these people?"

"Last week they all agreed Amber and Zach shouldn't even get extended visits and now they think they shouldn't have been detained in the first place," I said, anger boiling inside me.

"If something happens to these boys, I'm going to blame all of them," Jason said.

Our best hope now was that the county would appeal the decision.

———

A few nights later I was lying in bed with Roxy, consumed by our mounting losses with the courts, when I suddenly realized she was dead. Silently. In an unremarkable instant, my hand resting against her chest, she took her final breath.

Jason's parents were visiting. They stayed with the boys while Jason and I raced Roxy to the emergency vet, but I already knew that my one constant companion for the past thirteen years was gone.

The next morning, I couldn't pull myself out of bed.

"Stay," Jason said.

So I lay a little longer. I called a few friends. I cried. Strangely, actual grief felt like a respite from the anticipation of grief. I think Roxy somehow knew it was the right time to leave—that if the boys left and she'd died after, I wouldn't have been able to handle it. I felt an unexpected peace in her departure.

When I came downstairs later that morning, still a tender mess, Ethan was roaming the house room to room, calling, "Where Roxy go? Where Roxy go?"

In that moment I knew I would soon be doing the same, wandering from room to room, calling out their names in an empty house.

Chapter 17

Bruises

Shortly after the boys went to bed that night, we got a call from Ramona. "The county is not going to appeal the ruling." Her tone was serious, coming from the speaker, as we stood on either side of the island in the kitchen. "I'm sorry. I know this is not the outcome any of us wanted."

Less than two weeks earlier, the county argued that Amber and Zach weren't yet ready to resume full responsibility for their children, the Children's Law Center attorney agreed, and the court ruled in their favor. But now, after losing their case on appeal, they reversed course, abandoning both the boys and their own legitimacy. Instead of trying harder to keep the boys safe, they decided to save themselves, arguing for the case to go unpublished—so it couldn't be used as precedent in other cases. We took this to mean they also didn't think the decision held water—but they were more concerned about protecting the credibility of future rulings than the future of two children. The future of our children.

"Thank you for letting us know," Jason said.

"Ramona," I started, pausing to gather my thoughts. "You agree with us, right? I mean, we are acting in the boys' best interest, not our own, right?"

"One hundred percent," she said, without hesitation.

"Thanks. I just . . . it's just, sorry," I stammered, searching for the words to express what I wanted to say. "We love Ethan and Logan. Our fear is for their safety. We're grown men. We can deal with heartache if they're going back to parents who are ready to keep them safe. But if their parents hurt them, I don't know what we'll do. And so help me God," I declared, my voice cracking, "every person in America is going to hear about it." As the tears welled up in my eyes, Jason put his arm around my shoulders and squeezed my body next to his.

"The uncertainty is what I dislike most about my job," she said.

"That and DCFS," Jason added with bitter sarcasm.

"I wish we could assure safety, or sobriety, or deliver tickets out of poverty, but nothing is ever guaranteed. The best thing you can do when they leave is to let Amber and Zach know you are there for them. Let them know they can call you if they ever need a break." I wanted to wash my hands of Amber and Zach, and their entitlement, but walking away meant losing the boys forever and my heart wasn't ready for that.

"You're right, Ramona," Jason said. Any chance we stood of having a relationship with the boys relied on Amber and Zach seeing us as allies.

I thought I'd never fall asleep that night, but the second my head hit the pillow, I was out. The Band-Aid had finally been yanked off, just as I'd prayed for a few weeks earlier. It wasn't the outcome I wanted, but the misery of the unknown had ended. The dread of loss lingered, though.

———

It was clear throughout the remaining weeks of August that Nadia was under a lot of pressure to get the boys more visits with their birth parents so when they reunified, they wouldn't be returning to strangers. Her typical behaviors had gotten even worse. She would call Jason three or four times to confirm the same information, only each time she'd change one detail of great significance, like the date or time of a visit. Jason reworked his schedule countless times to accommodate Nadia's mistakes and his patience was wearing thin.

One afternoon in late August, I walked into the kitchen to find Jason standing in front of the stove, holding his cell phone in the palm of his hand, with Patty by his side. As I crossed through the doorway, he shouted, "Oh my god. You are so incompetent." He looked at the phone and then at me, taking a gulp. "She hung up."

"Who was that?" I asked.

"Nadia."

"Whoa," I said, taken aback by his uncharacteristic reaction.

Turning to Patty, Jason asked, "Do you think I went too far?"

"I would've slapped her," Patty announced. Jason and I tried not to laugh. But it was like when a child drops an F-bomb, it's not actually funny, but it's also hilarious. Patty had become an extension of our family, like a sweet, loving grandmother to the boys and a kind therapist to Jason and myself. She'd been an example of patience, despite the taxing interactions with Nadia. Someone with less grace would've cracked sooner.

"What happened?" I asked.

"This was the third time she's called in the last hour to schedule a visit for tomorrow with Amber and Zach," he said. "I told her multiple times, the boys have a dentist appointment at eight thirty in the morning, so the earliest I could get them to Amber's was ten o'clock. And she said, 'Great. I'll tell her to expect you at nine o'clock.'"

"She kept talking over him and just refused to listen," Patty chimed in.

"So that's when I called her incompetent," Jason said.

"Well, we've all said it behind her back. I guess it's time one of us said it to her face," I joked.

By the end of August, the county had approved weekend overnight visits and our request for an HSA was finally granted—too late to have any bearing on the case. The driver would arrive on Friday morning to take the boys to Amber and Zach's for the weekend, and we would pick them up on Sunday evening. Each goodbye felt like practice for the big one we knew was coming. We sent clothes, diapers, Desitin, and a copy of the boys' nap and eating schedule.

The real sorrow was seeing the boys' stable, predictable life uprooted every weekend. Amber ignored the schedules we shared, and over the next few weeks Ethan returned with dark bags under his eyes, looking tired and distressed, not typical toddler exhaustion from playing too hard, but like every moment had brought stress and discomfort. As soon as we'd arrive, Logan would clutch his sticky arms around my neck in a viselike grip and Ethan would immediately run out to the car. Back at our house, they'd fall apart. Logan was a puddle of emotions, crying and screeching for no reason. He'd even begun hitting Jason and me. Both boys began having regular tantrums and rashes from being left in wet diapers too long. Each time I applied ointment to a chafed butt cheek, I'd wince, imagining the pain my little guys felt and worrying that soon it was possible no one would be treating their rashes. Ethan was almost two and a half so we tried potty training him, hoping maybe we could help him avoid the ongoing flareups of neglect. Our mistake was buying a child-size toilet that played music when you flushed the handle. Instead of relieving himself, Ethan used the toilet as entertainment. "We play potty now?" he'd ask.

I wondered what they were experiencing and witnessing while they were with Amber and Zach. They didn't have the language yet to describe what was going on. How could we protect them, prepare them for their return? I felt helpless.

But in spite of everything, the boys continued to awe me with their resilience. Logan, now nineteen months old, could run almost as fast as his brother. One afternoon he was playing in the family room and tripped and fell into the coffee table. We knew toddler boys are synonymous with falls, bumps, and bruises, and we'd covered every sharp edge in our house with rubber protectors, but when Logan's left cheek hit the padded corner of the table, it still left a bruise. We took a picture, filed an incident report with Nadia and Patty, iced his cheek, and didn't think any more about it until a few days after their next visit with Amber and Zach, when Nadia emailed us stating Amber had accused us of abusing Logan. The photo attached to her email was *the same picture* I'd taken, in our living room, and filed with the incident report.

The allegations stung. Jason and I were the ones who'd comforted her sons for the past sixteen months, while she would go weeks without calling and months without seeing them. And now she was accusing us of hurting the boys? It was infuriating. I didn't want praise for our service, but we didn't deserve lies.

What hurt most was having our character questioned. How do you prove you didn't do something you're being accused of? Who is going to believe you and who isn't? I remembered my friend Kelly's fear that her child was going to be taken when her sister called Child Protective Services out of retaliation—the torment of being under suspicion. Amber knew we loved the boys, how good we were to them. I thought she appreciated all we'd done for them, for her. If anyone knew how it felt to have your parenting questioned, it was her. Why would she do this to us? I didn't know how I was ever going to look at her again.

Yet, even though Nadia said Amber was the one who made the allegation, I was suspicious. I didn't trust Nadia. Maybe Amber had asked Nadia how the bruise got there, and she didn't tell her what happened? That he fell, that we filed an incident report? Maybe Nadia hadn't even read our report? Maybe Amber hadn't even said anything at all, and this was Nadia's way of retaliating for the escalating animosity between us? Was this her way of saying "fuck you" for calling her incompetent?

The same picture showing evidence of our diligence was being used to suggest we'd caused harm. Anyone on the lengthy email threads could easily make the connection that the residual bruise Amber had seen on Logan's left cheek was the same bruise from the accident we'd already reported. But Nadia and her supervisor would not reply to our emails or phone calls asking how to mitigate Amber and Zach's fears over the boys' safety and how to make the two weeks until reunification as smooth as possible for the boys, and everyone involved.

The reunification hearing was scheduled for October 19, but shortly after 9:00 a.m. on the 17th Nadia called Jason and alerted us that the hearing had taken place three days early. Reunification had been approved.

The boys were required to go back to Amber and Zach immediately.

"Does that mean they're leaving today?" I asked him, my hand beginning to shake as I topped off the milk in Ethan's sippy cup.

"Nadia's going to confirm a time that works with Amber for us to drop them off," he said. I could see the hurt in his eyes. My husband had been so strong for me, and for Ethan and Logan, but this call was a sucker punch.

I didn't want to risk upsetting him, so I just asked, "What can I do?"

"I'm going to take them to the doctor's as planned, but if you could pack up their stuff that would be great."

"Of course," I said, "I'll get some bags and start in Ethan's room." I turned to face the cupboard where the shopping bags were kept and he grabbed my hand.

"Hey," he said, turning me around. "I love you." I moved into his arms, our embrace like two wounded trees leaning on one another for support.

"I love you too."

Jason left with the boys an hour later for the doctor's and I went upstairs to pack their rooms. Six weeks after the appellate court's decision, and after a few weekend overnights, we were no longer Ethan and Logan's dads. I folded their clothes and bedding, gathered their toys—feeling completely numb. I couldn't imagine surviving a week without their voices ringing through the house, without their hugs and snuggles, their weight in my arms, so familiar now I hardly knew myself without them. Packing up their things felt wrong, like I was removing all traces of them, obscuring how their arrival had altered the trajectory of my life, consumed my identity. My movements began to feel robotic. I was on autopilot filling shopping bag after shopping bag, tucking my favorite pair of Ethan's overalls, navy with white lobsters stitched on them, on top of an adorable tee that read "Someone in Des Moines Loves Me," a gift from Jessica, a friend from Iowa. I had to pack because that's what needed to be done. I thought only about how many more Mickey Mouse toys I could fit into each bag instead of the emptiness that would soon permeate the house, and my heart.

For Child Protective Services, this was a file closed. A family reunification success story. But what about the human lives the detention uprooted? What would happen to Ethan, Logan, Savannah, Amber, and Zach? How long until the five of them felt like a family again? How long until Ethan and Logan looked to Amber and Zach for comfort before searching the room for Jason or me first? Who would be there supporting them in their recovery, as the stress of parenting kicked in? In an email to the minors' counsel, Kris had talked about Zach's anger, how he yelled at and berated Amber. How he had dropped their infant son. Would they be protected from his rage? What would the coming weeks, months, years look like for this family? Had their situation truly changed from when the boys were first detained? What about the boys whose love shone a light on corners of my heart I'd never known were there? The joy of watching them discover and learn new things? The curtain had closed on our kitchen dance parties, and I wouldn't be there to distract and end a meltdown.

There was no way all the bags of clothes and toys were going to fit in the car, but that didn't stop me from packing them. I needed to be useful while I waited for Jason and the boys to return.

I dreaded calling my mom. She knew they were leaving, but none of us knew today was the day.

"Hi, honey," she said, as she always does when she answers my calls.

"Mom, the boys are leaving today."

"What? I thought they weren't leaving for a few more days."

"So did we. The court held the hearing early and ruled they needed to go home immediately."

"Ohhh," she gasped, quietly, as if she didn't want me to hear.

"Jason took them to see the doctor. There's no way their parents will stay on top of appointments. They couldn't even visit them regularly," I said, expressing my anger to the first person who ever made me feel safe.

"I'm so sorry, honey."

"I know. There's nothing we can do," I said, my voice cracking. "We tried everything we could think of."

Mom wanted to fix all my problems and cure my pain, but this time she couldn't.

———

Before I knew it, Jason was home with the boys. I prepared lunch, and he let me know Ramona had offered to drop them off with Amber and Zach.

"That's really thoughtful," I said.

"At first I said no, but then I called her back and accepted her offer," he said. "I just don't know how we'd be able to leave them there."

"I don't even want to see Amber after she made those allegations," I said, returning to cutting grapes for the boys' lunch. "I'm glad Ramona's taking them. But she's got a little car. There's no way all their shit's going to fit in it."

That afternoon Josephine came by with her two daughters to say goodbye, while the boys were eating, cackling back and forth in their dueling high chairs. Logan was repeating his new favorite word, "Ewww," over and over again, while Ethan belly laughed at his little brother. Josephine's youngest, seven-year-old Jenevieve, had brought a stuffed bunny for each of the boys and a hand-made card with a picture she'd drawn of her and the boys. The note read, "I love you, Ethan and Logan. From Jenevieve." The card sent me over the edge, and I ran into the hallway out of the boys' line of sight. The tears burst from my eyes. Josephine followed me, wrapping her arms around my chest. We hugged and shared tears, emotions our common language. I struggled to catch my breath, afraid of being heard by the boys, and then began drying my eyes as soon as Silvia, her twenty-year-old daughter, saw me.

"I'm sorry," I said, wiping away tears and snot from my ugly, crying face.

When the boys entered our lives our community became so much closer. Our parents, crisscrossing the country to visit, to babysit, to grandparent. Old friendships reignited with friends who also had children. Kati, whom I'd met a dozen years earlier working on campaigns, was also a newlywed and a new mom. Her son Jackson was just two weeks older than Logan. We'd shared parenting lessons and plastic glasses of rosé on Sunday afternoons by the pool. She, like so many of our close friends, had lived this journey with us. Trisha had babysat numerous times and Chris and Cody had brought pizza or tacos for dinner monthly. Our large circle of close friends had been there for every birthday party and mini celebration. The boys had pulled our village closer, tighter, and gave us a greater appreciation for the love enveloping our lives. I couldn't believe they were losing this community that had embraced them so open-armed. The boys' departure was as abrupt as their arrival sixteen months earlier.

Ramona was supposed to pick them up at four o'clock, but Amber asked that they be dropped off at six instead, so she could walk to the store for cigarettes before they arrived. I was happy to have more time.

The four of us were playing in the living room when Ramona arrived. Jason and I loaded the bags into her car before carrying the boys out. They were happy, giggling, and entertaining one another. Completely unaware of where they were going or that this time, they weren't coming home.

I placed Logan on my hip, the heaviness of loss saddling my heart. In the river of life, loss is an unexpected waterfall—savage, powerful, inescapable. Sometimes it hits with no warning, upending everything, a tree to the front of the Jeep that stopped Jaime's heart instantly. Other times you sense it lurking, fearful of what lies around the next bend, holding your breath, whispering a prayer for survival, *please, world, be kind to my boys*.

As Jason was buckling Ethan into his car seat, Ethan whipped his head around.

"Where Lo go?" he demanded.

Thank God they have each other, I thought, putting Lo into his seat.

Then the car was pulling away.

They were there.

And then they were gone.

Chapter 18

The Hardest Goodbye

We watched as Ramona's car drove down our street and turned left out of sight, taillights disappearing into the night.

"Fuck," I said softly, turning to look at Jason.

"Let's walk down to Larchmont and get ice cream," he suggested.

So often during the past sixteen months we'd been afraid to speak our feelings to one another. I was afraid my denial would meet him at acceptance or his bargaining would be met with my anger. But on that walk, stepping over the many-hued tapestry of leaves that had fallen on the sidewalk, leaves that had once taught Ethan his colors, we were both just sad. Two scoops of Salted, Malted, Chocolate Chip Cookie Dough from Salt & Straw couldn't even lift our spirits.

We ate on a bench across from the ice cream shop and an older gay couple walked by, two men, one carrying a Chihuahua who seemed thrilled to be in his companion's arms instead of walking. The four of us exchanged smiles, and I said to Jason, "Roxy would have preferred to be carried too."

"Yeah, but she went and fucking died," he said.

I jolted and then met his eyes. He smiled, the same smile I'd fallen for years earlier spreading across his bearded face. We both laughed at the dark humor, because really, what else was there to do? We were two childless fathers sitting on a bench eating ice cream. Crying was the only alternative.

————

The first few days without the boys, I was on edge every time I left the house. I didn't want to see anyone who would ask how I was doing. Or go anywhere I might bump into someone who didn't know the boys were gone, fearing they'd ask, "How are Jason and the kids?" Even strangers could set off my tears, a mom walking her baby in a stroller or a barista with rich blue eyes like Ethan.

My clients all knew what had happened and they were leaving me alone. The idea of building a marketing campaign for a product seemed so insignificant. I was aimless. I wasn't a nurse or a surgeon. If I skipped work for a few days, no lives would be lost. My inbox was solely receiving spam. The only calls coming in were from Mom, my sister, and a few close friends, but I couldn't bring myself to answer the phone. I didn't want to talk about it. I didn't want to keep replaying losing the boys.

At home, the silence felt like sympathy; the one-hundred-year-old walls had stopped creaking out of pity. Sadness lingered like a bad houseguest. I was angry the boys were gone. Angry at Nadia. Angry at the county for not fighting the court's ruling. And I was afraid. Frightened of what I didn't know. Were the boys okay? Were they getting enough food? Were they hurt or hurting? Was Amber comforting their tears and soothing their worries? Were they missing us as much as we missed them? Were they crying for us? Did they think we abandoned them? Mostly, I felt helpless. Jason and I had spent so much time and energy caring for the boys, making sure they were safe from physical and emotional harm, and now our job was over, and I couldn't accept the demotion.

I got up early and went to Spin class, always taking the last bike in the farthest row from the front, wanting to be present without being seen, to participate without having to engage. One morning, I signed up for a class with Shannon, a hard-riding, athletic brunette who always pushed us to tackle both hills and sprints. Her curly hair and freckles reminded me of the Irish girls I'd grown up with in Brockton. I felt like we were old friends, even though we'd never exchanged more than a few hellos. About halfway through the class she told us, "The next song is a three-and-a-half-minute climb. Take a drink and set your resistance to twenty-five." I followed her instructions as the first few notes began to play. I recognized it immediately. It was the Snow Patrol song that played on *Grey's Anatomy* every time Shonda Rhimes wanted us to cry.

"Find the beat," Shannon instructed, counting along with the tempo. "One-two, one-two, one-two. All right. We're gonna hold it here for thirty seconds."

This was a perfect song for a hill climb. It's slow but not too slow. It has a sobering effect. I'd always thought it should be played at bar close or during the ninth inning at Fenway so all the Red Sox fans can relax and stop getting into fights on the T.

"Let's add ten to the resistance in three-two-one," Shannon hollered over the music into the mic strapped to her head.

One-two-three-four, one-two-three-four, I counted to myself, starting to feel the added resistance in my quads.

"Give me ten more and pick up the pace. Let's go. Out of the saddle for ten-nine-eight."

I sprang from the seat, centering my weight above the pedals and pressing harder with each stride. The chorus kicked in, the song gained intensity, and perspiration rolled off my shoulders, down my arms, and splattered on the floor.

"Give me ten more on the resistance and we're going to hold it here for sixty seconds," Shannon called out. I cranked the knob to the right and wiped the sweat off my face.

"You know, this song was popular when I was running cross-country in college," she said, sitting back in her saddle. "One day, while

I was out for a run, a car hit me from behind. The impact fractured my skull, broke both my legs, and shattered my spine in two different places. Doctors didn't think I'd ever walk again." It didn't seem possible that she was talking about herself. This woman, making me burn calorie after calorie, was a stud, a jock.

"This song always reminds me of that time in my life, going from the hospital to the rehab center, all the hours of physical therapy I had to put in. It was such a difficult time. I wanted to run, but my legs wouldn't work. There were nights I lay in bed crying and feeling sorry for myself, asking God, *Why?* But I woke up every morning and put in the work. Because hiding in bed is not who I am." Shannon paused for a second. "Sorry, I don't know why I'm telling you all this. I guess I just thought, maybe one of you needed to hear it."

I rode hard for the rest of the class, the dimly lit room and the sweat streaming down my face masking my tears. For forty-five minutes I felt like maybe she was talking to me, that there might be a time when I too would walk again. But when I got back to our empty, silent house, I wasn't so sure.

The days without the boys seemed endless. Some afternoons I'd go to the gym, even though I'd already done a Spin class in the morning. I just needed to be out of the house, away from the quiet, distracted by the sounds and the people. I needed to escape the flash floods of panic and sorrow that drowned my spirit. The faces of strangers, looking away instead of seeing through me, brought me comfort. Friends checked in. Jessica, who had a seven-month-old daughter, offered to fly out from Iowa. Trisha dropped off cookies.

A few days after the boys left, the HSA driver arrived at our house to pick them up for a scheduled weekend overnight with Zach and Amber. No one had told her the boys had already reunified.

"This shit happens all the time," the driver said, laughing and shaking her head. "One hand doesn't know what the other is doing."

A week after reunification, Jason made plans for us to visit the boys in the afternoon. He called me from his office a few hours before the visit. "I just got off the phone with Kris. She said Amber and Zach are a mess and keep asking her for money. They've basically told her she can only see the kids if she gives them money."

"What the fuck?" I said. "Kris is the only member of that family who has been there for the boys."

"I know," Jason said. "She also asked Amber about the allegations she made against us, and Amber was totally confused. She had no idea what Kris was talking about. But get this, Amber told her she also received an email from Nadia saying *we* had blamed *her* for the bruise on his face."

"Fucking Nadia," I responded.

"Fucking Nadia," Jason agreed.

"So, she emailed both sets of parents—the foster and birth parents—claiming each had accused the other of child abuse?" I asked, needing to make sure I understood Jason correctly.

"Yeah," Jason confirmed. "How messed up is that?"

"Should we say something to Amber when we see her? To clear the air?" I asked.

"I don't think we have to. Unless she brings it up. Kris told her what really happened."

"That is insane. How is what Nadia did not considered retaliation or something? She gives social workers a bad name," I said.

"Yeah. She makes Kendra look like Mother Teresa," Jason joked.

We arrived at Amber and Zach's apartment shortly before three o'clock. Ethan was sitting shirtless on the couch in a pair of red shorts Jason's mother had bought him, watching *Finding Nemo*. This was the first time I'd been inside the apartment. I scanned the small living room, mentally taking note of what I saw the way I imagined a caseworker might. It was dirty, but far from unsanitary. The room was dim even in broad daylight. A huge TV hung on the wall. In the flashes of light from the screen I could see there were no covers on any of the electrical outlets.

Ethan sprang from the couch, adorably charging to greet us at the door. He hugged our legs and beckoned us to pick him up. Savannah was sitting on the floor in a food-splattered onesie, gnawing on a Duplo building block we'd sent with the boys a week earlier.

"Hi, pretty girl," Jason said, waving to her from the doorway. She smiled and wiggled side to side before letting out a gurgle, opening the floodgates for saliva to pour from her lips.

"Oh, it looks like someone's teething," Jason said with a smile.

"Where's Logan?" I asked Amber.

"He was driving me crazy, so I put him to bed," she said, sounding annoyed. What did she mean by that? Was he being punished? He was a toddler who just had his life turned upside down; it was expected that he'd act out. When you remove a child's stability and dismantle their routine they become as insufferable as a car full of *influencers* on the ride home from Coachella.

Of course it was Logan who was "driving her crazy." The child she'd spent the least amount of time with, and whom she barely acknowledged at visits, was the one she was punishing. I believed in my heart, if one of the kids was going to end up hurt or abused, it was going to be Logan.

"Zach's at work. This is what we do all day," she said with a smile.

Why did she just say that? Her words, the starter pistol to my mind's race. *What did she mean by it? Is she looking for sympathy—that she's a stay-at-home mom of three kids under the age of three? Or does she think sitting in a dark room in front of a television screen every day is parenting?* There was a park a few blocks away she could have easily walked to. I wanted to scream, *These kids need stimulation. Take them outside!*

"Well, at least the kids have good taste in movies," Jason said lightly, taking a seat on the floor next to Savannah as Dory swam across the screen above her. I didn't know if he was as confused as I was by her comment or if the look on my face signaled him to change the subject quickly. Either way, his humor kept the mood light.

I sat down opposite him, with Ethan running back and forth between us. We had brought another six bags of clothes and toys, which we placed on the laminate floor by the front door. Ethan ran over and began digging through the toys. "How long has Logan been napping?" Jason asked Amber, who had taken a seat on the couch.

"Like two hours," she said, oblivious to our hopes of getting to spend time with him too.

"Do you mind waking him so we can see him?" he asked.

"Sure, I'll go get him," she said, and disappeared into the bedroom.

Amber returned moments later with Logan in her arms. He was rubbing his eyes with his forearm, his cheeks pink with creases from his blanket. He looked at us startled, like he didn't believe what he was seeing, and then burst into tears.

Amber put him down and he ran back and forth between Jason and me, sitting in our laps, giving us tight hugs. I was so happy to see him, but he was almost manic, like he was making sure this wasn't a dream. I wondered again if he felt betrayed by us, abandoned. We were his safety, his stability, the foundation of everything he'd ever known, and then one day we were just gone. I wished I could explain to him how hard we tried. I wanted him to know I was just as heartbroken, that I was furious with the judges who failed him and Ethan. I wanted him to know we missed him desperately. But those aren't conversations you can have with a nineteen-month-old. For the rest of the visit, Logan was glued to our laps. If a toy caught his eye, he would get up briefly to snag it before racing back to the safety of Jason's or my embrace. Children don't have the vocabulary to articulate their feelings, so actions are their tell. Logan was nestling so deep into me, I thought he was trying to go through me.

We stayed for about ninety minutes, not wanting to overstay our welcome. When we got up to leave, Lo started sobbing. I'd never seen him so upset. He clutched my leg, his face red, tears pouring down his cheeks. I bent down to hug him, afraid that if I picked him up, I'd run out the door with him. He grabbed me around the neck, and I could feel his wet tears on my temple. I couldn't let myself cry. I needed to be strong for him. Amber picked him up. I kissed him on the cheek and told him, "I love you, Logan. I will see you soon." Once I turned toward the door, I couldn't turn back because my tears had already started.

I bawled the entire ride home. This goodbye was even harder than the last.

Chapter 19

Thanksgiving

Thanksgiving at Peggy's had become a tradition. She and her husband, Lloyd, would host around eighteen of their closest friends at their home in Redondo Beach, for a feast with copious amounts of food, good wine, and heartfelt laughter. On our way to the South Bay we stopped by Amber and Zach's apartment hoping to catch them and drop off some cookies Jason had baked before they left to celebrate at Rita's. They were gone before we arrived, so we left the Tupperware container outside their door and Jason texted Amber to let her know. I had wanted to see the boys, but I was relieved to not have to say "goodbye" again.

Driving to Peggy's the previous year, I had worried about Ethan or Logan destroying one of the irreplaceable artifacts Peggy had collected on her journeys around the world fighting slavery and human trafficking, but this year I felt a sense of unease about seeing our village.

It had been five weeks since Ethan and Logan left us, and I didn't want to hear "I'm sorry about the boys." Or to answer the questions, "Have you heard from Amber? How are the boys doing?" I wanted to skip past that part and arrive at the point where we all just understood we were not going to be a family, and I needed my friends to be distractions, helping me numb myself from the pain.

When everyone was seated, plates overflowing with turkey and sweet potatoes, butter and gravy being passed around the table, Peggy began her tradition of asking everyone to share what happened this past year that made them thankful. A few friends spoke before it was my turn, including Attila, one of Peggy's college friends we'd gotten to know through her holiday parties and Fourth of July barbecues. He offered a grounding perspective. "I lost my arm to cancer this year, but not my life. And every day I get to spend with friends and my beautiful wife, Lisa, is one I'm truly grateful for."

Then it was my turn. I thought of all the things that had happened to me, to us. How a year and a half ago I'd practically skipped into foster parent training, eager to build my family, with the man I loved. I'd embraced fatherhood with nerves and enthusiasm, but mostly enthusiasm. I survived a crash course in parenting, learning how to mitigate meltdowns and ease the pain of teething. I had earned the battle scars of fatherhood—a few strands of gray hair and some extra pounds. I was awed by a series of firsts: first words, first steps, first time sitting up. I wiped liters of snot from small runny noses, applied hundreds of Band-Aids, and fell completely in love with the boys who called me Daddy. Two babies, with their tiny hands and mini feet, their blue eyes and wide smiles, needed us to love them, to keep them safe. Jason and I stepped up and we loved every second of it—tucking them in at night and peeking in at them sleeping peacefully, playing Matchbox cars and building blocks. There's no greater feeling, I have learned, than the warmth of a child's smile first thing in the morning. The joy and comfort they find in your presence, the consistency and stability of your love. But that was all over now. There were no high chairs this year at Thanksgiving, no sippy cups to fill, no one who needed me to cut their turkey into tiny, bite-size pieces. My boys were gone.

"This year sucked," I began. "Except for Attila not dying, of course. I am really grateful you're still here, brother," I said, the crack in my voice betraying my emotions. "Sorry," I said, wiping away the tears that had started to roll down my face. I looked up to find Peggy and

Lloyd shedding tears of their own on the opposite end of the table. My vulnerability allowed them to release their own, their loving eyes no longer hiding their emotions. They were hurt and angry too. They also missed the boys, feared for their safety, and wanted Jason and me to be whole again. "I know I have a lot to be thankful for, but this year, it's just you all, my friends."

There was a pause when I finished speaking, and then Jason asked, "Oh, are you done?"

"Yeah," I said, sheepishly.

"Oh, I was waiting for you to mention how thankful you are for your loving and handsome husband," he jabbed.

"Sorry. I thought that was a given," I said, trying to save face—but, in that moment, I really was only thinking about myself.

"Right, I see," Jason said, in that passive-aggressive way that obviously meant he didn't.

He wasn't acting like himself. He seemed tense and annoyed. When it was his turn to say what he was thankful for, he just said, "This year, I'd like to take a pass."

After dinner, when Jason and I were alone in the dining room clearing some wineglasses from the table, I asked him, "Is everything okay? You seemed a little upset during dinner. Did I do something to piss you off?"

"No. Amber's been texting ever since we got here," he said. They'd maintained regular contact, texting frequently since our last visit. He kept their messages warm and upbeat. I was always imagining a potential disaster that might be taking place, but Jason could compartmentalize his fear.

"It's not our job to monitor them," he'd said to me. "But the best way to protect the boys is to keep the lines of communication open. Be available. Be the people Zach and Amber call if they need help."

His approach bore out that day.

"She's freaking out because Ethan's got a fever," he said.

"How high?" I asked.

"I don't know. She doesn't own a thermometer," he said, sounding irritated. I couldn't tell if he was annoyed with me or her, or the whole situation. "I guess it started yesterday. It sounds like he's got a flu. But she's freaking out. I told her to take him to the emergency room, but, you know, she doesn't like hospitals."

"In her defense, every time she's at a hospital, they end up taking her kids away."

As the day wore on, they exchanged a few more messages. Jason offered to pick her and the kids up and take them to Children's Hospital, but she said they'd take him when Zach got home from work.

The next day we slept in, ran some errands, cleaned our bedroom closet. Jason was texting with Amber throughout the day for updates on Ethan's fever and had reached out to Kris, to loop her in. By midafternoon, Ethan wasn't doing any better. Jason pressed her for what the doctor had said, but Amber only replied, *He gave us a prescription, but I couldn't afford to fill it.* When Jason read her text to me, I got angry.

"She's lying," I declared. "There's no way she even took him to the doctor because his prescriptions are free." Ethan and Logan were covered by Medi-Cal, the state's health insurance for low-income children. The only money we'd ever spent on their health care was for parking at the pediatrician's office. "He needs to see a doctor."

"Should we take them?" Jason asked.

"Yeah. But don't they have a car?"

"Zach has it, and he's at work."

"Okay. Let's take her to Children's Hospital."

My gut was telling me Amber was lying, and it pissed me off. We would have gladly left Peggy's yesterday to take them to the ER, but she had assured Jason they were going to take him. On the other hand, at least there was something we could do for Ethan now.

We picked Amber and the kids up at their apartment in Glassell Park around seven that evening, buckling the three car seats into the

SUV we had purchased when we thought we might end up with Savannah too. On the ride, I asked Amber, who was in the passenger's seat while I drove, if she had brought Ethan's prescription with her. "I'd be happy to cover the cost of filling it."

"No. I forgot it," she said.

I *knew* she was lying.

"We don't have any money for food," she added. "Zach only makes twelve dollars an hour and his check barely covers our rent."

"I'm sorry," I said, unsure what more to say. I wasn't going to offer her money. I knew she used access to the kids as leverage with Kris, so I changed the subject. "How does Zach like his new job?"

"It's fine. He works Monday through Friday and when he's home on the weekends he's always tired and just wants to sleep. I have to keep the kids quiet so he can sleep all day."

In the waiting room, we sat with one kid in each grown-up's lap—Savannah with Amber, Ethan with Jason, Logan with me. When Ethan's name was called, Jason stood up, but Amber stayed seated. Jason never looked back and was already greeting the nurse when I nudged Amber.

"Amber," I said. "You should probably go in."

She looked startled, as though she hadn't yet adjusted to the fact that we were no longer the boy's primary caretakers. At that moment, we were just friends helping a mom out while her husband was at work. We couldn't authorize any medical attention or care. The baton of parental responsibility had been passed back to her. She followed Jason and Ethan, Savannah in her arms.

I played with Logan in the waiting area. His blond curls, which hadn't been trimmed since he left us over a month ago, were dangling over his blue eyes. He was standing on my lap, pulling at my hat and kissing my cheeks. We sang "Itsy-Bitsy Spider," and he explored all the books that had been left out for kids in the waiting area. When Jason texted to say it was going to be a while, they were going to run some tests, I decided to take Logan to the grocery store to pick up some food and supplies for his family. With Logan in the shopping cart, I stocked up on all the boys' favorites, mac and cheese, waffles, oatmeal, bananas, milk, diapers, and I grabbed some ointment for diaper rash, just in case.

Loading bags into the car, buckling Lo into his seat, I thought of Amber's long-ago request in the church parking lot that we be the boys' godparents. For a second, I felt a wave of hope. We couldn't parent the boys, but maybe we could still protect them. We could do what we'd promised to do—love them, commit to their well-being.

When we got back to the hospital, Ethan's fever was down, and he was sleeping in Jason's arms. The doctor said Ethan had a bad flu, but that he was ready to go home. On the drive back, Amber was chatty, telling us about the pressure she was getting from the boys' social worker to enroll them in preschool.

"But I don't want to," she said. "People do messed-up stuff. I don't want strangers watching my kids."

I could see Amber's protective instinct for the kids. I knew she wanted to love and care for them. But she didn't know how. Sitting in a dark apartment in front of a TV screen all day wasn't healthy for her or her children. But nobody had ever shown her how to parent. She'd been mistreated and abused by those who were supposed to protect her, and the system had failed her, over and over.

"Amber, I get what you're saying. But teachers are like doctors—specially trained, certified. Parenting is really hard, and we all need a break sometimes," I told her, reminding her that it would be good for her to have time to herself—that self-care is an important part of recovery.

She stared out the car window. "I don't know," she said. "People can be so creepy."

When we arrived at her apartment, Jason and I helped Amber carry in the three sleeping children and unload the groceries. The container of cookies we'd dropped off the day before was empty and stacked in the sink on a pile of pots and dishes. I opened the refrigerator to put the milk away. There were a few uncovered plastic plates of leftover spaghetti on the shelf next to a two-liter Mountain Dew, with a half-empty bottle of ketchup in the door. Inspecting the fridge hurt, like a strong tug at both ends of the knot in my stomach. We hadn't even hosted Thanksgiving dinner, yet our fridge contained Tupperware full of sweet potatoes and turkey, leftovers Peggy had sent home with us. Amber had no money for food and was resistant to accepting help from professionals. How was she going to feed her family? If she'd accepted the county's offer for preschool, the children would get fed there. She would get a break and they would all benefit, but in her mind, the system had done enough harm to her already. She wasn't going to risk any more.

———

Jason and Kris were texting the whole time we were at Children's Hospital. She drove down the following morning to visit Amber, Zach, and the kids. She arrived with treats and played with the boys and Savannah for a while, then took the bedsheets and some clothes to a nearby laundromat. When she returned, they invited her to spend the night.

Sunday afternoon Kris called us, hysterical. She had gone out to buy some groceries because all of the food we had purchased on Friday had been eaten. When she got back to the apartment, Amber was smoking outside, with Ethan playing on the grass. Inside, Logan, now twenty months old, and Savannah, just ten months old, were in the bathtub unsupervised.

"I tried to tell her why this isn't safe," Kris said through tears and gasps for air, "but she told me I was overstepping. 'I know my daughter, she's fine,' she yelled at me."

I paced the house, angry, terrified, helpless. We had to do something. But what? Jason and I were approved foster parents; we were mandated, like teachers and nurses, to report any child abuse or suspected harm we discovered. But did this qualify? And did it matter that we didn't see it ourselves, that we were relying on Kris's account of what had happened? Besides, would it do us any good to reach out to Nadia? If she even read the email, she wasn't likely to do anything about it.

Later that night, Jason and I talked it over and decided to draft an email to Brandon Nichols, the interim director of LA County's Department of Children and Family Services, someone I'd met through my advocacy work. We explained what Kris had told us about Logan and Savannah being left alone in the bathtub and that we had no confidence in Nadia, our county social worker, so reaching out to him was our only hope of getting someone to help Amber and the kids. But reaching out to him was more than that, it was our Hail Mary. There was no one higher in the county child welfare agency and now the boys' case was on his desk. Hitting send filled me with relief. I didn't know Brandon well, but I knew he cared deeply about the well-being of the thousands of children in his charge, and most importantly, he was extremely competent. We'd never sleep again, never be able to live with ourselves, if we neglected to speak up against a preventable disaster. But there would be consequences. Amber was going to be furious that we'd betrayed her. She trusted us and we snitched on her.

Brandon replied immediately. He thanked us for our candor and concern, and said he had dispatched a new social worker to look into the case. He took every step I'd hoped he would.

The following night, Kris called to let us know a social worker had visited Amber and the kids. Amber was furious. She told Kris she never wanted to see any of us again.

Our efforts to protect Ethan and Logan had cost us our relationship with them. Yet, if fighting for the boys' lives, fighting to keep them safe, meant giving up being in their lives, the choice was clear.

Chapter 20

By the Throat

Something you don't think about when you're grieving is how uncomfortable your pain can be for others. It had begun to feel like a lot of our friends were walking on eggshells around us, tiptoeing, afraid of how we were going to react if the topic came up.

One night, Kati, her husband, Joe, and their son, Jackson, who was almost two years old, stopped by to say hi after having dinner at a nearby restaurant. My relationship with Kati had bonded our families together over the past year and a half. We'd gone from friends to family, and Jackson was the surprise nephew I cherished. He had wavy brown hair with natural blond highlights that would've cost a fortune at a salon in West Hollywood and the most unexpected, deep, gravelly voice that stopped you in your tracks. He always spoke slowly and deliberately, the bass of Barry White echoing through his two-year-old vocal cords. I had suggested countless times that he'd be a natural to voice cartoons—once he learned to read, of course.

We were standing in the living room when Jackson noticed a framed picture of the boys sitting on an end table. He looked at me, pointed to the photo, and asked, "Where kids go? They go night-night?" I could see Kati's whole body tighten, biting her lower lip with her top teeth.

They had lived this journey alongside us, and while she was hurting for me and Jason, I knew she too was grieving the boys.

"The boys aren't here, Jackson. But we've got a bunch of toys for you to play with," I said, trying to deflect and distract him.

I looked at Kati, who mouthed, "I'm sorry."

"There's nothing to be sorry about," I said. "He misses his friends."

"I know," she said, then she reached into her purse and pulled out a bottle of cabernet. "We brought wine."

Even though my family had suffered huge losses, I had no tried-and-true rituals to get through the grieving process. Grief took me by surprise every single time, like an attacker jumping out in the dark. Grief shouldn't have been a stranger, but no matter how many times we'd met, I was still wary of its power and the endless depths of its void.

When Jaime died, I was terrified that if I allowed myself to feel my grief it would take me down, so I ran from it. I threw myself into my work, my relationships, anything to avoid confronting the pain of losing someone I loved so much. But the truth is, I wasn't protecting myself at all. You can't hide from grief. It's the lion of emotions. You can't outrun it. One minute you're bopping along and the next you're pinned under its claws, unable to breathe, praying for a quick ending to the pain. Grief sneaks up when you least expect it, a song playing on the radio, the scent of a familiar perfume in a crowded room, finding a Lego wedged between the couch cushions.

This time I was resolved not to hide from grief or any other emotion that threatened to pounce. Whenever frustration or anger or heartache snuck up on me, I sat with the emotion and gave myself the grace to feel my pain. There were days I missed the boys so much I couldn't get out of bed. I'd tell my clients I was sick, so I didn't have to face anyone and could just cry alone or punch a pillow until the emotion passed like the shifting tide.

Grieving the loss of loved ones who aren't dead carried its own complexities. Alive and well are not synonyms. Did the boys cry for us the way we cried for them? Were they angry with us for disappearing? We never would have abandoned them, but we knew there would be consequences if Amber found out we were responsible for telling the county about the bathtub incident. Did we make a mistake emailing Brandon? Should we have looked the other way? I tried telling myself stories to justify our actions, but grief made me second-guess my own narrative. I kept repeating, *I could not have lived another day if something happened to one of them and we had done nothing.* It became my mantra.

I felt helpless, almost pathetic, because no matter how fiercely I wanted to protect Logan and Ethan, I had no control over anything. It wasn't my job to protect them any longer. While they were in our care we lived under the incessant gray cloud of uncertainty, but I always knew they were safe. Free from abuse and neglect. I wanted to see them, to hold them and tell them I loved them. Worse, we didn't have any clue how they were doing. I was living in constant fear for their safety and praying for someone to intervene.

We heard from Kris from time to time. Amber would occasionally allow her to see the boys, but it was usually in conjunction with a demand for something—free child care, groceries, or, most often, money. Kris told us Amber and Zach had been evicted from their apartment, and they'd moved with the three children back into Rita's house, the place where so many of Amber's problems began, where they'd been living when the boys were removed from their care, where dog shit had been left on the floor. I wondered if a social worker was still checking in on them. Did the county even know they had moved?

The federal government requires reporting on whether or not children reenter foster care within twenty-four months of reunification.[1] This process was designed as a way of measuring the success of the services provided to the families in care. But how would they know if something was off? Who would know if Amber or Zach started using again? Who would know if the kids were hungry? Hurt?

The children were too young for school. Amber was unlikely to accept the county's offer of free day care; she thought those workers could be "creepy." She was resistant to hospitals. Their lives would never intersect with a mandated reporter, professionals legally bound to communicate signs of abuse or neglect. Who would call Child Protective Services if they needed intervention? I couldn't count on Rita, who had failed to protect Amber when she was a child.

I knew when the boys came into our lives that one day we might have to let them go. If losing them meant we had given Amber and Zach the space to heal and become the parents their children deserved, then it was a risk I was prepared to take. I wanted a family and to have children of my own, but not by stealing someone else's. I never rooted for them to fail, even though their actions determined my future. Had Amber and Zach turned a page, learned about parenting, and gotten treatment for their mental health challenges, I would have found beauty in the system. I would not have overlooked its many dents and scratches, but seeing someone achieve the life they always wanted is hard to cheer against.

Our story was as unique as it was common. Every day, seven hundred kids enter foster care—the reunification clock begins ticking, but too few will beat the buzzer, returning home. During the most intense time of a family's life, underresourced and overworked frontline workers are asked to make life-altering and often trauma-inducing decisions about the children's future. Is their home safe? Would they be better off living with relatives or foster parents? Which services are best suited for a child with a host of serious challenges? Is there even space available in those programs or did they close due to budget cuts? Do we have a therapist who doesn't have a waiting list? And what about the parents? Which program will help them reunify with their children? Can they get into recovery or learn the skills of parenting that were absent from their own childhoods? All the while we expect judges with hundreds of cases on their dockets to make fair and just decisions in the fifteen to thirty minutes allotted for each case.

The national system has fifty executives, the governors of each state, who certainly don't win reelection on the outcomes of kids who've been abused or come from unsafe homes. Each new administration shepherds in their priorities and expectations for the field, but few have ever backed their goals with adequate funding. The system is broken, but the blame doesn't lie with the workers, it lies with the policy makers. It also lies with the public, who don't cry out for more support for the families suffering in our communities. When we lock up adults, where do their kids go? When we allow drug companies and doctors to overprescribe opioids, what happens to the children of those who've become addicted? So many of society's challenges flow directly into the river of foster care.

Fostering is a public service. It's not for everyone and it shouldn't be. Jason and I had stepped up to answer our community's need for caregivers. We wanted to foster and ultimately adopt, but when adoption didn't materialize, the consolation was supposed to be that we had helped a family heal. When children are removed from their parents it's likely the most difficult time in that family's life. For children the upheaval is traumatic, and for parents it's pretty much rock bottom. Foster homes are supposed to be a safe, kind, consistent landing place for kids while they wait for the adults in their life to sort out their issues. I knew that wasn't always the case, but it is always the goal. That stability and safety are supposed to give birth parents peace of mind, knowing their children are well cared for so they can work on themselves and heal. But that wasn't how it had worked out.

I put my faith in a broken system, and it failed. I had envisioned a future in which we would always be in their lives, but Ethan and Logan were sent back to a home not yet ready for them and there was nothing more I could do to protect them.

I didn't believe Amber and Zach were capable of keeping them safe, and telling myself they were safe and cared for was just lying. I was frightened for them, but especially for Logan. I kept having the same dream, night after night, that Amber had hurt him. I'd wake up, drenched in sweat, and crying. Inside I was destroyed. The helplessness left me physically ill, wanting to vomit. Amber had never displayed anything but a lack of interest in Logan and the way she talked about him *driving her crazy* when we had visited their apartment was just off. It wasn't right. He was a toddler just being a toddler. My feelings of powerlessness were defeating.

Jason felt the same way. It had been a couple of months since the boys left, and we were both still struggling to establish our routines. We had enjoyed the rhythms and responsibilities of parenting. I loved preparing big dinners, setting the table, and eating together as a family. And he navigated the boys' social-emotional development with the skill of Simone Biles on the balance beam. But all of that was gone now. We had gotten a taste of the life we wanted and watched it disappear. Jason would be turning forty in six months, and the question neither of us wanted to ask was, how long do we wait? How long do we wait for Ethan and Logan, and now Savannah, to come back into foster care? I had no doubt it would happen, but it could be years, long after they'd forgotten about us, the fun we shared, and the love we felt for them. What if we decided not to wait? Would we foster again? With a 55 percent reunification rate, there was no guarantee we wouldn't find ourselves right back in this situation a few years from now. I didn't think I could go through this again. We could try private adoption, but we had friends who'd been waiting for years to be selected by an expectant mother. I didn't want to wait. Surrogacy was no guarantee either. In addition to the cost, which exceeded the price tag of my first home in Iowa, miscarriage was a concern. I wanted what every person wants when they take the risk to love—a guarantee.

I wanted the impossible.

Meanwhile, Jason and I were in a rocky place. We tried to remember the couple we'd been on our wedding day, floating up the aisle to the sound of a string quartet playing "Crazy in Love," the couple who loved spending time together, who could make traffic fun. We took a road trip up the coast, spending a few nights with friends in Santa Cruz and then over to Monterey and Carmel-by-the-Sea. On the ride home, I

brought up the topic we'd been carefully avoiding since the boys reunified. "Do you have any thoughts about what to do next? I mean, as far
as becoming parents is concerned."

"I don't want to give up on the boys," he fired back. His tone made
me defensive, like I'd been accused of being disloyal to Ethan and Logan.

"Me neither," I said quickly. "I never want to turn our backs on
them. But what do we do? They aren't in foster care right now, and we
have no guarantee they're ever coming back in."

"They'll be back in care," he said, matter-of-fact.

"But how long do we wait?" I could feel the temperature rising in
my body.

"As long as it takes," he said. My back straightened and my shoulders
stiffened.

"In the meantime, do we want to consider surrogacy again? Or private adoption?" I asked.

"Maybe," he said. I could feel my breath getting faster.

"Which one?" I asked, with the intensity of an interrogator.

"I don't know," he said. "Probably surrogacy."

"What if we get pregnant, and they come back into care? We'd have
four kids. Or five if we're going for twins." I felt desperate, hopelessly
craving clarity that seemed impossibly out of reach.

"Well, we are not going to say no to them, so that would mean we'd
have a lot of kids."

"Could we have that many kids? What if Amber gets pregnant
again?" I was bombarding him with all the what-ifs that had kept me
awake night after night since the boys left. "We couldn't afford to have
that many kids in LA. Where would we go?"

"I don't know," he said. His calm was usually the day to my night,
the rich to my poor, the Han Solo to my Princess Leia. "We'll have to
cross that bridge when we get to it." Jason's *one day at a time* answer
was perfectly rational, but to me it was more frustrating than when the
volume on a commercial gets unnecessarily loud.

"I want to know now!" I had already begun screaming before I realized I was even upset. Suddenly I was a little boy again, tantruming about things beyond my control. Things I wanted but couldn't have, yearning for safety and protection, for comfort and assurances. I wanted Jason to solve this for me, for us, like he'd solved all of the boys' problems.

I wanted to know it would all work out. I wanted answers.

I wanted our children.

I pulled the car off the freeway and onto a dusty country road, my vision blurred by anger. I was seething. I put the car in park and turned to face him. "Why can't you just make a decision?" I wailed through tears, unfairly asking him to do what I was incapable of doing myself. I was ragged, and in my deep-set need to self-protect, I was unleashing on the one person who understood, who held the story with me—who held me, period.

Jason sat quietly, motionless in the passenger's seat. I sobbed, finally wailing, "Fuck. Fuck. Fuck. Fuck. Fuuuuuck," at the top of my lungs, punching the steering wheel with each word. We sat in silence for a minute. It felt like a century. Without saying anything, Jason reached over and grabbed my hand. I turned to him, my head hanging low. He leaned in and pulled me toward him. I placed my head on his shoulder and began to catch my breath. The release allowed anger to loosen its hold on me, making way for shame, which arrived within seconds, parading in like a debutante to the cotillion. I was embarrassed, no, mortified, for lashing out at Jason, the only one who truly shared my pain. He deserved more from me.

But shame was the price of growing up in a family where the unspoken code seemed to be: *It happened. You know it happened. I know it happened. But no one else needs to know.* In high school, I remember crying at my grandmother's funeral. An older relative came up to me and my mother and said in a disapproving tone, "If it's too much for him, he doesn't need to be here."

"He's fine," my mother barked without hesitation.

She was trying to protect me, but I had already received my aunt's message loud and clear—children cry, not grown men. At fifteen, I knew I was expected to act like a man, so I choked back my tears and learned to bottle my emotions. Twenty-five years later, I was a grown man, unlike any I'd known as a child, but I still didn't know how to speak my feelings, to be with them. They had me by the throat.

I apologized to Jason, and he didn't make me feel any less for my childish actions. He just said, "It's okay. This is all hard."

———

In those months after the boys went home, Heather reached out regularly. I wondered if she'd had meltdowns and rages after Joanna died. I remembered something she'd told me once about the morning the cops came to her door to tell her Joanna was gone. They said she and Jerry needed to grab their infant son and jump in the police cruiser to go identify their baby girl. Shock left her unable to process the news. As she approached the car, her son nestled tightly in her arms, she began yelling at Jerry to install a car seat in the police cruiser so the baby would be safe. In the darkest moment of her life, her instinct to protect her child was as sharp as ever.

"It's hard, Marky," she said. "Time is the only thing that helps you heal." She told me about a girl in the grief support program at Joanna's Place. "Her mom died when she was four. Then she's thirteen, and her dad dies. I see someone live through that, and I know how strong we are."

Heather had decided to foster a distant cousin's baby. I was amazed by her resilience in the face of such unimaginable pain. There was nothing she could do to change what happened to Joanna. She couldn't bring her daughter back or fill the void that loss left in its wake, but she had found a way through it by helping others who had been impacted by grief.

"Sometimes we do hard things because we can."

She paused, making space for her or me, I couldn't tell.

"All I mean is, there are lots of kids out there who need love. Take your time."

The scenario Heather had painted—that we'd feel ready to love again—seemed impossible. We'd finally taken down the cribs, but Ethan and Logan were still with us every second—their pictures on the wall, remnants of their wardrobes hanging in the closet. We felt them everywhere. In the maddening, searing quiet of the house.

We'd been parents for eighteen months, and now we weren't. I didn't know how to stop loving them, or how to stop being who I had become.

A father.

Chapter 21

Purpose from Pain

Christmas was staring us in the face like the barrel of a loaded gun. Every time I thought about celebrating without the boys or going home to Massachusetts for the holiday, I was filled with dread. I didn't want to be Debbie Downer sitting in the corner pouting while everyone else celebrated. *Nice stocking. Too bad Santa didn't bring one for Ethan and Logan.* I didn't want my agony to poison the day for my family, and I didn't want to have to talk about it. The anxiety of being around family that Christmas called up the memory of the morning Jaime died, which had been branded on my mind like a face tattoo.

After my mother's frantic call to let me know what had happened, my roommate, Kelly, drove me to Baltimore, where I boarded a Southwest Airlines flight home. I sat in the first row, in the seat closest to the door so I could be the first one off the plane. When the doors opened, I tore up the Jetway like I could somehow outrun the terror. The second I emerged into the airport I heard my brother's deep voice bellowing "Marky" from the other side of the boarding area. I didn't expect him to be there, but in that moment, there was no one in the world I wanted to see more. Paul was standing next to my dad, and as soon as they spotted me, the two of them began maneuvering through the crowd like

defensive backs trying to tackle a receiver. I ran to them and the three
of us, grown men, hugged in the middle of the airport in Providence,
Rhode Island. I buried my head into my father's chest sobbing, "I can't
believe she's gone."

But seeing my father and brother was the easy part. When we arrived
at Auntie Cheryl and Uncle John's house just over the Massachusetts
border, where the whole family had gathered, greeting everyone felt like
walking a gauntlet. Mom met me outside. No words were exchanged;
there was nothing we could say to change the reason for my unplanned
visit. We just held each other, crying in the long driveway of my aunt's
dream house. My aunt and uncle had built their home on a small hill,
selecting every detail from the granite countertops to the chandelier
in the foyer and the hydrangeas in the garden. They had created the
perfect nest, to raise and shelter their daughters, Keli and Jaime. My
cousins' bedrooms always seemed palatial compared to the one I shared
with my brother. They had plush carpeting and fancy dressers that
weren't made by my dad in his toolshed. Jaime's house had always been
a place of refuge for me, bathed in the warm light of our family's love.
But that day, anguish had cast a dark shadow over my sanctuary.

Entering through the side door of the house to the kitchen, I found
Uncle Jimmy seated at the table with his wife, Auntie Sharon, standing
behind him. When they saw me, Jimmy mouthed my name and put
his hand over his bloodshot eyes. Sharon just looked down at the floor,
hiding her tear-soaked face. We were all hurting, mourning our shared
loss. However, seeing me arrive, knowing Jaime was usually one step
ahead or two behind, made her absence even more real. They knew I'd
lost the best friend I'd ever known. All the plans we'd made, the dreams
we shared, were suddenly gone.

"Is that Mark?" I heard Auntie Cheryl call out from the family room.
"Mark?" she called to me. "Get him in here," she commanded. I raced to
her, passing through the kitchen, stopping briefly at the center island to
kiss Grandma Mary and Auntie Mary on the way. Auntie Cheryl lifted
herself from the couch to greet me as I walked in the room, the sweet

blue eyes I'd only ever seen sparkle now sunken and red from tears. As our arms locked around one another, we began holding each other up, the weight of our bodies supporting us from collapsing under an avalanche of grief.

"How can this have happened?" she whispered through tears and soft gasps for air.

"I don't know."

It was all I could say.

Out of the corner of my eye, I saw Keli making her way to me from the dining room, shaking her head slowly as she moved in for a hug. Her long dark hair—like her sister's—was sticking to her face, soaked with tears. Just eighteen months younger than Jaime and me, Keli was a younger sister to us both. There were no words I could offer to make anyone feel better and it wouldn't have mattered. We were all stunned, confused, and angry.

I saw my sister hovering in the corner. She had arrived shortly before me, and I was certain she had just ricocheted through the same gauntlet in which I was now enmeshed. I walked over to her, extending my arms and pulling her into my chest. We stepped into the formal living room, the one we were never allowed in as kids, Keli following behind as she had back then. We sat down on the sofa that was usually reserved for fancy guests, and out of sight from the rest of the family, the three of us sobbed like children, holding hands tightly as if we were never going to let go.

No one was going to object to us being in the off-limits room today, disrupting the vacuum cleaner streaks on the rug or shuffling the throw pillows. The spotless piano in the corner was purchased by my aunt so the girls could take lessons. Auntie Cheryl wasn't trying to stage-mom the next Alicia Keys; she just wanted her daughters to have the opportunities she was denied as a little girl in the projects. Neither of them enjoyed piano, but Jaime could perform a masterful rendition of Bon Jovi's "Never Say Goodbye." And saying goodbye is what brought me there that day.

Uncle John walked into the living room and stood in the doorway. I jumped up to embrace him. At six foot two, he had always been a giant to me, but in that moment, with his shoulders slumped in the wooden doorframe, we stood eye to tearful eye.

"She's gone, Mark. Our Jaime's gone," he wept. I could feel his chest jerk with emotion as he pulled me in tightly. This mountain of strength, crumbling in my arms as the absoluteness of Jaime's death settled into the spaces she once filled. The fortress he built, the safety it provided, was finite. I wanted to comfort him, but I didn't know how. And the tearing of my heart made me weak. One instant of recklessness had undone a lifetime of meticulous love and watchfulness. Our lives changed forever that day. But how much, we couldn't begin to understand. Something beyond our control had taken our Jaime.

"Never Say Goodbye," once the anthem of childhood rebellion, was now just empty lyrics, a melodic reminder that "Together Forever" was no longer an option.

We were the torn pieces of a once-whole portrait, tiny shreds scattered about. Jaime was gone, and I just wanted to run away. I wanted to break free. There was nowhere else I wanted to be, but being there also meant it was all real and I just couldn't accept the truth, the pain, or the hurt in the eyes of everyone I loved.

Over the next few days, hundreds of people paid their respects: childhood friends, teachers, neighbors, and distant family members making the trek to offer condolences. Kindness and compassion while you're grieving force vulnerability to surface, and I hated feeling vulnerable.

I hated that this loving family couldn't protect her.

I hated that she was gone.

I hated that the boys were gone too. I couldn't just run to the playroom and scoop them up into my arms, make them laugh until they lost their breath, or kiss their cheeks over and over. I couldn't allow myself to go home, to be this vulnerable, not that Christmas, maybe not ever. It was all too fresh, like a festering wound hidden under a thin layer of scar tissue. The boys had been gone for two months and I didn't want to feel exposed. I didn't have the strength to be raw with my family again. I didn't want to accept condolences from the people I loved most. I didn't want to have to repeat the story of the three judges, or the email we sent to Brandon, or share my nightmares about their safety. My family deserved more than my canned lines about their reunification, but I wasn't ready, not yet. I convinced Jason we should host our friends in Los Angeles instead and spend New Year's Eve in Hawaii.

A few weeks into the new year, I got a call from a friend at the Los Angeles County Board of Supervisors. She asked if she could connect me with a woman named Lisa Campbell-Motton, who was one of the directors of LA County's Probation Child Welfare division.

"Probation just secured a big grant from the state to recruit foster parents for the nearly one thousand teens in their custody," she explained, "and I was hoping you'd be willing to meet with her because of your work with the FosterMore campaign."

After what Jason and I had just been through, I wasn't sure I was the right person to be convincing anyone to become a foster parent.

Sensing my hesitation, she added, "Probation Child Welfare represents such a small percentage of the county's foster care population, and this is the first time they've ever had a budget for foster parent recruitment. In fact, they have never had a single foster parent who wasn't a family member or somehow connected to the young person. They're social workers, not marketers. They have no idea how to build a marketing campaign. Will you please go talk to her?"

A few days later, I found myself in South Los Angeles, sitting in a narrow, windowless conference room lit by those fluorescent bulbs that should be outlawed. The building housing the county's Probation Department was built in the 1970s and hadn't been updated since. The thin blue industrial carpeting lining the hallways and offices was worn through in patches from years of foot traffic. A dozen or so workers sat in cramped cubicles separated by towering file cabinets, where I imagined decades of paperwork held the untold stories of thousands of forgotten children.

I was told Lisa was running late. While I waited, I pulled up the presentation I had put together, but I couldn't get my computer to connect with their ancient projector. I glanced at the time on the top corner of my laptop. She was ten minutes late.

Lisa was warm and polite when she walked in a few moments later, but I got the sense she didn't want to be in this meeting.

I thanked her for taking the time and dove into my presentation, breaking down how advertising through social media could effectively pinpoint the most viable foster parent candidates. As her interest grew, so did a discomfort inside me. It was the same unease I had felt when I first saw the RaiseAChild banners towering over Beverly Boulevard. Did I really want to convince more people to experience the pain I was going through?

"To be honest," I said, turning from the laptop and abandoning my slides, "it's hard for me to make a case for anyone to become a foster parent right now."

Lisa looked at me, arching one eyebrow. She leaned in closer, clearly intrigued.

"My husband and I fostered two boys for a year and a half, and three months ago they were returned to parents who weren't prepared to care for them."

"I'm sorry to hear that," she said. From the way she looked at me, her soft brown eyes intently locked on mine, her lips pursed, I knew she meant it.

Then the whole story came tumbling out. I told her about Amber's indifference to Logan, our frustration with Nadia, and the three all-powerful judges whose decision I believed had put the boys and their sister in danger. "We tried everything. Called anyone who'd listen. We even consulted with a private lawyer, but the county just gave us the stiff-arm. We didn't become foster parents to take someone else's babies, but we couldn't just do nothing when we knew they weren't safe.

I've been so angry, sometimes I want to torch the system," I confessed. "I want to expose the hypocrisy of an institution masquerading as child welfare when in reality the children are treated like afterthoughts."

My passion and pain had taken over and I didn't realize I'd even raised my voice. I looked at Lisa, and for a moment I couldn't tell if she was going to throw me out of her office or hug me.

"I understand your frustration," Lisa said, folding her hands in her lap and nodding. "I've been doing this work for thirty years, and I have to light myself on fire to get any attention for our kids. This department is where children end up when they've been failed by every other institution. We are the backstop of a flawed system."

I was stunned by her frank acknowledgment of the county's failures. "Most of the teens we serve have been in and out of foster care their whole lives. They've bounced from foster home to group home until finally, they land here because they broke the law. We had a fourteen-year-old girl assigned to us the other day," she started, shaking her head. "Her mother was addicted to drugs. Dad left before she was born. She was a victim of human trafficking. This girl has been failed by every adult in her life and the systems that were supposed to protect her."

I hung tighter to her words than the *Mona Lisa* to the walls of the Louvre. She asked me to continue my presentation. When I was done, she told me there had been only eight adoptions of foster youth on probation nationwide, five of which had been handled by her or the people she supervised. She was a bright light in a dark place, hope in a sea of despair, the anti-Nadia. But Lisa and her team were greatly outnumbered and tremendously underresourced. They had more than one thousand teens in their care.

"Being placed in a safe and supportive home can change the trajectory of a teenager's life," Lisa continued. "Without it, too many will exit our care to find themselves homeless or eventually in jail. No one wants to talk about the kids who spend their childhoods in the system; foster care, group homes, juvie, probation, and then they turn eighteen and wind up in jail."

"A life sentence on the installment plan," I added, agreeing with her.

"Exactly," she continued. "Their involvement begins in childhood."

"Wow," I muttered, dismayed by the reality many of these kids encounter.

"The biggest challenge we face is that the teenagers we serve are the ones most people are afraid of. They don't want to know about kids who have it so bad crime becomes a means of survival. They join gangs for the safety it provides in their neighborhoods or to find the sense of belonging they never felt at home." I stared at her, nodding and rocking slightly in my chair, still processing the picture she'd just painted of the teens in her care. "They sell drugs or their bodies so they can eat, so they can survive. The teenagers who commit sex crimes were most likely victims themselves," she added. "It's a horrific cycle that, without intervention, just repeats and repeats."

I was shocked by her realness. No one working within the system had ever been so honest and straightforward with me. Lisa wasn't sugarcoating facts. Parents, families, neighbors, governments, society—we *all* fail these children every day.

"This is why we need more people involved in their lives," she said. I thought of Amber and how different her choices might have been if someone had stepped in when she was a child being neglected and abused. Instead she ended up trapped in a similar cycle of victim and perpetrator, clinging to her children for a sense of love and belonging, but wholly unprepared for the day-to-day reality of caring for them.

"We need people like you, who have friends on the Board of Supervisors. When you tell them about the challenges in the system, they listen."

Her words stung a bit, but she was right. Having your privilege called out is never comfortable, but I'd already learned she wasn't one to pull any punches, so I welcomed the awkwardness. If you are open to it, discomfort is the prelude to empathy, a prompt for growth and transformation. Besides, the discomfort I was feeling was nothing compared to the hopelessness of the young people trapped in the system. By their twenty-first birthday, one in four kids who age out of foster care have experienced homelessness and one in three have become a parent.[1]

The conversation with Lisa flipped a switch inside me. Ever since the boys left, I had been so overcome with grief and anger I couldn't see what I really wanted, what I really needed to begin healing: a path to create purpose out of my pain. I may have lost my boys, but maybe I could help other kids in a different way. I had to work with her.

Lisa told me contracting with the county was a bureaucratic nightmare that would likely take several months, but she was determined to figure it out. She promised to stay in touch, and I left the drab office invigorated.

———

We didn't hear from Kris, our only source of intel on the boys, throughout the spring. In some ways, the silence may have helped me feel a little less raw. Jason and I both got busier at work. To fill the silence at home, we started making our own fresh juices and completed a two-week food purification cleanse—the stuff gays in their forties do when they don't have children. With each morning that passed, it got easier to get out of bed and face the day, but some things still derailed me—spotting Logan's crib disassembled and tucked away in the closet behind our winter coats, or an iPhone photo memory showing Ethan's crystal blue eyes squinting while a smile lit up his face.

As more time passed my reaction to grief began to change. The lion of emotions that for so long had immobilized me under the strength of its claws didn't have the same power over me anymore. Or perhaps I was reclaiming my own strength. There were times when I still retreated to solitude, but I began to find joy in the memories we shared—Ethan and Logan banging tambourines at the farmers' market with Trisha, their smiles in the back seat of the car, hearing them giggle, or their voices calling me, Daddy. Reminiscence blanketed me with comfort and reminded me of the gift they were in our lives. But sometimes the memories conjured up a feeling of regret too. I wondered if I had allowed myself to fully experience the joy when these things were happening. I had been so worried about losing them, did I miss out on having them? The night in the hotel, when Logan took his first steps, I had my first panic attack. In those moments, when joy was so palpable, so present, was I? Was anxiety blocking joy? Did I stand in my own way?

Did my fear strangle my joy?

In June, a couple of weeks after Jason turned forty, I signed a contract with the Los Angeles County Probation Department and began working with Lisa to design a foster parent recruitment campaign for the youth in her care.

We spent the summer in focus groups trying to figure out what type of stranger would open their heart and their home to a teenager who had been convicted of a crime instead of slamming the door shut when they heard the word "probation." We talked with men and women of all ages, races, and income levels across Los Angeles County and by summer's end we had identified a very particular group as our best hope of finding homes for the teenagers.

They were predominantly women in their fifties. They had raised children and were often empty nesters. Many of them were single, divorced, or widowed, which, as I told Lisa, was great because it eliminated the barrier of convincing a reluctant or unwilling spouse. But the real common thread binding them together was the experience of being powerless in an effort to help someone they loved. For some, it was the loss of a childhood friend who had been removed from a dangerous home after the system stepped in. For others, most often teachers, there was a promising student whose ambitions were shattered by parental abuse or neglect. Night after night, we heard heartbreaking stories from women, many of whom had shouldered the pain of their grief for decades. They knew they couldn't change what had happened, but what we were offering was a way to write a new ending to their story by changing someone else's life. Perhaps this work would allow me to write a new ending to my story too.

Jason and I also began talking about a new chapter in our lives. As we approached the one-year anniversary of the boys' reunification, we decided it was time we began exploring parenthood again.

Chapter 22

Thank You

One Thursday morning in November, a little over a year after Ethan and Logan had left, I woke to a text from my friend Devin. I'd coached her through her decision to foster a year earlier and she was now caring for an infant. Her case plan had moved from plan A to plan B, and she was on the fast track to adoption. Devin's message read:

> *I'm not sure if you're ready for this, but my adoption worker mentioned she had three siblings added to her caseload—a six-year-old girl and two boys, ages five and two. She said these kids are 100% not going back to their parents, and she doesn't want to split them up. I hope you don't mind, but I told her about you and Jason, and she told me to reach out. She said they are healthy, smart, and sweet. She even called them "magical."*

I read her text five or six times and then put my phone down without writing back. Three kids. That part didn't throw me. Not that long ago I'd prepared to parent three. But when I pictured three kids, the only faces I saw were Ethan's, Logan's, and Savannah's. I couldn't imagine bringing new children into our lives when we were still grieving the ones who'd left. I couldn't bear the thought of opening ourselves up to another loss. I could still hear the echo of Ethan's belly laugh and see the faint vision of Logan's blond curls bouncing as he ran down the hallway. Yet how long could we wait to love and parent again? How long could we keep wondering if they were coming back? I thought about Savannah and her precious smile. She had probably taken her first steps by now. But if a guarantee was what it would take for me to gamble my heart again, this seemed as close to an assurance as child welfare permits.

When Jason came home for lunch, I read Devin's text to him while he made a salad. I didn't know what I wanted more—for him to say *yes* or for him to say *no*.

I watched him dress the salad and wash the knife and cutting board. Then he looked at me and smiled. "Let's find out their story."

"Are you for real?" I asked.

I thought of Jason throwing a Wiffle ball in the sunlight all those years ago, how I'd known he was born to be a father. He'd more than proven the truth of my hunch, over and over again.

"Just ask," he said, meeting my stare. "See if it's even legit."

"Really?" I asked. "You'd do it again?"

"Yes," he said, looking back at the salad. "Maybe. I don't know."

————

I texted Devin back that afternoon, and we spoke with her adoption worker, Eleanor, on Friday. Adoption workers are only assigned to cases after the court decides reunification is no longer the goal. Eleanor told us, "I've been doing this for twenty-one years and I've never fallen in love with any kids faster than I did with these three. They are so special."

On Monday we met with Eleanor in her office. She told us their names and showed us a black-and-white photocopied picture of each child. Aimie had just turned six. She had long, wavy dark hair and beautiful brown eyes. She was petite. In the photo she wore a dress and a long string of pearls around her neck, her lips pressed softly together in a shy, sweet smile. Eddie was ten months younger than his sister and had an infectious, toothy grin that forced you to smile back. Not even the low toner in the Xerox could dull the energy he was putting out. Joshua, the baby, was two and a half years old. His picture looked like it was taken at the DMV—a straight-faced glare at the camera—no smile under his buzz cut. But even the serious expression couldn't hide his dimples that were big as life.

When I asked about their parents, Eleanor said they were young. That life had dealt them a rough hand and that they'd had their own interactions with the system as kids. She said they loved their children very much, but their circumstances didn't allow them to do what was needed to care for them and keep them safe. I wanted to press her for details, but I remembered Kendra's deliberate vagueness and decided to focus on the kids.

By the end of the meeting, we were placed in a "potential match," the foster care equivalent of exclusively dating; we couldn't be offered other kids and they couldn't be matched with other foster parents. They had been living in Hemet, east of Palm Springs, a three-hour drive from Los Angeles, for the past year. They had been moved out of Los Angeles because our county, with a population roughly the size of Michigan,[1] didn't have a foster home large enough to accommodate three siblings. Thankfully, their social worker did her homework and found them a caring family in neighboring Riverside County, so they could remain together.

The sense of loss over Ethan and Logan still loomed, but we were also excited to meet Aimie, Eddie, and Joshua. Before we even knew they existed, Jason and I had decided to spend Christmas in LA with friends and leave that night on a red-eye for a much-needed vacation together. We wanted to reconnect and make some new memories. We called it our delayed honeymoon, spending New Year's Eve in Bali and then a week Australia. It was also our way of making sure we were still us, that the pain we shared had not destroyed the love we had for one another. Eleanor suggested we wait to meet them until we returned from our trip, so we didn't confuse the children and completely disrupt their holidays. We agreed and appreciated her consideration of their foster parents.

We talked about the kids throughout our vacation, like we'd already met them.

Driving through Point Nepean National Park in Victoria, we saw a road sign that read, "Slow Down," with the outline of four animals. "Pull over, I want to see this sign," I said excitedly. "Okay, that's a kangaroo on the bottom right and the top left is a crocodile, but what are the other two?" I asked Jason, as the car came to a stop on the side of the empty road. "Is one of them a dingo?"

"No, dingoes look like coyotes," he said, squinting at the sign and smiling with amusement. The simple yellow sign conveyed so many messages.

"If we see a crocodile, you better gun it," I warned him. "I've heard they can run thirty-five miles an hour."

"You're safe, babe." He placed his hand on my knee and looked me in the eyes. "This rental car can easily clear forty miles an hour." I tried to ignore his joke, but I couldn't fight back the smile it brought to my face. "The bottom left looks like an anteater," he offered, returning the conversation to the sign.

"Anteaters are real?" I asked, floored. "I thought they were make-believe, like unicorns or dragons."

"Maybe you should put down Instagram and pick up a *National Geographic* sometime," he teased. We both laughed.

"And maybe I should feed you to the crocodiles," I quipped back.

The heartbreak and the loss, the anger and the tears, everything we had been through had made us stronger. The time away together made me realize, we were still us.

"This would be an amazing place to bring the kids," he sighed, looking out the window at the lush wattle trees. "Imagine taking them snorkeling in the Great Barrier Reef or their reaction to that kangaroo we passed."

"Yeah. Except I wouldn't let them out of the car for fear something would eat them." He laughed and shook his head. My ability to worry, even about an imaginary adventure, was something he'd come to expect.

"Do you want to get out and take a picture with the sign?"

"And get eaten by one of those things? Are you out of your damn mind?"

The conversation got me excited and thinking about all sorts of things. What would they be interested in? Would they like dolls and trucks? My Little Pony and superheroes? Would they be afraid moving into our house? How would they sleep? I hope they aren't allergic to dogs. We bought them souvenirs, small backpacks from Australia with stuffed koalas and kangaroos.

A few days after returning from our vacation, we drove out to Hemet for our first meeting with the kids and their current foster parents, Victor and Sofia, a couple in their late twenties. They had begun fostering a few years earlier as a way to help families during a difficult time. Victor had a son from a previous relationship, and they were hoping to have children together, so adopting was out of the question. They welcomed us into their immaculate, Spanish-style home and introduced us to the kids. Joshua ran straight to Jason. When Jason lifted him up, he nestled his head against Jason's shoulder. I waved to Aimie, who was hiding behind Sofia's legs, smiling and sneaking peeks at us. Her long hair was pulled back into a ponytail with a white bow. Eddie stood next to Victor, smiling and fidgeting. He was excited and ready to play. We gave them the stuffed animals and the backpacks, and they immediately put them on. Eddie showed us the room he shared with Joshua, and we all sat on the floor together, playing with plastic trucks and Duplo blocks. Aimie had a game she'd made up that she wanted us to play, but Joshua kept showing us his dance moves, and Eddie wanted us to see every toy in his toy box. At one point Joshua put Jason's hat on his own head and nearly disappeared underneath it.

I had no idea what the kids had been told about us before we arrived, but I was struck by how open they were to meeting us. We only stayed for about thirty minutes, but during the ride home I pictured their faces, as though searing them into memory—Joshua's gentle eyes, Eddie's fiery smile, Aimie's long hair and dimples.

"I think we should put the boys in the big room next to ours," Jason said, "and Aimie can have the smaller one at the top of the stairs."

"Yeah," I agreed. "We should see if she wants us to paint it, to get rid of the blue."

"She should definitely get to decide the color and the decor," he added. I just smiled, knowing the only way she'd get to choose the color was if she selected the one he already had in mind.

We drove out to Hemet again a few days later. This time we took them to a park, then for dinner at Chuck E. Cheese, where we got our first lesson in being outnumbered by your children as the three of them took off in different directions. We explained only once why it was important to stick together, so no one gets lost, and they didn't leave one another's side again.

Finally, a week later, we picked them up to spend the weekend at our house. Friday night traffic was terrible leaving the city, and we arrived two hours late. They had no fear getting in the car with us or leaving their foster parents. They had a bond like nothing I'd ever seen. The safety and stability I'd found in my mother, they found in each other. If ever the boys had concerns, they looked to Aimie for reassurance. Siblings whose only consistency is one another often share a trauma bond, a special way of looking out for one another. Aimie wasn't afraid of spending the weekend with us, so the boys shouldn't be either.

Eddie was so excited on the long car ride. He couldn't stop asking us questions. "What did you have for lunch today? Have you ever seen a giraffe? How fast can you run?" The questions tumbled out, one on top of the other, with no time to respond. Then, all of a sudden, the car went quiet. All three kids had fallen asleep.

"I think the lightning round just ended," I joked, and watched the lights from passing cars flash over their peaceful faces.

We parked in the driveway, and I carried Joshua, while Eddie cozied into Jason's arms. Aimie held my hand as we walked to the door. Brian stampeded to the other side of the glass to greet us and the three of them screeched as if a monster had suddenly appeared from the dark. Aimie hid behind me, clutching my leg, and Joshua's grip around my neck nearly stopped me from breathing. But before the weekend was over, they had warmed to Brian, and he was playfully allowing Joshua to use him as a stepstool to get onto the couch. We spent most of those two days laughing together and jumping on the beds.

Eleanor approved their move-in date, and we had two weeks to ready the house. We bought and assembled three beds. Joshua's was shaped like a boat, Eddie's was a top bunk with a slide coming down the side of it, and Aimie's had a white canopy hanging overhead, a perfect fit for our princess.

In late February 2019, we loaded our SUV with three car seats, bags of clothes, and toys. I looked in the rearview mirror and saw three beautiful faces smiling at me. They weren't the three faces I'd expected when we bought this car, but it felt right. Three children who needed parents and two childless fathers, our once upon a time had begun. My heart was full again.

We were in a pre-adoptive placement. This would be our first of countless rides together as a family. Plan B, adoption by foster parents, was the goal. After six months of living together, the law would allow a judge to officially terminate the birth parents' rights over the children and our adoption would proceed.

———

Months passed and we celebrated milestones. Joshua turned three and potty trained overnight. He couldn't land on just one theme for his celebration, so Jason dubbed it "Young, Wild, and Three: a Paw Patrol, Batman, Spiderman, Baby Shark pool party." Aimie lost her first tooth and enrolled in a hip-hop ballet class. Eddie began playing soccer and discovered how fast he could run in a superhero costume. My parents and Jason's parents took several trips to spoil them. Mom would text, *Aren't you and Jason due for a vacation? I'd love to come watch my grandkids.* Our village of friends fell hard for Joshua's showmanship, Aimie's sweetness, and Eddie's sincerity. The walls of our house had a new soundtrack: Eddie's racing footsteps, Joshua's giggles, and Aimie's singing.

We worked with Eleanor on the adoption plan and Nicole, their county social worker, began making monthly visits. She was nothing like Nadia. Nicole would arrive with the correct paperwork, on time, and she listened. She had been a caseworker for about two decades and was responsible for training others. Before they moved in with us, she had logged hours upon hours each month driving from her East Los Angeles office to visit them in Hemet. The windshield time didn't bother her because they were safe and together—and that's what mattered most to her.

We ate as a family at the dining room table almost every night. The meals shared in those early months brought us all together, helping us each discover where we fit in, how we belonged. The kids, fighting for the spotlight, relished our presence and attention. If Aimie didn't like the vegetables, she'd tell a painstakingly long, uber-detailed story while hiding them on her plate, hoping we wouldn't catch on to her trick. Eddie would interrupt her about a dozen times to add details she overlooked, to change the subject entirely, or just to say the word "poop." Jason and I did our best to curb the interruptions and to share the floor among the three of them, but poor Joshua struggled to get a word in edgewise. The older siblings had no patience for his imaginary friend "Catboy" and didn't want to hear about his preschool classmate, Sebastian—or "the bastard," as he pronounced it. Within a few months they stopped calling us Mark and Jason and declared us Daddy and Pop. They may not have been the first kids to call me Daddy, but this time, I knew it was forever. Hearing the high pitch of their voices call out Daddy sent electric currents straight to my heart.

I was their dad, and they were my children.

The honeymoon was short-lived. They each had their own way of testing boundaries, whether it was having a tantrum in Target for a toy or crouching in the closet to be left alone. The tools I'd mastered with toddlers didn't work as well with older kids, but our therapist offered me some new, helpful strategies, and Jason was always there in a pinch. Our love for them was instantaneous and I think they knew it.

That summer they learned to swim in the yard, made dozens of sand castles at the beach, and took their first plane rides out east to meet their extended family. Seeing my sister dote over Aimie, French-braiding her long hair and regaling her with love and attention, was blissful. "Aimie's my only niece," she reminded us a thousand times. Watching all three kids immediately bond with their cousins in Pittsburgh made my heart sing. When Joshua crawled up into my lap, exhausted after a long day, I held him tight, kissed his forehead, and told him how much I loved him. This time I wasn't letting fear strangle joy. I wasn't worried about the what-ifs.

We all were falling in love. It was magical and it was right.

We were a family.

———

In the fall, Jason and I found ourselves preparing for another trip to the fourth floor of the Edmund D. Edelman Children's Court. Now that the children were in a safe, loving home longer than six months, a judge would terminate their biological parents' birth-given rights over their children. We found ourselves completing another set of JV-290s, the form that lets the court hear from foster parents. I told Jason I wanted to take the first crack at them, and that he could make any edits he wanted. I wanted our love to spring from the page like a jack-in-the-box.

The form asked mostly very direct questions about the children's medical, dental, and emotional health, allowing respondents to check a box indicating there's nothing new to report or provide an update in the limited blank space. The kids were healthy. In fact, Joshua had grown so much since moving in, his pediatrician said he could be written about in a textbook. But I wanted this opportunity to address the court.

I wanted the judge to know the children were so much more than just safe—they were loved, well cared for, and happy. That we were giving them opportunities to explore their interests and counseling to address any issues from their past or struggles with the transition into our house and our family.

The JV-290 is shared with all the parties to the case, so if their parents attended the hearing, they too would get a copy of whatever we submitted. I didn't expect them to show up at court. They knew they weren't getting their children back and this wasn't going to be a good day for them. The hearing would proceed whether they were there or not, but in case they did attend, I wanted the JV-290 to speak to them too.

I thought for a while about what I wanted them to know, how I wanted them to feel if they read this form. It was too late for them to get their kids back, but I hoped my words would help them find peace knowing Aimie, Eddie, and Joshua had become our universe. Their happiness and safety were the force moving us through our days. I wanted the joyful, well-adjusted kids I loved to shine through, so I wrote like a proud dad about Aimie excelling at school. How she skipped around the yard, singing loudly for all to hear. I wrote about Eddie's wild curiosity and sense of adventure, and Joshua's vivid imagination and the way he looked up to his brother and sister.

The morning of the hearing, Jason and I arrived on time and paid our six dollars in cash to park. As we made our way to the courtroom, I noticed a petite woman in her twenties with long dark hair and soft brown eyes stepping off the elevator. I elbowed Jason.

"That's got to be their mother."

"How do you know?" he asked.

"Look at her!"

It was like watching Aimie emerge from a time machine. She shared her dimples, Joshua's eyes, and the beauty mark resting lightly above her lip was identical to the one dotting Eddie's infectious smile. I hadn't expected to see her at this hearing, but nothing could have prepared me for what happened next.

Just after we took our seats, a young man with a shaved head, long dark beard, and visible tattoos on his hands and neck was escorted into the courtroom and began surveying the crowd. I knew this must be their father. I couldn't help but wonder what he was thinking. What he was feeling. How did he arrive at this moment? How different our lives must have been. If life had gifted him the same opportunities I'd been given, would he be in this situation?

My mind was racing, but he was laser focused. His eyes scanned the room, taking in every face, paying no attention to the judge or even his lawyer. He was looking for someone. He had a message to deliver. Our eyes locked and I realized Jason and I were his intended audience. My stomach sank. Unsure of what he wanted to say or how to react, I pursed my lips and forced a smile.

"Thank you," he mouthed slowly and silently.

I was stunned. All I could do was stare blankly back at him.

"Thank you," he mouthed again. "Thank you."

Wanting so badly to say something, but struggling for words, I mouthed the only thing I could think of to say. "Of course."

I would do anything for our kids.

I'd wanted safety to be as simple as a rainbow baby gate. A shelter against the bad things and the hard things. A bright, tangible border you could put up around your life. Your loved ones. Your heart.

I learned it's more complicated. Life isn't a safety checklist or a curated playlist of love songs. It's the breakup songs too. The loss and heartache and regret. The outcomes we can't predict and the things we'll never know for sure. Safety isn't the absence of suffering. It's the strength and courage we muster when we don't know how the story will end. It's the grace that lets our hearts go on risking when we think we can't take any more hurt. It's the question: *Could you do it again?* And it's the answer:

No.

Maybe.

Yes.

Epilogue

Ten months after Aimie, Eddie, and Joshua moved in, I was driving to present the foster parent recruitment campaign I'd built to a conference of probation officers, when Jason called to let me know he'd just gotten off the phone with a Los Angeles County caseworker. Ethan and Logan were back in foster care—Savannah too—after their social worker discovered signs of abuse.

"She hurt Logan, didn't she?" I asked.

"Yes," Jason confirmed, his voice soft and steady. I could tell by his tone he was trying to remain calm. We had predicted and feared this would happen. It was the *I told you so* moment I'd hoped would never come. "I don't know the specifics. All she'd say was that he was abused."

Rage hit me first. Rage for what the kids had endured. Rage for the ways the system had failed them by putting them back in harm's way. Rage that the system could easily fail them again. I knew Jason was as upset as I was, but his default was to lead with logic in any crisis, while I was still learning to ride my emotions without training wheels.

"Mark, they want to know if we'll take the three of them—Ethan, Logan, and Savannah."

"Holy shit" was the only thing I could think of to say. I'd wanted this call for so long, but that was before we'd met and fallen in love with Aimie, Eddie, and Joshua. And there was more to it.

Because Amber had won her appeal and the initial detention had been deemed inappropriate, what was now really the second detention would be counted legally as the first. In other words, the clock went back to zero. Reunification would be the foremost goal. The kids would again be in the limbo of visitations and six-month hearings, repeating all the losses and potential losses they'd already endured.

But my fury wasn't the point. If we said "yes," what would life be like for the six children? Where would everyone sleep? How would we arrange all the visitations and individual appointments with therapists and specialists? What would happen if the kids didn't get along, or were resentful of one another? What would happen if they got attached, and then Ethan, Logan, and Savannah reunified? What would it be like for them to be living on two different and unpredictable trajectories, to face different but simultaneous uncertainties?

"What do you think we should do?" I asked Jason, loosening my grip on the steering wheel.

"How could we ever say no?" he asked. "The social worker said our house is large enough to care for all six kids. They'd have to update some paperwork, but she said that's easy." He'd made up his mind. My exit was approaching. I checked both sides and steered to the right. I couldn't imagine them going to another family or being split up. But how could we manage the logistics of six kids, not to mention the emotional needs?

"They must be so scared," I said, my heart bogged by pain. "But six kids?" The thought of six children racing around the house was overwhelming and frightening. "We'll need to buy a bus just to go anywhere together."

"Should I tell her yes?" he asked.

"I guess," I muttered slowly, fear and excitement charging through my veins. I wanted to see them, to hug them and tell them how loved they are.

"I have to call Children's Bureau to let them know and I'll reach out to the principal of Aimie and Eddie's school to see about getting Ethan enrolled," Jason said. He'd clearly thought a lot of this through in the brief time between hanging up with the social worker and calling me. "Good luck with your presentation. I love you."

"I love you, too," I said, and hung up.

What the hell did I just commit to? I thought as I turned off the freeway. *This is insane.* Doubt cascaded through my mind. *Can we afford six kids? There are other great foster homes. But how could I let them go to strangers? Will they even remember us? Are we acting in their best interest or being selfish? How would I ever look Amber in the face? Or sit in the same room as her at a visit knowing she'd hurt Logan? What if they reunify again?* Things were going well at home. The kids were all settled in and were well-adjusted. They'd already experienced more upheavals and change in their young lives than most people will ever face. Was this fair to them?

Aimie had just had her first dance recital the weekend before. When she stepped onstage in her pink tutu and locked eyes with me in the crowd, smiles overtook both our faces, and I fought back a flood of tears. The once-shy, dimpled girl hiding behind her foster mom was now shining, brimming with confidence. After the show, she raced excitedly through the crowd and over to me. I lifted her up as she wrapped her skinny arms around my neck. Kissing her cheek, I whispered, "I love you, baby girl. I'm so proud of you."

"I love you, Daddy."

I arrived at the building where my meeting was to take place and my phone rang. It was Jason.

"Mark, I've got Amanda from Children's Bureau on the line," he began. Ramona had moved on to a new job and Amanda, whom we'd only met a couple of times, had taken over as the supervisor.

"Hi Mark," she said.

"Hi Amanda, do you think we're insane?" I asked, with a slight laugh.

"No. Not insane," she said, forcing a chuckle. "But I just wanted to talk this through with you both before you call the caseworker back." Her tone turned serious. "This is not a decision that should be made with emotions."

"I appreciate that," I said, as I shifted the car into park in a spot far enough from the door that no one would pull up next to me and interrupt my call.

"It's been a long time since the boys left your home, and we don't know what they have gone through or experienced. I hate to say this, but they are not the same babies they were two years ago. I spoke to the county worker, and she told me the boys had some aggressive behaviors."

I didn't want to hear what she was saying. I had already agreed with Jason, we should take them back. Also, it hurt to think of them suffering; I knew that my biggest fear, that they would be abused, had been realized. Her words reminded me of Patty saying that children who reunify often regress, and I thought about how the boys began biting and hitting after they started overnight visits with Amber and Zach. What had those behaviors morphed into? What if they hurt one of our other kids? At three and a half, Joshua weighed less than Ethan did when he arrived at our doorstep. One aggression could inflict serious physical hurt to him. As much as I didn't want to hear what Amanda was saying, I knew I needed to pay attention.

Jason and I were supercharged with emotion. Our instinct was to throw a protective wall around the boys and Savannah like we had for Aimie, Eddie, and Joshua. We wanted to keep them safe no matter the toll that took on us, to get them whatever help they needed to heal, and return them to the sweet, loving boys who left our care all those nights ago. Our home was big enough for six children. But a bed alone does not make a home. How would the two of us have the capacity to meet the emotional needs of each child? How would we reverse course for the boys and get Savannah the help she needed, while not disrupting Aimie, Eddie, and Joshua's progress?

"This isn't about how much you love them, it's about what's best for them," Amanda said. "And what's best for the family you've built with the children already in your care." Her words echoed in my ears, and I thought about our dinner table. Seeing Jason's crooked smile across the table, Eddie perched on his leg and Aimie glued to his side. Joshua lying across my lap, his mouth wide open, giggling loudly as he tried to protect his ticklish armpits from my fingers. Could we add three more children to this table, this family? Would the two of us be able to meet all their needs? Would it be fair to any of them? Maybe they'd be better off with other foster parents, who could give them their full attention?

We told Amanda we wanted to talk privately, and that we'd call her back shortly.

"Jason, I love the boys as much as you do, and I absolutely hate myself for saying this, but I don't think we should take them." My own words, a dagger jamming deep into my heart. Jason didn't say anything. I waited a few more seconds and added, "I just don't think it's fair to them, or to Aimie, Eddie, and Joshua."

Jason never agreed or disagreed with me. He just said, "I'll let the county know." I hated myself for saying no.

Sometimes the biggest act of love is to give up what you want in service of what is best for your children. To accept what you *can't* do on someone else's behalf.

For me, the hardest moment of being a parent was when I had to say, *I can't parent.* When I had to accept that the greatest act of love I could offer Ethan, Logan, and Savannah was to not parent them. The most sacrificing, selfless thing we could do was say, "No."

Does this story have a happy ending?

Yes and no.

In December 2020, just before Christmas, Jason and I became the adoptive parents of Aimie, Eddie, and Joshua. We survived a pandemic and a year of homeschool, and we all learned to Zoom. They introduced me to a new set of feelings and emotions, lighting up foreign spaces, once distant in my heart. The reward of parenting wasn't something I ever thought I'd get to experience as a young man. And now that I'd discovered it, I couldn't imagine my life without it. Watching Aimie shine onstage or in her classroom and nursing her tender heart as she learns to navigate big feelings. Delighting in Eddie's wonder-filled approach to each day and his amazement when that curiosity unearths a new finding. Seeing Joshua grow from an adventurous toddler to a kind little boy, quick to offer a hand or light up a room with a silly face or a clever remark.

As for Ethan and Logan, the children who first broke our hearts open wide, they spent a few weeks with Kris before going to live with another foster family. The stress was too much for Zach and Amber's relationship and they separated. They were both offered reunification services, but only Zach followed the court's directive. I don't know what happened to Amber, if she's living in Lancaster with her grandmother or somewhere else. Her life has been a roller-coaster ride, with high-highs and low-lows. My hope for her is that she's able to find peace, and stability to work through any challenges she's now facing, and that she doesn't miss out on the lives of her remarkable children.

After another year apart, the boys and Savannah reunified with their father. Our communication with Kris, our only source of information on the children, grew more infrequent. I don't know what their lives are like with Zach, where they live, or what they had to experience before they got to wherever they are now. Not a single day has passed that I haven't thought of them, and the lessons our time together taught me—how our capacity to love knows no limits, but our ability to keep our loved ones safe is bound. How quickly strangers can become family. And how sometimes, all the love in the world isn't enough to keep a family together.

Ethan and Logan, the first to call me Daddy, will forever be in my heart. I thought I'd never love again, that my heart was too ragged to be restored, but I was wrong. Love is an invitation to risk. A wave that floods the soul, rendering powerless those in her path. We can build the fortress, a shelter, but we exist at love's mercy, defenseless in her clutch.

I am still learning to accept where my feet are, what's in my control and what's not. I made the choice to embrace the love and joy of my family and to put my faith in the good of a system that failed the boys. It was painful, at times hilarious, but if asked to do it all over again—a million times, yes.

In fairy tales the bad guys are defeated, spells broken, chaos quelled. But not without a cost. Is any happily ever after truly happy? Both are real—the joy and the sorrow, the safety and the fear.

One afternoon Eddie and I were in the pool. There was a leaf floating on the surface of the water—something he doesn't like—so I ruffled my hand to push the leaf away.

He looked me squarely in the eyes. "You're brave," he said.

"Because I touched a leaf?"

He nodded. "Are you afraid of bees?"

"No," I said. "If you leave them alone, they don't bother you."

He studied my face. "Are you afraid of losing your mom?"

I realized he wasn't asking about my mom dying. He meant losing her the way he lost his mom, after a judge's ruling, after the night they were taken away.

I thought of Heather racing to put a car seat in the police cruiser the morning after Joanna died. Of Kris making the call to find a different placement for the boys. Of my aunt and uncle waking to a knock on the door and the news of Jaime's death. Of Amber seeing another investigator come into her home and learning her children were once again being removed. Of my mom, the little girl, kneeling beside her mother's coffin, saying her final goodbye.

I thought of us having to say goodbye to Ethan and Logan.

Of us not being able to take Ethan, Logan, and Savannah back into our home as they reentered the system.

"I think we're always afraid of losing the people we love," I tell him. "I think that's what love is."

I think of Eddie's birth father, who when faced with losing his children, thanked the very men whose hearts they would fill.

"It's being a little afraid," I say, "and still deciding to love the best and biggest way we know how."

Acknowledgments

The list of people I'd like to acknowledge is longer than the queue for Taylor Swift tickets. At the very front is the man who encourages me, loves me, and always supports me (sometimes begrudgingly), my husband, Jason Daley Kennedy. Thank you for making each day an adventure, each moment a blast, and for reminding us to breathe. My heart belongs to you.

Aimie, Eddie, and Joshua, you three are the greatest gifts in my life. If joy had legs, it would be you all. I am so lucky and so tremendously honored to be your dad. You make me proud every single day. I love you always.

A very special thank-you to my inspirational cousins, Heather and Jerry Mullin, for allowing me to share the most horrific event of their lives in the hope that it can inspire a movement of people to get involved and help children and families living on the brink. Heather and Jerry's strength and capacity to love are a lesson for all humankind. I love and admire you both so much.

Lara Love Hardin. Lara Love Hardin. Lara Love Hardin. You deserve a million shout-outs. Mama Love, you believed in me, saw the beauty in this story, and took a chance. I cannot thank you and your team at True Literary enough for being my friend and my agent. Thank you to Doug Abrams and everyone at Idea Architects for your help and support, especially the story-shaping, narrative-driving Wenonah Hoye. I am so grateful to have had your brilliance in my ear multiple times a week. Esme Schwall Weigand, you are a lyrical genius, whose invaluable contributions made this book possible. Your words are a superpower.

The person who gave me the chance to put this story on paper was Michelle Herrera Mulligan. I am eternally grateful for this opportunity and for Michelle's incredible support and guidance throughout the process. I'm also indebted to the amazing team at Atria and Simon & Schuster, Erica Siudzinski, Mona Houck, Shida Carr, Sara Browne, Debbie Norflus, Dayna Johnson, and Lisa Sciambra. Thank you also to Joseph Papa for your help and support.

Throughout my life I've been spoiled by the love of my parents, Donna and Paul Daley. Mom and Dad, you encouraged me to dream, inspired my creativity, and taught me to believe in the promise of to-morrow. I feel like Rocky knowing you're in my corner. My siblings, Paul and Cheryl Ann, were my first and remain my best friends.

I am so grateful for Teri, Paul's smartest decision, and Brian, Cheryl's partner, not to be confused with our dog—who I am also extremely grateful for—along with his baby sister, Adele.

Throughout the writing process, I went to great lengths to make sure the facts, figures, and studies cited in this book were accurate and told the full story. While I sought help and input from some of the leading academics in the field, if any errors are found, they are solely my responsibility.

The first time I heard Sarah Font of Penn State speak, I wanted to be her friend. Sarah walks the walk and explores the most complex issues facing child welfare. I am so grateful to you, Sarah, for reading count-less drafts and ensuring I presented the most accurate data available.

Sharing a meal with Emily Putnam-Hornstein, PhD, of the University of North Carolina–Chapel Hill, is a master class in child welfare policy. Emily, thank you for sharing your wisdom and time, and for opening your network to me. Which leads me to Julia Reddy (soon-to-be PhD). Thank you, Julia, for your thoughtfulness, brilliance, and help getting me wonky.

My family is huge, loving, and so tremendously fun. I love you all, the Daleys, Kennedys, Greens, Wools, Macalones, Nees, Hosfords, Maleys, Cullinans, Mullins, Dhooges, Haases, Garners, Kennys, Ulatowskis, Gradys, Widmaiers, Eleys, Winters, Szuminskys, O'Connors, Madigans, Grosses, and our Pittsburgh matriarch Grandma Bea.

I won the in-law jackpot. Jay and Patricia Kennedy are the pot of gold at the end of a long rainbow. They are the absolute best and in my next life, I want to be one of their grandchildren.

In addition to the countless DoorDash drivers who provided a critical service to me while writing this book, I have so many friends and family who supported me—proofreading chapters, providing feedback, babysitting, and letting me share stories about them. I want to thank David Daley, Keli and Tommy Hosford, John and Kathy Macalone, Rachel Griffin, Hilary Carr, Steve O'Dell, Sarah Homier, Kate Foster, Javier Morgado, Ira Gilbert, Jill Nagle, Kelly Satish, Oscar and Kristin Grajales, Margie Sullivan, Chay Carter, Tiffany Anderson, Kevin Hager, Margaret Coyne, Naomi Schaefer Riley, Dr. David Wolff, Aimie Billon, Nicky Chang, Devin Alexander, Sofi Palacios, Kristian Denny Todd, Sullivan M. Daley, Mike Maley, Connor Nee, Patrick Nee, Jillian Nee, Tommy Nee, and Mary Nee, and Truc and AD Rastogi.

Peggy Callahan and Lloyd Sutton, your friendship means the world to me and your existence has quite literally changed the world for so many others. You two are the perfect combination of "profound and profane."

My oldest friendship remains one of the greatest I'll ever know, Kristen Conrad Garrity. You are the face of loyalty. I am so grateful for you, Chris, Cole, Eva, and Carol.

Jimmy Wynn, you have been a mentor, a friend, a brother, and now an editor to me. The universe truly gifted me with you.

There are some badass women I cannot imagine my life without. I am awed by their brilliance and their grace, their passions and their strength, but above all, I am deeply honored by their love: Kathleen Cerniglia Hipps, Jennifer Lavin, Jessica Vanden Berg, Trisha Griffiths

Kosalka, Lisa Johnson, Kim Pieper, Erin Seidler, Christina Wool, Angelique Pirozzi, Dawn Smalls, Jennifer Hanley, Monica Leung, and Beyoncé Knowles-Carter (friendship forthcoming). I love you all so much.

This book would have taken another year to write if Kate DiRienzo Payne were not in my life. You are incredible and I'm so grateful for you.

There often comes a point in working with people where your admiration turns to adoration. Lisa Campbell Motton, Paige Chan, Nathaniel Foster, Alex Rush, Jeff Zinn, Dave Margowsky, Yali Lincroft, Jeannine Balfour, I adore you all. Thank you for your leadership and your friendship. Speaking of people I adore, my work family, Nicole Cadena, Kristen Pratt, and Jennifer Perry—our calls would be so much shorter if you all weren't so damn funny.

When I was living this journey, I didn't know about all the work being done to improve the system or the names of any of the thoughtful, hardworking, and innovative leaders driving change within the California Department of Social Services. I am honored to work with Kayla Granderson, Kristy Macy, Danielle Mole Gabri, Daniel Wilson, Rebecca Buchmiller, Sarah Rogers, Dianna Wagner, Johnny Cuestos, Kimberly Wrigley, Kendra Elmendorf, and so many more. I am also grateful to the staff at Children's Bureau for their support throughout our journey.

A very big thank-you to Joe Hipps for sharing his Kati (and other Katie) with me. I am grateful to have you, the incredible Katie Giarla, and your team at Fifth Season as my partners in bringing this story to television. In addition, I am ecstatic and so grateful to have the incomparable Alan Poul and Sam Champtaloup from Boku Films driving this forward, along with the phenomenal Samuel D. Hunter. A very big thank-you to Sylvie Rabineau and Elizabeth Wachtel at WME for their help (and hand-holding) throughout this unbelievable process.

I want to mention my forever friends who will never hold this book, but will always hold space in my heart, Allison Kerr, Katherine Hamm, Joanna Mullin, Jaime and Cheryl Macalone.

Lastly, I want to thank people who still read books and you who listen to the audio version, too, that counts. Thanks.

Notes

CHAPTER 1: PROTECTION

1. U.S. Department of Health and Human Services, Administration for Children and Families, Administration on Children, Youth and Families, Children's Bureau, *Child Maltreatment 2016*, 2018, https://www.acf.hhs.gov/cb/report/child-maltreatment-2016.
2. U.S. Department of Health and Human Services, Administration for Children and Families, Administration on Children, Youth and Families, Children's Bureau, *The AFCARS Report* #24, 2017, https://www.acf.hhs.gov/cb/report/afcars-report-24.
3. Daniel Webster et al., "CCWIP Reports," University of California, Berkeley, California Child Welfare Indicators Project, 2023, https://ccwip.berkeley.edu.
4. Nadine Burke Harris, MD, *The Deepest Well* (New York: Houghton Mifflin Harcourt, 2018), 39.
5. Children's Bureau, *The AFCARS Report* #24.
6. Ibid.

CHAPTER 3: BABY FEVER

1. U.S. Department of Health and Human Services, Administration for Children and Families, Administration on Children, Youth and Families, Children's Bureau, *The AFCARS Report* #24, 2017, https://www.acf.hhs.gov/cb/report/afcars-report-24.
2. U.S. Department of Health and Human Services, Administration for Children and Families, Administration on Children, Youth and Families, Chil-

dren's Bureau, *The AFCARS Report* #29, 2022, accessed May 24, 2023, https://www.acf.hhs.gov/sites/default/files/documents/cb/afcars-report-29.pdf.

3. U.S. Department of Health and Human Services, Administration for Children and Families, Administration on Children, Youth and Families, Children's Bureau, *Child Maltreatment 2016*, 2018, https://www.acf.hhs.gov/cb/report/child-maltreatment-2016.

4. Carolyn A. Greene, Lauren Haisley, Cara Wallace, and Julian D. Ford, "Intergenerational Effects of Childhood Maltreatment: A Systematic Review of the Parenting Practices of Adult Survivors of Childhood Abuse, Neglect, and Violence," *Clinical Psychology Review* 80 (2020): 101891, https://doi.org/https://doi.org/10.1016/j.cpr.2020.101891, https://www.sciencedirect.com/science/article/pii/S0272735820300799.

CHAPTER 4: LOVE AND RISK

1. Kids Data, "Exit Status Four Years After Entry into Foster Care," accessed June 7, 2023, https://www.kidsdata.org/topic/521/foster-status-4yr/table#fmt=687&loc=2&tf=79&ch=21,22,23,24,25,26&sortColumnId=0&sortType=asc.

2. California Penal Code, §11165.13 (2000).

3. Ibid., 40–41.

4. Ibid.

5. Ashley L. Landers et al., "Abuse After Abuse: The Recurrent Maltreatment of American Indian Children in Foster Care and Adoption," *Child Abuse & Neglect* 111 (January 2021), https://doi.org/10.1016/j.chiabu.2020.104805.

6. Sarah A. Font, "Child Protection Investigations in Out-of-Home Care: Perpetrators, Victims, and Contexts," *Child Maltreatment* 20, no. 4 (July 2015), https://doi.org/10.1177/1077559515597064.

CHAPTER 6: JAGGED THINGS

1. U.S. Department of Health & Human Services, Administration for Children and Families, Administration on Children, Youth and Families, Children's Bureau, *Child Maltreatment 2016*, 2018, https://www.acf.hhs.gov/cb/report/child-maltreatment-2016.

2. Jill Duerr Berrick, *The Impossible Imperative: Navigating the Competing Principles of Child Protection* (New York: Oxford University Press, 2018), 28.

3. Children's Bureau, *Child Maltreatment 2016*.

4. Sarah A. Font, Sheridan Miyamoto, and Casey N. Pinto, *Child Sexual Abuse and Exploitation in Pennsylvania*, Center for Rural Pennsylvania, Pennsylvania General Assembly, January 2020, 119.

5. Berrick, *The Impossible Imperative*, 26.

6. Peter J. Pechora et al., "Educational and Employment Outcomes of Adults Formerly Placed in Foster Care: Results from the Northwest Foster Care Alumni Study," *Children and Youth Services Review* 28 (2006): 1459–81, doi:10.1016/j.childyouth.2006.04.003.

7. Kids Data, "Exit Status Four Years After Entry into Foster Care," accessed June 7, 2023, https://www.kidsdata.org/topic/521/foster-status-4yr/table#fmt=687 &loc=2&tf=79&ch=21,22,23,24,25,26&sortColumnId=0&sortType=asc.

8. Carolien Konijn et al., "Foster Care Placement Instability: A Meta-Analytic Review," *Children and Youth Services Review* 96 (January 2019): 483–99, https://doi.org/10.1016/j.childyouth.2018.12.002.

CHAPTER 8: A HOME FOR LITTLE WANDERERS

1. U.S. Department of Health and Human Services, Administration for Children and Families, Administration on Children, Youth and Families, Children's Bureau, *The AFCARS Report* #24, 2017, https://www.acf.hhs.gov/cb/report/afcars-report-24.

2. Alicia Summers, PhD, National Council of Juvenile and Family Court Judges, "Disproportionality Rates for Children of Color in Foster Care," https://www.ncjfcj.org/wp-content/uploads/2012/06/Disproportionality -Rates-for-Children-of-Color-2010.pdf, 9.

3. Elizabeth Hinton, LeShae Henderson, and Cindy Reed, "An Unjust Burden: The Disparate Treatment of Black Americans in the Criminal Justice System," Vera Institute of Justice, 2018, https://www.vera.org/downloads /publications/for-the-record-unjust-burden-racial-disparities.pdf.

4. National Partnership for Women & Families, Issue Brief, April 2018, https:// www.nationalpartnership.org/our-work/health/reports/black-womens -maternal-health.html.

5. Angela Hanks, Danyelle Solomon, and Christian E. Weller, "Systematic Inequality: How America's Structural Racism Helped Create the Black-White Wealth Gap" (Washington, DC: Center for American Progress, 2020), https://americanprogress.org/issues/race/reports/2018/02/21/447051/sys tematic-inequality/.

6. Marian F. MacDorman et al., "Racial and Ethnic Disparities in Maternal Mortality in the United States Using Enhanced Vital Records, 2016–2017," *American Journal of Public Health* 111 (2021): 1673–81, https://doi.org/10 .2105/AJPH.2021.306375.

7. National Indian Child Welfare Association, "Setting the Record Straight: The Indian Child Welfare Act Fact Sheet," https://www.nicwa.org/wp-content /uploads/2018/10/Setting-the-Record-Straight-2018.pdf.

8. Bryan Newland, *Federal Indian Boarding School Initiative Investigative Report*, Department of the Interior, Washington, DC, April 2022, https://www.bia.gov/sites/default/files/dup/inline-files/bsi_investigative_report_may_2022_508.pdf.

9. Carlisle Indian School Digital Resource Center, https://carlisleindian.dickinson.edu/teach/kill-indian-him-and-save-man-r-h-pratt-education-native-americans.

10. Child Stats, Forum on Child and Family Statistics, https://www.childstats.gov/americaschildren/tables/pop3.asp. Children's Bureau, *The AFCARS Report* #24.

11. U.S. Census Bureau, U.S. Department of Commerce, *The Hispanic Population in the United States: 2017*, 2017, accessed May 26, 2023, https://www.census.gov/data/tables/2017/demo/hispanic-origin/2017-cps.html.

12. Children's Bureau, *The AFCARS Report* #24.

13. Shamini Ganasarajah et al., "Disproportionality Rates for Children of Color in Foster Care, Fiscal Year 2015," National Council of Juvenile and Family Court Judges, Reno, NV, September 2017, https://www.ncjfcj.org/wp-content/uploads/2017/09/NCJFCJ-Disproportionality-TAB-2015_0.pdf.

14. A. Summers, S. Wood, and J. Russell, "Disproportionality Rates for Children of Color in Foster Care," National Council of Juvenile and Family Court Judges, Reno, NV, 2012.

15. W. Clarke, K. Turner, and L. Guzman, "One Quarter of Hispanic Children in the United States Have an Unauthorized Immigrant Parent," National Research Center on Hispanic Children & Families, October 2017, https://www.hispanicresearchcenter.org/wp-content/uploads/2019/08/Hispanic-Center-Undocumented-Brief-FINAL-V21.pdf.

16. Emily Putnam-Hornstein et al., "Community Disadvantage, Family Socioeconomic Status, and Racial/Ethnic Differences in Maltreatment Reporting Risk During Infancy," *Child Abuse & Neglect* 130, no. 4 (August 2022): 105446.

17. Clarke, Turner, and Guzman, "One Quarter of Hispanic Children."

18. Peter J. Pechora et al., "Educational and Employment Outcomes of Adults Formerly Placed in Foster Care: Results from the Northwest Foster Care Alumni Study," *Children and Youth Services Review* 28 (2006): 1459–81, doi:10.1016/j.childyouth.2006.04.003.

CHAPTER 9: THE STORY OF MY LIFE

1. County of Los Angeles Department of Children and Family Services, Child Welfare Services Data Fact Sheet FY 2015–16, https://dcfs.lacounty.gov/wp-content/uploads/2020/02/Factsheet-FY-2015-2016.pdf.

2. X. Zhou, J. McClanahan, S. Huhr, and F. Wulczyn, "Using Congregate Care: What the Evidence Tells Us," Center for State Child Welfare Data, Chapin Hall, University of Chicago, July 2021, https://assets.aecf.org/m/resourcedoc /chapinhall-usingcongregatecare-2021.pdf, 9.

3. Fred Wulczyn et al., "The Dynamics of Foster Home Recruitment and Retention," Center for State Child Welfare Data, Chapin Hall, University of Chicago, September 2018, https://fcda.chapinhall.org/wp-content/uploads /2018/10/Foster-Home-Report-Final_FCDA_October2018.pdf.

4. U.S. Department of Health and Human Services, Children's Bureau, *Child Welfare Outcomes 2019: Report to Congress*, 2019, accessed May 29, 2023, https://www.acf.hhs.gov/sites/default/files/documents/cb/cwo-report-to -congress-2019.pdf.

5. T. Shaw, "Re-entry into the Foster Care System after Reunification." *Children and Youth Services Review* 28 (2006): 1375–90.

6. Marybeth J. Mattingly and Christopher T. Wimer, University of New Hampshire, Carsey School of Public Policy National Fact Sheet #36, Spring 2017, https://scholars.unh.edu/cgi/viewcontent.cgi?article=1303&context=carsey.

7. Stephanie Cuccaro-Alamin et al., "Risk Assessment and Decision Making in Child Protective Services: Predictive Risk Modeling in Context," *Children and Youth Services Review* 79 (August 2017): 291–98.

CHAPTER 10: HOUSE ON FIRE

1. Movement Advancement Project, "Foster and Adoption Laws," accessed June 8, 2023, https://www.lgbtmap.org/equality-maps/foster_and_adoption _laws.

2. Danielle Taylor, "Same-Sex Couples Are More Likely to Adopt or Foster Children," United States Census Bureau, September 17, 2020, https://www .census.gov/library/stories/2020/09/fifteen-percent-of-same-sex-couples -have-children-in-their-household.html.

3. U.S. Department of Health and Human Services, Administration for Children and Families, Children's Bureau, Fact Sheet for Families, June 2021, https://www.childwelfare.gov/pubPDFs/lgbtqyouth.pdf.

CHAPTER 11: LOVE IS NOT ALL YOU NEED

1. Adoption and Safe Families Act of 1997.

2. Laura Radel and Emily Madden, "Freeing Children for Adoption within the Adoption and Safe Families Act Timeline: Part 1—The Numbers," Office of the Assistant Secretary for Planning and Evaluation, U.S. Department of

Health and Human Services, February 2021, https://aspe.hhs.gov/sites/default
/files/private/pdf/265036/freeing-children-for-adoption-asfa-pt-1.pdf.

3. National Association of Counsel for Children, "State Models of Children's
   Legal Representation," 2022, https://secureservercdn.net/50.62.198.124/zmc
   .c18.myftpupload.com/wp-content/uploads/2022/07/Model-of-Rep-Chart
   -2022.pdf.

CHAPTER 15: NO BLOOD, NO FOUL

1. Social Security Administration, "Disability Evaluation Under Social Security," sec. 12.00: Mental Disorders—Adult, https://www.ssa.gov/disability
   /professionals/bluebook/12.00-MentalDisorders-Adult.htm#12_04.
2. S. E. Kimberlin, E. K. Anthony, and M. J. Austin, "Re-entering Foster Care:
   Trends, Evidence, and Implications," *Children and Youth Services Review* 31,
   no. 4 (2009): 471–81, https://doi.org/10.1016/j.child youth.2008.10.003.
3. Megan Miranda et al., "Implications of Foster Care on Attachment: A Liter-
   ature Review," *Family Journal* 27, no. 4 (2019): 394–403.
4. E. Putnam-Hornstein, "Report of Maltreatment as a Risk Factor for Injury
   Death: A Prospective Birth Cohort Study," *Child Maltreatment* 16, no. 3
   (2011): 163–74, https://doi.org/10.1177/1077559511411179.

CHAPTER 20: BY THE THROAT

1. Adoption and Safe Families Act of 1997.

CHAPTER 21: PURPOSE FROM PAIN

1. "Child Welfare and Foster Care Statistics," Annie E. Casey Foundation, last
   modified September 26, 2022, https://www.aecf.org/blog/child-welfare-and
   -foster-care-statistics.

CHAPTER 22: THANK YOU

1. "Quick Facts, Los Angeles, California," U.S. Census Bureau, last modified
   July 1, 2022, https://www.census.gov/quickfacts/losangelescountycalifornia.

Index

About the Author

Mark Daley is a social activist, entrepreneur, and foster-turned-adoptive father. Daley has more than two decades of experience in message development, communication strategy, and public policy, including as a communications director and spokesperson for then-senator Hillary Clinton's 2008 presidential campaign. He has worked with more than thirty members of Congress, numerous governors, and other elected officials. He is the founder of One Iowa, the state's largest LGBTQ+ equality organization, and TheFosterParent.com, a national platform to connect interested families with foster organizations. Daley lives in Southern California with his family.

About the Author

Mark Daley is a social activist, entrepreneur, and foster-turned-adoptive father. Daley has more than two decades of experience in message development, communication strategy, and public policy, including as a communications director and spokesperson for then-senator Hillary Clinton's 2008 presidential campaign. He has worked with more than thirty members of Congress, numerous governors, and other elected officials. He is the founder of One Iowa, the state's largest LGBTQ+ equality organization, and TheFosterParent.com, a national platform to connect interested families with foster organizations. Daley lives in Southern California with his family.